# *Ḏamurruŋ'puy Mälk*
## Saltwater Skin

Mary McCarthy

*D̲amurruŋ'puy Mälk*
Saltwater Skin

For the Yolŋu people of Arnhem Land
and for the continued preservation of languages and culture for all
Indigenous groups of our earth and future generations.

And for Mayzie
my goddaughter

*Ḏamurruŋ'puy Mälk Saltwater Skin*
ISBN 978 1 76109 154 4
Copyright © text Mary McCarthy 2021

First published 2021 by
**Ginninderra Press**
PO Box 3461 Port Adelaide 5015
www.ginninderrapress.com.au

# Contents

| | | |
|---|---|---|
| Author's Note | | 8 |
| Preface | | 9 |
| People and places | | 12 |
| 1 | On arrival | 15 |
| 2 | The first week | 26 |
| 3 | 'Mary, can we visit you?' | 33 |
| 4 | Cyclone | 42 |
| 5 | New friends | 50 |
| 6 | Adoption | 57 |
| 7 | Walkabout | 64 |
| 8 | Mayrparr | 68 |
| 9 | Magic Yapa | 75 |
| 10 | Yolŋu essence | 86 |
| 11 | Gutharra | 92 |
| 12 | Ṉilatjirriwa guḻun | 101 |
| 13 | Hunting nyoka | 107 |
| 14 | Gunga – Part 1 | 114 |
| 15 | Uluru | 122 |
| 16 | Gunga – Part 2 | 131 |
| 17 | Old Yapa | 137 |
| 18 | Dharpa Buŋgul | 144 |
| 19 | Old Yapa leaves our world | 150 |
| 20 | The past | 160 |
| 21 | The spirit of Yalakun – Part 1 | 163 |
| 22 | Marrŋgitj | 168 |
| 23 | The marrŋgitj's mother | 175 |
| 24 | Baymarrwaŋa | 181 |
| 25 | Living between worlds | 189 |

| | | |
|---|---|---|
| 26 | Return to Yurrwi | 196 |
| 27 | The spirit of Yalakun – Part 2 | 200 |
| 28 | Djutjutjnha, Waku | 206 |
| 29 | Yirritja Ḏärra' Buŋgul – the spirit of Yolŋu Rom | 220 |
| 30 | Ḏarraku matha – my language | 233 |
| 31 | Mimi, Warrabunbun and the Marrngitj dharpa | 240 |
| 32 | Yoga and Yolŋu – the collaboration of two ancient worlds | 250 |
| 33 | Bäpi Munduku<u>l</u>' | 255 |
| 34 | Ḏiltjipuy Mirritjin' – bush medicine | 262 |
| 35 | The spirit of meditation | 269 |
| 36 | The ochres of Munduku<u>l</u>' | 274 |
| 37 | My last day on Yurrwi | 283 |
| | Statements by Yurrwi women | 287 |
| | Glossary | 295 |
| | References | 310 |
| | Acknowledgements | 312 |

We live our culture by singing and dancing, sitting in shade, not inside. Hunting *weṯi*,* *djanda, guya, miyapunu, nyoka, maypal*. We pass our tradition onto the *djamarrkuḻi'*. Family sharing is important. *Gurul* never ends, sharing *rrupiya, ŋatha*. That's the Yolŋu way.

When people die we always sing, we have *Dhuwa ga Yirritja buŋgul*. Yolŋu come from everywhere, from Elcho, Yirrkala, Ramo, Gapuwiyak, our extended family gather to show respect because we are all connected.

We have a *yindi' buŋgul* to help that person pass to spirit but even though they are gone, their spirit remains. It is still here.

When we grow old we pass our knowledge on to the young children. Our culture is strong.

*Ga Balanya*.

*Wäwa* Jo Djembaŋu, 2004

You must tell this story because not many people come here and live with us. So you can let them know about us. You must use their real names in the story so we can remember them; those who are gone now, too. Also there may be people who read the story and know someone. Maybe they came here long time ago and met them. Then they can say, I know that person, that's my *yapa* or my *waku* or my *wäwa*.

That story will help them connect with their family again. You should write that story, *Yapa*, so we can remember.

*Yapa* Jessie Murarrgirarrgi, 2016

---

* Yolŋu words and their translations are listed in the Glossary, page 295.

## Author's note

This book contains names and images of Aboriginal people who have died. In Aboriginal communities, it is usually important not to name or show images of the recently deceased. However, all names and images in this book are shared with permission of the Yolŋu people of Milingimbi community.

# Preface

Within the first two years of living on Milingimbi Island, I knew I wanted to share a story about what I was experiencing in this rare world. I had a strong urge to let others know about this life. Late at night when my work was done, I wrote down my experiences, thoughts and my feelings. I put down just about every word that anyone had shared with me. After eighteen months, though uncertain of my decision to go, I left my island home and returned to life as a yoga teacher and my work to support others on their journey to well-being on the north coast of New South Wales. I took trips to Sydney to share my work there. I began to write my journals into a book and frequently listened to Yolŋu music and recordings of *buŋgul*.* Most evenings I spent hours staring at all the photographs I had taken. This way, I felt close to the spirit of the Yolŋu. Once I began to settle back into my life on the north coast, I became painfully aware of how torn I was without my Yolŋu family, how culturally shocked I was living back in New South Wales. I realised my journey in Arnhem Land was not yet complete. And so I returned to my teaching position, my home and my family on Yurrwi, Milingimbi Island, in July 2006.

*Ḏamurruŋ'puy Mälk: Saltwater Skin* is by no means an anthropological, political, or linguistic account of a life had with Yolŋu. It is not a claim to know Aboriginal spirituality in Australia. Nor is it an intimate account of school teaching, or the many things perceived as 'negative' about Australia's original people. I make no claims to be an expert or an authority. The Yolŋu women helped me with the use of language throughout the book. It is simply intended to help readers learn and respect my Yolŋu kin, culture and languages. This is my story, although without this life with Yolŋu, this story would not exist. I share from my heart and my own personal experience, a story about the power of love, born out of my passion for spirit, healing, yoga and Yolŋu. It is a story about deep connection with Yolŋu kin, land, spirit and their profound effect on me.

This story is not to discount or deny the illness, sorrow, death and complex issues that exist in our communities. It is not my intention to romanticise life there. Quotes that I share from various books are in no way stating that all Aboriginal people share the same way of being or the same views. I am simply sharing readings that I came across on my journey that gave me various perspectives on what I was living.

My experiences with Yolŋu have transformed my life and given me some insight into the most ancient culture on our planet. As a young girl, I wanted to live with Australia's original people to experience something of their unique world. It was reading the book *Walkabout* when I was about fifteen years old that triggered this yearning. By the time I took this journey, though, I was shocked and saddened by the fact that so many traditional elders had now gone and language and culture with them. On Milingimbi Island, it was very hard to watch the elders I got to know pass from this world. Still, though, I want to share my experience with others. I've sat in many airports around the world, sometimes late at night, and often shared my experiences with people I meet there. I find that European travellers are always eager to learn, and sadly Australians in general are shocked to see photos of a rich culture they never knew existed in their own country.

As it turns out, this book has taken many more years to write than I planned, partly due my continuing work in other parts of Arnhem Land, and my continued teaching of and studies in yoga, and also because the book has evolved, as I have too, I hope. I know that my diet, yoga practice and various attitudes are very different now.

Over the years, I've had conversations with Yolŋu regarding the book. In 2013, I returned to Milingimbi to discuss the draft of it with as many Yolŋu as I could. I returned again in 2014. I've been given permission to share these stories. It has been complex because so many of my loved ones have left this world now and in general, once a person has passed away, they are no longer called by their name for some time after their death, and people who share the same name are given another name to go by. I've done my best to communicate with those involved in the stories and in some instances I have changed names for reasons of privacy.

People have changed – my sisters no longer smoke cigarettes, and some people have made a large commitment to a religious path.

We live in a world of diversity, of different languages, cultures and spiritual expressions. Today, differences have become so great that separation is stronger than wholeness, separation not only from each other but also from nature. We need to celebrate diversity and help grow a unifying thread of connection. Culture and stories are important for everyone. The spirit of one's voice may have a different tone, it might have a different language and a different way of looking and being in the world, but the essence is equally valuable, no matter our culture, our skin or our background. We live in a time when, more than ever in our world and on our planet, healing is needed. An important consideration to make, I feel, is that an incredibly complex rich, diverse and deep knowledge already exists in our land and First Nations people, an academic knowledge that can lead all of us into a sustainable future for our planet if we open to it and are willing to listen, learn and truly collaborate together.

May *Ḏamurruŋ'puy Mälk: Saltwater Skin* open minds and hearts and help us grow in understanding and respect. May we all be inspired to be true to ourselves, live beyond our wildest dreams and realise how deeply connected we all are, so that together we can create harmony.

Mary E. McCarthy

# People and places

Kinship terms (*wäwa, yapa*, and so on) indicate relationship to the author.

## Darawundhu – Bottom Camp

| | |
|---|---|
| Dorothy Mawukuwuy Linda Slim | *yapa* sister) |
| Dorothy Muwalkmuwuy | *yapa* (sister) |
| Elizabeth Yibi Yibi | *yapa* (sister) |
| Esther Rarrinya | *waku* (child), schoolteacher |
| Jessie Murarrgirarrgi | *yapa* (sister) |
| Jo Djembaŋu | *wäwa* (brother) |
| Margaret Maṯay | *waku* (child), schoolteacher |

## Gätni – Garden Camp (where author lived, including Djambaŋ mala – Tamarind women)

| | |
|---|---|
| Bridget Lalawan | *waku* (child), Melissa's daughter, school |
| Clancy Bandhamarra | *wäwa* (brother) |
| Daphne Nimanydja | *waku* (child), Djambaŋ, daughter |
| Dorothy Buyuminy | *waku* (child), Djambaŋ |
| Dorothy Guwalkuwalk | *waku* (child) (from Yalakun) |
| Gwendoline Bambaniwuy | *yapa* (sister), Nimanydja, Bäpa Joe's daughter |
| Jennifer Munguḻi | *waku* (child), Djambaŋ |
| Jerome Gulikuli | *gaminyarr* (grandchild), school student |
| Joe Mawunydjil | *Bäpa* (father: minister, and author's adopted father) |
| Joshua Buŋgalkthun | *waku* (child) Nunydjulu's son, school student |
| Judith Maḏupinyin Ganyawu | *gäthu* (brother's child, niece) |
| Wendy Mipururr | *gaminyarr* (grandchild) |

## Djambaŋ and school

Judy Munymuny (Guminda)    *waku* (child), Djambaŋ
Melissa Natuyŋa    *yapa* (child), Nimanydja, *Bäpa* Joe's daughter
Nancy Djämbutj    *waku* (child), Djambaŋ
Rebecca Nunydjulu    *yapa* (sister), librarian Nimanydja, *Bäpa* Joe's daughter
Roslyn Djuwandayŋu    *gäthu* (niece), Djambaŋ and school
Sandra Djalili    *waku* (child), Djambaŋ and school
Terry Malmaliny    *wäwa* (brother) (from Yalakun)

## Milingimbi Community Education Centre (CEC – the school)

Elizabeth Ganygulpa    *gutharra* (grandchild), school administration
Elizabeth Milmilany    *mukul rumaru* (poison cousin), school LPC Language Programme
George Milay    *wäwa* (brother) artist, school groundsman
Gwen Boyukarrpi (number 2)    *gutharra* (grandchild), schoolteacher
Gwen Warmbirrirr    *waku* (child), schoolteacher
Margaret Gamuti    *waku* (child), Djambaŋ
Marilyn McGregor    assistant principal
Mitch Porteous    Stuart's son, visiting community, secondary student
Savannah Ganima    *yapa* (sister), school student
Stuart Porteous    schoolteacher
Jenny Robins    schoolteacher

## Damuyani – Top Beach Camp

Keith Lapuluŋ    *waku* (child), artist, teacher, musician, Elder

## Murruŋga Island

Laurie Baymarrwaŋa    *dhuway* (father's sister's child; cousin; husband)

**Mimi spirit**

Unnamed

**Quotations**

| | |
|---|---|
| Elizabeth Ganygulpa | *gutharra* (granddaughter) |
| Lapuluŋ Dhamarrandji | *waku* (son) |
| Laurie Baymarrwaŋa | *dhuway* (father's sister's child; cousin; husband) |
| Mark Yiŋiya | *galay* (mother's brother's son or daughter; wife) |

**Marrŋgitj**

Unnamed                traditional healer

**Places and clan names**

| | |
|---|---|
| Birrkili | a clan nation |
| Ḏiltji | Bush Camp |
| Ḏipirri | homeland close to Milingimbi |
| Djambaŋ | tamarind tree (Milingimbi) |
| Djiliwirri | homeland for *Wäwa* Jo |
| Galiwin'ku | Elcho Island |
| Gamaḻaŋga | a clan nation |
| Gapuwiyak | Lake Evella |
| Gätni | Garden Camp |
| Gurryindi | a clan nation/language |
| Maningrida | settlement in proximity to Milingimbi |
| Marraŋu | a clan nation |
| Mewa | Army Camp (Milingimbi) |
| Ṉilatjirriwa | name of billabong (Milingimbi) |
| Ŋamuyani | Top Beach Camp (Milingimbi) |
| Ŋarawundhu | Bottom Camp (where author was adopted, Milingimbi) |
| Ramingining | community close to Milingimbi |
| Yalakun | homeland community close to Gapuwiya |
| Yirrkala | Arnhem Land |
| Yurrwi | Milingimbi |

# 1

# On arrival

> I am going to tell you a story of Milingimbi, to who it belongs and the meaning of some place names. Milingimbi is not the whole island: it is only one place – the well – where the mission stands. There is the bush camp, where the water is. We call the whole place Milingimbi, but really there are lots of small places, each with its own separate name. The Macassan Well belongs to the Yirritja moiety. It was made by a snake called Mundukul. He came flashing lightening, from Worral. When he was at Worral, he was Balmawuy tribe. [But] when he got here was the Walamangu tribe.
>
> – Tom Djawa, interview with linguist Michael Christie, Milingimbi, c. 1970s, *The Native Born*

I peer out the dusty plane window, my senses awake to the red earth below. Blue-green waterways meander across Arnhem Land like a snake and the ocean glints ahead.

'That's Milingimbi,' the pilot yells over the whirring propellers of the light aircraft. He wears a black cap, sunglasses and headphones, so I have almost no idea what his face looks like.

I spy the low-lying island ahead, just off the mainland. I'd read that it was roughly nine kilometres by eleven but, from thousands of metres up, it looks tiny. The island is covered in lush, green scrub, but as the plane hovers, I spot what must be saltpans and a billabong. I am the only passenger on this five-seater plane from Maningrida to my new home, Milingimbi, some five hundred kilometres north-east of Darwin.

As the plane descends, I see houses dotted along red dust roads on the edge of the sea. My skin prickles. I know I'm being drawn into an unfamiliar world, moving out of the one I spent my whole life in and into an ancient one that is completely new to me.

The heat hits my face as I step onto the tarmac and dust tickles the back of my parched throat. I can smell the bush, woody and damp. I walk towards a large tin shed, the only building in sight. A mixture of nerves, knowing and excitement swim in my belly. I'm going home, were the words running through my head on the plane from Sydney to Darwin.

I see a petite woman waiting on the tarmac in front of the tin shed. I nervously slide my hand down my mauve dress to smooth any creases and wonder if I am dressed modestly enough. I was informed, when I was in New South Wales, that dressing modestly is very important in this community and that the women wear long skirts, no thighs showing, and they love bright colours.

'Have you got enough stuff or what?' the large, bearded man, who has appeared by the plane, yells at me. His eyes bulge as he hurls all my bags onto a metal trolley.

My sense of awe at finally being here is shattered by his gruff manner and I begin to worry about what might unfold.

I let out a long exhalation and hurry over to the woman, neatly dressed in a white blouse and grey skirt, glasses perched on her nose tip.

She smiles. 'Welcome to Milingimbi, Mary.' Her voice is deep and warm.

I relax a little. I had spoken to her on the phone when I was back in Byron Bay, so I know that Marilyn McGregor is the Assistant Principal at Milingimbi Community Education Centre (CEC), the school.

We heave my heavy purple bag and backpack, daypack, computer and bag of food into the back of the troopie (four-wheel drive). Marilyn steers the lumbering troop carrier onto the tar road and I look out at the tall gum trees and green scrub through the window. Suffocating heat presses in on me. My make-up is slipping down my face and my white T-shirt and dress are drenched with sweat.

I cast about for something to say to Marilyn and notice a tiny yellow and brown woven basket between the two front seats. 'That's a lovely basket,' I say.

'Yes. The women here weave well,' Marilyn says, her eyes steady on the road ahead.

I want to ask Marilyn how long she has been here and if she has woven a basket. I admire the smooth pandanus weave. I want to make one of them. I wonder what Marilyn will think if I ask to teach yoga classes at the school.

We pass a large oval on the right and a cluster of houses on the left. The houses are red and yellow corrugated iron with wooden verandas. Smoke rises up from a burning fire near a large tree. An old white ute sits in front of a blue house. Beyond the houses is a cluster of trees and shrubs and I catch a glimpse of grey in the distance, perhaps saltpans.

'That's Bush Camp,' Marilyn points to the left. She glances at me, smiling. 'And this is the school.' She has a motherly quality that is encouraging.

I think of my own mum for a moment. She's been gone a long time now. I bet Marilyn has a husband and a few kids.

She stops the truck in front of a yellow, corrugated-iron building. On one wall is a painting of a tree with a fish lying under it and a sign reading 'Milingimbi CEC Yurrwi Island'.

Her arms rest on the wheel and she pushes her glasses up off her nose with one finger. 'Look over that way. Behind that yellow building is the early childhood section, where you'll be working in the morning. From there, you'll walk across the grass to the secondary section in the afternoon.'

I nod, staring at the school. So this is the place that has brought me back to teaching in a school setting after fifteen years away from it. My intuition was sharp from a very young age. It grew through vivid dreams in my teens and the deaths of my loved ones. Through my connection with nature and the creek I spent hours at on the golf course across the road from my Sydney suburban home, my intuitive nature came alive. Down there, perched on a rock in the shade of the trees, I sniffed the damp air where dank leaves mottled the ground. I touched the brown cool water with my fingertips and it rippled. In this womb of nature, I experienced a force I couldn't name. The force moved through rocks, trees, sky, water, air, birds and it moved through me. I felt connected to all these elements and knew I was a part of them. We were joined: inseparable.

These experiences led me to become interested in meditation and take on studies in the healing arts. In addition to teaching English for Specific Purposes to adults both in institutions and privately, I've spent these past years studying and teaching meditation and working extensively as a kinesiologist, hypnotherapist and energy worker with people of all ages and backgrounds. We are all intuitive and there really is nothing to do to activate this quality within ourselves; it is naturally there if we care to take notice and practise using it.

For me, though, it was nature, dreams and death that woke me up to my insight. For a long while, I was scared of what my intuition was showing me, I wondered why I needed to know such painful things and so I had some resistance to it. I also felt judged at times because there have been a lot of negative connotations with being intuitive in our culture. Now I realise it is a great tool that we can all access and be a support in our decision-making process every day. Each person has their own path and their own way with their insight, and the form the information comes in is unique for each of us.

I wipe the sweat from my face, no longer concerned about my make-up. I have longed to live in an Aboriginal community since I was about sixteen. It's the end of February 2003 now and I am finally here. The teacher the school was expecting was unable to come, hence my late arrival in first term. I wonder if I am crazy to imagine that the Yolŋu will teach me anything about spirit and healing. I'm certainly not going to ask Marilyn what she thinks, no matter how friendly she is.

Marilyn drives us further down the road and I gasp as the ocean comes into view – a slice of magnificent blue-green, almost emerald in colour.

'Oh wow, that looks so inviting, I'd love to jump right in there,' I say.

Marilyn pulls a face. 'And you won't,' she scoffs light-heartedly, placing her hand on her heart. 'There are crocodiles.'

'I guess there would be,' I say feeling a bit disappointed. How weird, I think, all this water and no chance of a swim.

Marilyn refocuses and points to a concrete ramp leading into the sea. 'This is the barge ramp, where we collect our food off the barge. It comes from Darwin and that's the shop over there.' Marilyn turns and points behind us to a large brick building.

'Where is everyone?' I ask. I haven't seen a soul, except that grumpy man at the airport. I am sure he is probably a lovely man, though. Must be the heat affecting his mood.

'Oh, around somewhere,' Marilyn says nonchalantly. 'It's unusually quiet, though.' Her brow crinkles for a moment.

To the left of the barge ramp there is an old red mud-brick building, a few houses facing the sea and a massive tree. My eyes fix on the tree; its solid trunk, thick branches and roots spreading like long gnarly feet. It emanates a strong presence and I wonder if it's the tree from the painting I just saw at the school. If so, it must have some significance. I can almost see the old people sitting around it singing and telling stories. My impulse is to jump out of the truck and sit under this mighty tree like I did under the Bodhi tree when I was at Bodhgaya in India. But what would Marilyn think?

'This is Dum Dum and that's Top Camp down there past the old mud-brick building that used to be an art centre. There are five camps where people live,' explains Marilyn and pats her face with a tissue. 'That's the clinic near the sea there.' She points to the right of the barge ramp. 'And Bottom Camp.' Marilyn lifts her glasses and wipes around her eyes with the tissue. 'Past Bottom Camp, there are some boundaries for sacred business, so don't walk there.' She turns to look at me, her hazel eyes large and round through the glasses.

'Of course! No,' I say, hoping I don't accidentally wander over a boundary.

What would happen if I did? The thought of being at sacred business is very enticing, though. I would love to know something of sacred business, if I am allowed. Judging by the deep presence of that magnificent tree, it seems that spirit is alive on this land. How exciting!

I yawn and raise my hand to hide it. I hope I can remember all this very useful information Marilyn is telling me. She is patient and thorough in her delivery and her presence is calming my fears. I suddenly feel exhaustion creep in after my journey. Marilyn puts the vehicle into gear and backs away from the emerald sea, then pauses a moment longer.

I still cannot see anyone around and I can't wait to meet some Yolŋu people. On my way up here, I enjoyed sitting between two Yolŋu children in the middle of the back row of the Air North plane from Darwin to Maningrida. Until my first trip to Yirrkala two years ago, I had never met a Yolŋu person, just read about them, and I saw David Gulpilil in the movie *Walkabout*. It was filmed in the desert, yet I know he is Yolŋu and from Ramingining.

'And that's Ramingining over there across the water,' says Marilyn, as if reading my thoughts.

My skin moves eerily. I look fixedly at the sea again, wondering what ancient stories it holds. I exhale deeply and taste the salt on my lips. So this is the land of the Saltwater people. And here I am.

I remember the words of the *yidaki* player I met about a year ago back in Sydney.

'Hey, sister!' the *yidaki* player had shouted as he entered the back room of the Newtown café. Deep dark brown eyes, long wavy black hair, his eyeballs leapt out and he pointed directly into my heart. 'Where's your land?'

I sat immobilised by his sixth sense. Instantly, the craving for sticky date pudding that had been gnawing in my belly moments before was forgotten.

'Well, at the moment I live in Byron Bay,' I answered awkwardly.

'No!' he waved his finger around. 'Where's your land sister, your people, you gotta go there.'

My heart thumped as his words sank deep into me. I can still remember the feeling of his stern gaze.

'You are Saltwater,' piped up the large, curly-haired Aboriginal man standing next to me.

I took my eyes off the *yidaki* player, turned and looked up at this man. He was big, but a frail lightness emanated from him.

'I'm a shaman,' he revealed, taking my hand and casting his eyes over my palm.

'Saltwater, well, that feels right,' I murmured, not really knowing where my answer originated from. A flash of panic swirled in my gut and goosebumps rippled through my skin.

It was Scotty who had brought me to that café. Six feet four, lean, good-looking, with electric blue eyes and a tattoo of the rainbow serpent on his arm. He is a muso with a tribal allure and plays the *yidaki*. I met Scotty on the nine-month yoga teacher training course in 2000 in Byron Bay. Byron Bay was where I dreamed my husband Shaun and I would go and live and build our mud-brick home but the magic Byron was where I landed after our marriage ended.

In addition to falling in a heap and surrendering to grief, meditation and yoga postures helped. One thing about practising yoga is its ability to bring to light the truth, like it or not. There is a level of comfort in knowing something is right but that does not necessarily remove the agony from it. Yoga can shift stuck emotions. It is not about denying one's feelings but acknowledging them. Now that our life together was over, what would I do? I recall the mixture of relief, panic, grief and yet excitement that dwelled in me.

It was my love of yoga and a desire to transform 'me' that led me to the yoga teacher training in Byron Bay after my marriage break-up. I had been teaching meditation for years and practising and teaching some yoga asana (postures). However, yoga teaching was not my focus at all now that I needed to take care of my own well-being. Yoga had already been a great support to me through many losses in my life and I figured that after a marriage break-up I had a lot to learn and, through this full-time practice and study of the eight limbs, I would have a chance to find balance again. And there I met Scotty. He had travelled up to Arnhem Land and been adopted by the Yolŋu people in Yirrkala. A distant memory twigged in me as soon as he spoke to me in the classroom at the Yoga Arts Centre.

I shivered in the cool night air as we stepped out of the Newtown café onto the streets of Sydney that night, the *yiḏaki* player's words in my head. I remember being aware of a lightness filtering through my bones and a strong sense of being in the right place at the right time.

Marilyn pulls up outside a big, red, corrugated-iron clad pole house, surrounded by long grass and a palm tree. She drives in off the road and parks under a carport at the back of the house. 'This is your place.' She climbs out of the troopie and slams the door. 'This is the laundry.'

I climb out to see a washing machine and sink on a concrete slab in the corner.

The house is a long rectangle shape with the front of the house facing the street, but no front door. The doors are on each side of the house each with a set of stairs. We climb the concrete stairs from the back up the right side of the house. At the top there is a small veranda and birds chirping in a tree brushing against the corrugated iron.

'No *ganydja*. No *rrupiya*. No *ŋänitji*,' the sign on the screen door reads. Seems weird, I think.

'There is a phone through here, I think.' Marilyn must have seen my angst. She opens the door and we walk through the hallway into the large lounge room, with an open bench into the kitchen.

At the end of the bench there is a grey patch on the yellow wall where I imagine the phone once hung.

'Oh, it's gone.' She sighs, her shoulders sinking down.

I wonder what happened to the phone but I don't ask. My breath quickens and my heart beats faster as I spy three steel bolts nailed one beneath the other in a row on the door across the room. This is the door on the left side of the house. It also leads to the backyard and to the clothesline.

Marilyn remains calm. 'Just relax.' She looks me in the eye. 'I'll see you at school in the morning, at about seven-thirty.'

Are you for real? I want to ask Marilyn, but I smile weakly. 'Okay.'

I can't believe how romantically I have dreamed of this life up here. Right now I am stuck on what I see on the surface – the bolts on the door, the sign about 'grass' and the space on the wall where the phone once hung. A pool of fear and regret whirls in my guts.

I farewell Marilyn and open my daypack on the mottled green bench. I take out the ingredients for a cup of tea: a purple cup, small pot, tea bags and some long-life milk. Thanks be I have them. I fill the saucepan Marilyn has lent me and put it on the electric stove to boil. I pull a red apple out of my daypack and bite into it, its crunch loud in the quiet of the kitchen.

I shudder as I remember again there is no phone. 'Mary, breathe!' I say out loud, taking a deep breath.

I look around at the yellow walls with deep blue doorframes. The floors are green linoleum. I haven't seen lino since my childhood home. There is an old cane lounge and two tired-looking cane chairs in the lounge room. The windows are covered in dusty wire mesh and look like they have never been cleaned. This could be a great home, I think, once I have scrubbed it up. I'm decorating the room in my head, but really I'm afraid. What the hell am I doing? It's years since I've taught in schools and I've never lived in a remote community for any length of time.

I take another deep breath and speak out loud again to put a stop to my mind running away with terror. 'Mary! I know you are afraid – terrified, in fact – but you…I can do this. I want to do this and I'm doing it.'

I sip my tea, wipe away a tear and think back to the soothing sound of the sea at my Byron Bay studio.

My mind wanders back to an important experience in 2001 that triggered this whole journey. Scotty had introduced me to Jonathan outside Fundies Café in Byron Bay. Dark hair, large eyes, handsome face and smooth golden skin, Jonathan lived and worked in Yirrkala and, like Scotty, had been adopted by an elder and played *yi̱daki* too.

'Whatever happened to Arnhem Land, anyway?' I had asked out loud in my meditation only that morning, and then there I was standing before a guy who lived there.

'Ask and you shall receive,' Jonathan had replied, looking me straight in the eye after I had shared my meditation experience with him. An air of strength and wisdom exuded from this guy.

Wow, this is a profound moment, I remember thinking. A flush of goosebumps pulsed on my skin. From that meeting, I was led to my first trip to Yirrkala.

'Come with an open heart,' were the words Jonathan had said to me before my arrival in Yirrkala in 2001. And here I am in Milingimbi two years later. I followed my heart here to this island, so now I must accept the choice I'd made, keep opening my heart and jump into this new life here.

I sit on the bed and place my hands on my chest and breathe slowly in and out, noticing the movement of the breath in my lungs and allowing my mind to become quiet.

I lie down in the dark, smiling up at the glowing green stars that dot the ceiling. The last teacher must have stuck them there. The dream I had the night before I left my beachside pad comes to mind. I had fallen asleep listening to the sound of the sea lapping on the shore after watching *Rabbit-Proof Fence* with my ex-boyfriend. It was a clear and simple dream revealing patches of blue sky, green gum leaves and brown-red earth. A black forearm and hand reached through these colours and beckoned me, though not in the way I am accustomed to. The hand was cupped, palm faced down and the fingers moved toward the wrist. A wave of peace washed over me when I awoke.

'That's how the islander people beckon you,' my friend Dave in Byron Bay had explained to me the next day as we spoke on the phone.

'They're calling me,' I smiled.

'I am on Milingimbi Island,' I say out loud now. Tomorrow I start being a schoolteacher again.

I think back to all the kids I taught in the past. I loved the little ones for some years before I moved into adult education. I always felt teaching came naturally to me. I summon my own strength. It's in me somewhere beneath my fears and I call on spirit for help too. I close my eyes and try and feel the earth beneath me. I ask to align with it and with the Yolŋu here. I give thanks for permission to be here on this land, in this community. I intend to earn respect in this community, to sleep well and not get eaten alive by sand flies and mozzies. I smile at my house, this community, my family and friends.

I smile because I got on that plane and I'm here.

# 2

# The first week

Knowing Love, I will allow all things to come and go, to be as subtle as the wind and take everything that comes with great courage. As my teacher would say to me, Life is right in any case. My heart is as open as the sky.
— From the final scene of the film *Kama Sutra: A Tale of Love*, directed by Mira Nair

I follow the worn trail of damp grass, past a frangipani tree and through a couple of backyards, and try not to look into the houses. Marilyn pointed out the track yesterday and told me that the first red pole house is where a long-term teacher named Nikos lives. I come to a thick forest of bamboo where yellow leaves form a soft floor on the damp ground. I walk through the bamboo and past the smoky remnants of a campfire.

When I step onto the tar road, I pass a blue house and a brown and white dog rushes out barking and growls at me. I stop and shakily breathe the tepid air. The dog slinks to one side, hackles raised.

'*Yow*,' comes a voice from another house.

'Hello,' I say and hesitate before walking on. I reach the school and my stomach flutters with anxiety as I open the office door.

A woman with dark wavy hair stands behind the counter. 'There's no water,' she announces. 'The main pipe's broken, so a plumber will be flown in from Darwin and the children will be sent home. There's some water in the urn. Make yourself a cup of tea in the staffroom.' She points in the direction of the next room.

I enter the staffroom to find a few Yolŋu women sitting on an old cane lounge chatting in Yolŋu language.

I smile and look over at them. 'Hello, I'm Mary,' I say.

Everyone has stopped talking. '*Yow*,' they nod and smile.

Then a guy walks in with brown shoulder-length hair.

'Hi, I'm Mary,' I say.

'I'm Jon. I'm the music teacher.' He shakes my hand.

Just ten days ago, I was teaching a yoga class in Byron Bay; now I'm afraid of dogs and unsure how to behave with the women around me. What am I doing here? I watch my fear as it rises up again. There is no certainty with this choice I have made, no guarantee that life will unfold perfectly as a result but I chose to do this and, fear or no fear, I will do it.

Marilyn bustles through the door with a cheerful smile. 'Good morning, Mary. I'll take you over to your room. You can meet Gwen Boyukarrpi.'

We walk down a path and across a grassy area to a yellow, corrugated-iron building with colourful handprints painted on the door.

'This is *gopu* class. Come in,' Marilyn says, holding a bunch of papers in her hands.

A few children are playing with the jigsaw puzzles and Lego. Marilyn whispers to Boyukarrpi to send them home and they scurry off. The room is quite dark and the windows covered with paper.

'Gwen Boyukarrpi, this is Mary McCarthy,' says Marilyn.

'*Yow*,' says Boyukarrpi. She is sitting at her wooden desk with a big folder in front of her. She turns toward us but does not look directly at me. She has strong broad shoulders, smooth skin, and curly hair.

'Hello,' I say. 'I'm really happy to be here.'

'Mary's come from Byron Bay. McGregor Street, actually, same as my name. Marilyn McGregor. Right, Mary?' she giggles.

'Yes,' I laugh too, but mine is nervous.

'This is Margaret Maṯay,' Marilyn says and waves her hand to the other woman sitting at a low table on a tiny chair gluing some of the kids' pictures onto a large sheet of red cardboard.

She has high cheekbones and a petite nose. Her hair is tightly swept off her face in a bun and she wears a loose, flowing, floral dress showing strong toned arms.

'*Yow,*' Maṯay says, studying me carefully.

'Now, Mary will be with you in the mornings, and then she'll go over to the secondary school. But today, because of the plumbing, you can do some planning. See you later,' she grins and slips out of the room.

'*Ma'*!' says Boyukarrpi.

I watch Marilyn leave the room and wonder what *ma'* means. I am feeling excited to be here, but I am nervous as well. I am not sure what to say, or where to begin in this new world. I know I have come to teach ESL (English as a second language) but I have no idea how it will work. I want to be respectful. The women are very quiet, yet they exude a strong presence. For a while there is silence and then we slowly begin to talk about the daily routine here in the early childhood section.

At four p.m., we pack up and I head across the grassy area, happy to head home and sit down in the quiet.

At lunchtime at school today, I'd spoken on the phone with the previous teacher who taught in the classroom I'm in now and also lived in this same house. She told me they had been broken into several times. My home feels even less safe now. I throw my yoga mat on the floor, drink a big glass of water and munch on an apple. I plonk down on the mat with my back against the wall and let out a big sigh. Everyone down south says I'm a brave woman for taking an adventure on my own but I'm not, I'm scared out of my wits and still resisting the change in my life to a degree. I'm supposed to be married with a kid in Sydney right now. On the other hand, though, when I slow down, breathe deeply and feel into my heart, I feel perfectly safe. I'm not sure what any burglars would take, anyway. I doubt they would want books on teaching English and yoga, whoever 'they' are. I laugh out loud.

I arrive at school and sit on a wooden bench near a bottlebrush tree in front of the staffroom. A man with grey tufts of hair around his ears and a huge grin on his face comes up to me.

'You must be Mary. I'm Stuart, and it's great to meet you.' He reaches out his hand to me.

I look up and extend my hand to his. He is wearing white pants and a white shirt and has several bits of red material wrapped around his wrist.

'Yes, I'm Mary,' I reply.

'You must be feeling such a multitude of things. Actually, I live next door to you and if there's anything at all that I can do to make you feel comfortable in this change, I will. Why don't you come over for dinner on Friday night and we can talk about everything?'

What are you, an angel? I think and this is the beginning of my friendship with Stuart Porteous.

'What does *gopu* mean?' I ask Boyukarrpi the next day as I enter the classroom.

'Fish *muka*,' she says, tossing a piece of Lego into a box.

'*Muka*?' I repeat but she doesn't respond.

About twenty children, five and six years old, play with Lego and puzzles on the floor. The dim room is alive with their chatter and squeals of laughter. I sit on the edge of a table under a whirling fan and look around at the crayon drawings of crocodiles, fish and crabs on the wall. Yolŋu alphabet cards stretch across the top of one wall and the English alphabet on another. There is an old blue bookshelf piled with books that have spilled onto the carpet. Tins of red, green, yellow and blue coloured pencils sit on a trolley next to Boyukarrpi's desk. Tins of thick grey pencils sit on a separate shelf. Maṯay is sharpening them. Low long desks are grouped together with tiny orange and blue chairs tucked under them.

Two girls and a boy run up to Boyukarrpi, pull her black and red floral skirt out and hide behind it. Their big eyes peek out at me. They giggle so hard their tiny bodies shake.

'*Nhini, nhini,*' says Maṯay, waving her hands, filled with pencils, in the air.

'What does that mean?' I ask.

'Sit down, *muka*.' There's that *muka* word again. It reminds me of *Ardho muka Svanasana* in Sanskrit, down face dog, a yoga posture, but I am sure they are not related. Then again they could be; both are ancient languages.

'Oh, that's a good one,' I respond, watching kids running around the room, laughing, some blowing bubbles with gum and others chewing on the ends of coloured pencils. There are more boys than girls. They laugh and run after each other, playing tag at a high speed. Most are wearing shorts and T-shirts. The girls have an array of pigtails, plaits and hairstyles with colourful clips in their thick black hair.

Boyukarrpi and Maṯay stand and gather the kids together. I notice that Boyukarrpi is quite tall and her curly hair sits just above her shoulders. I sit on the floor at the back of the group wondering why I am wearing big boots and socks on my feet in this heat. I look around at the others. No one else is wearing shoes. Boyukarrpi claps her hands and starts to sing; her eyes are big. She seems shy, yet warm and affectionate with the children. They huddle close by her feet and cling to her dress. I wonder how many other non-Indigenous teachers have worked in this room with Boyukarrpi before me and I wonder how she feels about it.

It is not long before a little girl with thick curls and dark sparkling eyes plonks on my lap. She has a pink butterfly clip in her hair and she runs her tiny fingers lightly down my cheeks and my nose, her eyes intently scanning my face.

'Lello,' she says, moving the palm of her hand gently down my hair.

'Yellow?' I laugh. No one has ever told me I have yellow hair before. Well, maybe in Japan.

A round-faced boy with one front tooth missing runs up, stops dead in front of me then reaches out and twirls his long fingers around my earring. *'Nhä dhuwal, nhä dhuwal?'* His eyes laugh.

'I'm sorry. I don't understand,' I say, and then I realise that he doesn't understand me either.

He skips away and my heart tightens at the prospect of teaching English when I have no Yolŋu language or even a concept of it. I have taught English to people of all ages and many nationalities, but this feels different, not just another language. This is another world, like no other I have experienced.

For now, I try not to worry about teaching and simply delight in the fact that these children are being taught in their own language. I am moved by the children's lightness of heart, their freedom of expression, openness and affection. I witness a rich spirit brimming from their eyes. There is something different about the teacher–student relationship too. It doesn't feel like the usual classroom etiquette; it feels like a big family in here.

The little girl in my lap settles back against me and begins to repeat the Yolŋu words her teacher is saying while she points to a picture of a buffalo, a crocodile and a kangaroo.

Back home, I nestle onto my mat, back against the wall. I'll start practising in a minute but for now, flashes of the children's smiles throughout the day are vivid in my mind I remember vividly the day I graduated as a schoolteacher.

I had stood under the fig trees at St Joseph's College, Hunter's Hill, in Sydney with my boyfriend Maury and my parents; my best friend Cheryl, her man and parents were there too. Cheryl and I were excited and elated about our lives that graduation day. I had just accepted my first teaching job. We stood holding onto each other, nerves running through our bodies but feeling very mature in our long black capes. Mortar boards covered our heads. I remember thinking that I would teach for a while. My love, Maury, and I had been going out for over three years; he had already asked me to marry him when we were nineteen. The picture in my mind went: we would get married, have a few kids, get a house and, well, that was it really. What more could I want? There was really nothing else to want. Teaching in an Aboriginal community had faded from the top of my dream list. Beneath this exhilaration, though, there was something uncomfortable slithering around, a twist, a knot pulsing in my gut that said perhaps something about it all was a lie. I had pushed down those growing gnawing feelings that wanted to be heard. Mary, Mary, listen. Life is not all it seems. Listen, Mary. That feeling of doom was eating away inside me, wanting to drag me down like it did before when my nana died and black sorrow like thick sludge had spilled into my heart. I resisted. No no, not that. No, not death, not change.

'Mary McCarthy.' Hearing my name shook me out of my thoughts. Maury squeezed me close, beamed a big smile that went straight into my heart, and I glided up to receive my teaching qualification.

Children's laughter outside brings me back to Milingimbi. How my life changed so radically from that day. It became nothing like I expected at all.

# 3

# 'Mary, can we visit you?'

*Yurrwi latju wäŋa*
Yurrwi beautiful island

It's Saturday morning. I'm awake early. I try to will myself back to sleep but due to years of early morning yoga, I'm usually awake at dawn. I sit on the bed with my back to the wall, sipping hot tea. I can only see a smattering of green leaves through the dusty wire mesh on the windows. Clouds are looming. It looks like rain and the air is thick, steamy and making my skin clammy.

While people refer to two distinct seasons, wet and dry, I've been reading that there are six seasons here that describe an annual cycle of natural events. February–March, which is right now, is the wet season, known as *Mayaltha*; March–April *Midawarr*; May–August *Dharratharramirri*; September–October *Rarranhdharr'*, October–November, pre-wet season, is *Dhuludur'*, and December–January is *Bärra'mirri*. In addition to climatic shifts, flora and animal life changes occur and interweave, creating a rich integrated system that Yolŋu are a part of and live by, through hunting and collecting bush food and medicine, and through ceremony. The school year has a month break in June, the dry, and is the most pleasant time in terms of temperature. Christmas time is very hot and there may or may not be rain.

I like being up high in my big pole house. It feels somewhat strange, though, as there seem to be lots of people in the Yolŋu houses across the road. It is quiet outside right now but for the birds. I let out a sigh, realising I have made it through my first week back as a schoolteacher after so long away from it – not from teaching but from school teaching. I have a lot to learn and there is a lot to do. I'd forgotten how demanding a schoolteacher's life is.

I take another sip of tea and reflect on the week. There were a few highlights. First of all, it is nothing like any other teaching job I have ever had. Okay, I taught English in Japan for some months, where I spent early mornings being screamed at in horror by the toddlers under my tuition. They'd never seen a blonde white girl. Other days included being dressed up in expensive elaborate kimonos by the Japanese women as they learned English with me in their family shop, then afternoons with solemn senior secondary students, doing more school after school. Not to forget sitting around a large wooden table holding up my Greenpeace magazine to the twelve nuclear scientists before me at the nuclear power plant.

Yes, that was different, but this is another world again. My task with the Year One and Two students is to teach some oral English. This is a bilingual school, so in the first years of schooling the focus is on the student's first language. I am to teach half an hour of oral English to the class as a whole daily, then take small groups for oral English throughout the day. *Walking Talking Text* is our programme and, in addition, I'm to join in and work as a team teacher with Boyukarrpi and Maṯay to plan the rest of the curriculum. The onus is that the younger students remain speaking in Yolŋu language as much as possible until Year 3. At least so far this is my understanding of it.

On Thursday afternoon, I sat in the secondary classroom on the edge of a table, listening to the students. I'm becoming more familiar with the Yolŋu term *balanda*. I'm a *balanda* here. The students have *balanda* names like Shaun and Leon. I would love to learn their real names but I can imagine they would be difficult to pronounce, as difficult as it would be to learn English for them, I guess.

Bill, the principal, stood at the whiteboard with a black marker in his hand. He encouraged the students to talk about what they do after school.

'*Huntinglil*,' one of the boys said, his teeth bright white.

Bill wrote down the word 'hunting'.

'*Maranydjalk*,' the boy spoke again.

'What's that?' I asked.

'Stingray *muka*,' he smiled.

Everyone giggled. *Muka*, I repeat under my breath. I've discovered that *muka* is like saying 'indeed' or 'definitely' and it can be a question or agreement indicator. I really am in another world. Stories about hunting stingray and barramundi, and cooking mud crabs on the fire at the edge of the sea, I find very intriguing.

At Friday's assembly, the student's singing went straight to my heart. Tears ran down my cheeks as I sat huddled with the Year One students on the steps of the AV room listening to them sing. Giggles and sheepish smiles filled the room. The kids are very shy and find it hard to stand in front of an audience; in fact, they prefer to turn their backs to everyone and face the whiteboard as they perform.

Yesterday afternoon, I expected the arrival of an order of some fresh vegies but, as it turns out, they won't come until Tuesday. My helpful neighbour Stuart, dressed in a crumpled blue shirt, explained exactly what I must do in regard to food, travel and life on the island. I stood in the administration office feeling somewhat overwhelmed but then I found two parcels in my pigeonhole.

'Yay!' I exclaimed out loud. I hugged the phone. Hopefully, when I plug it in it will work. I yanked a parcel from dear Kate out of the wooden slot with the label 'Mary McCarthy' on the bottom. Kate lives in Byron Bay. A toss of blonde hair, ocean blue eyes and queen of the surf. We became close friends on the 2000 yoga teacher training.

I walked to the shop and resorted to buying some frozen vegies and cheese. I sat on the lounge room floor and opened Kate's present. I felt a bit teary but am glad and sad to be here at the same time. My identity, or the person I perceive myself to be, is dissolved as I begin a new life yet again. Kate sent me a green journal with 'Mary's Journey' written in pink ink on the cover. She had taken the time to write some inspiring reflections, such as, 'Love by the way you walk, the way you sit and the way you eat. Love connects us.' There was a photo of us doing Trikonasana* on the deck of her Broken Head home. It's a perfect pressie for recording my moments here.

After a yoga practice, my mind is steady and I feel grounded in my body on this island again.

Today is a new day. 'Today is cleaning day!' I declare out loud. Finally, I get up and gather my cleaning instruments: a mop, a bucket, scrubbing brush (all three need cleaning before I can use them), bottle of baby oil, bottle of Dettol and some soap. I would not normally use such cleaning agents but I have been advised that the ingredients, mixed together, will keep insects at bay. I don my long shorts and an old black singlet, wrap a purple scarf around my head, get down on my hands and knees and scrub the grotty bathroom lino floor and shower recess. Red dust tinges everything in this house.

Last night, I woke to the sound of mangy dogs howling. I know they are mangy because I see them on my way to and from school – skinny, half-hairless creatures, lying around scratching fleas, licking wounds and growling at me. Yet they are much loved by the Yolŋu. I had tiptoed barefoot down the hall and stared out at the dark, moonless sky from the lounge room window. Doubt clouded my mind and I asked myself if the choice I'd made to come here was the right one or one that would perhaps isolate me.

I have left my studio home and left the complicated relationship I had with Carlo, my Italian/French boyfriend. I left behind my long-held dream of having a child, although, if I am honest with myself, there's still a tiny part of me that hopes for a miracle. For some years, I had expected my life and energy to flow in the direction of motherhood. Perhaps, though, it would be good for me to put my attention on my own learning and on something larger, beyond my own life now.

I am cleaning the kitchen sink when the water runs out. 'Oops!' I yelp.

'Mary, you there?' I hear Bill the principal's clear deep voice.

* For explanation of yoga terms, see Glossary (page 295).

I wipe dirty sweat from my brow, throw a long blue dress over my shorts and singlet and pull the lounge out from where I've jammed it against the door at the end of the lounge room. I laugh as I unbolt the three locks. They seem less scary now. 'Come in.'

'I won't come in.' Bill stands at the bottom of the stairs.' He wears a large, brown Akubra hat and long sleeves.

I wonder if protocol is the reason he won't come in. 'Excuse my Dettol appearance,' I say, self-consciously.

'The lawn looks good,' he remarks, indicating the freshly mown backyard. He is a tall, distinguished-looking man. He reminds me of a sea captain with his well-manicured grey beard. I can imagine him enjoying a gin and tonic and drawing back on a long wooden pipe.

'Yeah, there's lemongrass, a pawpaw tree and a banana tree. I'm excited about growing some food,' I reply, catching sight of my dirt-filled nails.

'The clothes line is tragic, though,' he says and we crack up laughing. 'I think someone ran into it in his troopie,' he says.

We stare at the mangled frame of metal leaning up out of the ground.

'Oh well, I can still hang clothes on it.'

'Here's some cleaning stuff, and I'll be back with four chairs and a table in a while. Oh, also, next week I've organised an induction meeting for you with Paula, one of the Yolŋu teachers and myself. We'll discuss some important things for you to know about school and life here.'

'Thanks so much.' I wave as he jumps in the school troopie and backs out onto the road.

I splash my face with cold bottled water from the fridge and sit down on the floor. The middle of the lounge room floor seems to be my favourite spot, or with my back against the wall on my yoga mat, and occasionally I sit on the lounge. Pen in hand, I begin to write my shopping list on a large notepad. 'Toilet paper, rice crackers, red split peas, kidney beans, tomatoes, turmeric, cumin, oats, frozen berries, beans, garlic, sweet potato, broccoli, carrots, apples, oranges.' My list must be faxed to Darwin by Tuesday and my food will arrive on the barge a week later. I'm a long way from the pristine organic diet on the north coast of

New South Wales but happy that I get some food. I wonder when I will get to eat some bush food.

Thrilled about my phone being connected, I call my Aunty Margot in Sydney. 'Oh Mary, it's you,' her joyful voice comes through the phone. 'It's so nice to hear from you. How are you going up there?'

Then I call Jonathan. He's in Yirrkala and has two visitors staying from Japan. 'Hi, Mrs Milingimbi, how're you doing? Bet you're wondering what the hell you're doing there?' he asks.

'Well, sometimes,' I hesitate.

'Personal space is a big adjustment. Nothing will be passed, nothing will go unnoticed,' Jonathan warns.

'Great! I'm a private one,' I say, feeling a bit sheepish.

'The Yolŋu will take you beyond it and it's very liberating,' says Jonathan. 'Your insights are crystal clear, Mary, trust that.' He's always straight to the point.

Thank God for Jonathan and Aunt Margot.

'*Yow, yow*, Mary. Mary.' I hear a call at the door and then a knock, not just one knock but a continual thumping on the wall outside.

'Okay, okay, I'm coming,' I yell.

Two tall, thin Yolŋu girls are standing at the door. 'Can we visit you?' they ask in unison.

'Yes, come in. What are your names

'Loretta and this one Francis.'

I wonder what their real names are. They have lovely smooth skin.

One girl picks up a cloth and starts wiping the bench.

The other sees the bubble-gum pink nail polish on the arm of the chocolate armchair. 'Mary, this one, can I?'

'Let's relax.' I pat the lounge.

They sit down next to me and we paint our toes.

'*Latju*,' says Francis. She wears a hot pink T-shirt with long, dark blue shorts. Her hair is thick and crinkly. With eyes wide, she blows a large bubble with her gum and admires her pink toes.

'*Latju*?' I repeat.

Her bubble bursts and gum spreads over her thick lips. '*Yow, latju* (beautiful).'

Loretta lightly touches my pigtail and then dangles my earrings with her fingers. She is wearing a blue T-shirt that has *manymak* written on it.

I get up and make us a cup of tea. They paint their fingernails, giggle and chatter in Yolŋu. My ears enjoy the sound of their words. I pull some cold oranges out of the fridge.

We sit down again and share the oranges and some dates. The gum must be stuck somewhere inside her mouth, I decide.

'Where's your mummy?' asks Francis, munching on an orange. The juice slides down her long fingers.

'In heaven,' I answer, pulling a date seed out of my mouth.

'Where is your dad?'

'In heaven too.' I point upwards.

They look at each other. 'Where's your husband? Where you babies?' both girls ask.

Good questions, I think, remembering my fruitless efforts to conceive. I wonder how to convey this to the girls, but I say, '*Bäyŋu.*' This is one of the first words I have learnt in Yolŋu *matha* this week.

As our nail polish dries, they tell me that they live just up the road and then in the middle of our conversation, Loretta says, '*Yow, marrtji.*'

'Sorry, I don't understand.'

'We…are…going,' she draws the words out.

'Oh, that was quick,' I say as they run down the stairs and disappear.

I wonder if this visit means everyone will come around. I hope so. I want to meet the people of this community.

I flit about wiping down benches, sweeping the kitchen floor and sing to my heart's content. I sing about dreams, about love, about the weather and I love to chant or hum a mantra. I dreamed of being a singer. Eons ago, I sang almost daily with my brother Johnnie. We talked often about starting a band. I sang on the grassy headland at Broken Head at a friend's wedding and in various singing groups. I'm uplifted and my mind clears when I sing.

After a productive day, I roll out my mat, stand with my feet together and place my palms in Anjali mudra over my heart centre. I'm not focusing so much on the pumping action of my heart, but I'm connecting with my inner feelings. In yoga, the image of a lotus flower opening and closing in the heart centre is often practised. In Anjali mudra, we bring the heels of the palms together and the fingers together, but the knuckles stay apart. The palms are apart like the bud of a lotus. I connect with my heart and the breath and open to what I can learn in my yoga practice and aspire for a calm mind. I take some time to connect with my breath and enjoy stillness.

From there, I move into Surya Namaska and from Ardho mukha svanasana, I step forward and hang in Uttanasana. Unrolling up into Tadasana, I find my centre again, stand still and watch the movement of my breath in my chest. From there, I move into my next sequence of standing postures, some seated postures, twists and maybe an inversion. In the heat, my body becomes light and fluid and, following an hour or so of postures, I sit with my breath for fifteen minutes then lie in Shavasana.

Where is your mummy, your babies, your husband? Thoughts of the day enter my mind. It's not the first time I have been asked these questions this week. It clearly mystifies the Yolŋu that I am alone. I wanted to reply, 'I don't know.'

I roll over and rest on my side, briefly reflecting on those deep losses I have endured, deaths of loved ones, separation from siblings, and the loss of potential motherhood. My ex-husband now lives thousands of kilometres over the ocean. We have very little contact. Disconcerting that one can live so intimately with another for almost thirteen years and yet return to being complete strangers again. Rain begins to spatter on the tin roof and I breathe it in like a cleansing shower.

For some years, it felt like my heart had abandoned me and for a while I wondered if it would return. If there's one thing I've learnt, though, it's that with each of these losses, something new has always emerged. And now, the new is presenting itself to me here on Milingimbi

Island in the form of the land and the Yolŋu people. The Yolŋu call this island Yurrwi and so shall I. I remember that though life had to change radically, I have wanted this experience since I was a young child.

Paulo Coelho said in his book *The Alchemist*,

> And when you want something, all the universe conspires in helping you to achieve it.

I wanted this, I followed the signs, and now I'm here and it is time to do some planning for school. I sit and place my hands on the 'earth' with my mind on my breath for another minute.

# 4

# Cyclone

A great Spirit Being of the Yirritja moiety of central Arnhem Land takes the form of a snake. The name of this snake cannot be spoken in everyday talk, only by the initiated inside the sacred ceremonial ground. When anyone sees one of these this species, they refer to it by the general term for snake, Bäpi. The Spirit Being is said to make lightening with its tongue, clouds with its breath and rain with its spittle. This happens when it emerges from its home and stands erect in the sky.

– Mamalunhawuy, Milingimbi, in *Australian Dreaming: 40,000 Years of Aboriginal History*, Jennifer Isaacs

Well, it's proving to be a bit of an adventure, Yurrwi Island. Last night, Tuesday, my ninth night living in a remote community, Stuart, his son Mitch, Bill the principal and Mark (another teacher) picked me up in the school troopie to go on a food pick-up. It was pouring with rain. In the dark, the huge red and white barge lit up the whole barge landing area with brilliant white lights. Perkins Shipping had arrived with food for everyone – well, for those who ordered it, and the shop. For me, it seemed a big event really.

Stuart in his usual inspired and cheerful way took us up to meet the captain. Fear shot through me as we climbed up a tiny ladder and walked along a skinny, slippery walkway in the hammering rain. I felt the force of the wind and rain on my face. My stomach churned as I crept along, thinking of all those hungry crocodiles lurking there below. I could feel them, or decided I could anyway. Soaked to the skin, we loaded box after box into the troopie and tuckshop van. I reflected on my order that will arrive next week. I wished I had added some Japanese soba noodles, seaweed and chocolate to it. This is all very exciting. I have never had to get my food off a barge before.

Needless to say, I slept like a log after the barge adventure.

The wind is wild. Rain is teeming down this March day, and it feels like the wet season to me. In March and April – *Midawarr* – daily storms are meant to be less frequent now but there can still be heavy rain with rolling thunder and lighting. The winds change direction. The north-west wind now becomes a north-east wind. It's a good time to catch fish like barramundi, and dugong and mud crabs. Plants are fruiting and towards the end of *Midawarr* will be ripe.

One minute the earth is bone dry, then drenched, then bone dry again. The change seems instant. The trail I take to school every day is very slushy. I walk through puddles that seem like streams by lunchtime and waterholes by home time. Well, that is an exaggeration. I have grown to love this tropical rain, its smell, its taste on my tongue and the sound of it drumming on my tin roof.

Rain is always welcome in this stifling heat. Warm tropical rain pelts down and then slows to a light drizzle. Just before it arrives, a ripple of air fans the sweat sliding down my limbs, bringing exquisite cool relief, momentarily. But damn it, the searing heat intensifies and is extra scorching immediately before and after the downfall. Hot steam rises up off the black tar road. Spots of black mould form on the walls at home and everything is damp with a musty smell. Mosquitoes multiply by the hundreds. Sweat constantly streams down my skin. In the rain as I walk, my clothes become instantly soaked, heavy and plastered to my skin, but somehow an umbrella seems pointless. I wonder if they will ever dry. I wonder a lot of things here in this new life on my island home.

Yesterday I arrived at school and the phone lines were down and there was no power. I walked into the staffroom and found this note written on the board by the principal:

Winds moving at 110 kilometres an hour. Cyclone expected in Darwin, Maningrida and possibly Milingimbi.

The room was empty of anyone to ask about it.

'Where are the kids?' I ask Boyukarrpi as we stand in an empty classroom.

'*Wäŋaŋur,*' she answers.

'At home?' I know this word now.

'*Yow. Wata ga wandirr, yindi*'. Big wind is coming,' she says.

'*Wata*,' I say, repeating a new word.

Today I arrive to find the word 'Cyclone' written on the board. I lean in closer, squinting my eyes to find more words either side of it that may have faded or been accidentally rubbed out. But no.

There are a few kids in the classroom so Boyukarrpi and I sing some songs. She leads them in a song about a *weṯi* running away from a hunter and I lead them in 'Where is Thumbkin' in English. They sing the Thumbkin song in both languages. I notice the kids call Boyukarrpi Gwenie. Wriggling and singing their lungs out, these children are so expressive and beaming with joy. I want to be an exciting on-the-ball teacher for them. I'm going to make some tangible resources. Boyukarrpi, Maṯay and I can make an assessment kit for their speaking and listening skills.

Bill and Marilyn visit our classroom. Bill stands stroking his beard and says, 'If the cyclone happens, we'll be picked up in the troopie and evacuated to where I'm not sure. Ramingining? There'll be no school tomorrow.'

'Perhaps,' adds Marilyn, 'all teachers need to be at school in the morning so we'll all be together if the cyclone hits.'

Intriguing, I think. I have no clue about the implications of this news. I have never been in a cyclone before. Right now, ignorance, as they say, is bliss.

I leave school and amble home. The sky is grey: the air, eerily still.

Stuart's son Mitch appears and cycles around me, skidding his bike to an abrupt stop. 'Ready for the cyclone, Mary?' he says, laughs and his head tosses back, curls on his head wild.

'How do I do that?' I ask but he zips ahead through a long puddle, the tyres on his bike causing a fountain of muddy spray.

I shrug, looking down at the mud on my Blundstones. Then it dawns on me: I need chocolate. I haven't had any since Byron Bay. I head for the shop. Kids are splashing about in the puddles. The green field looks so lush next to the red dirt, flooded road, like a watercolour painting. It doesn't take much to delight these children. I love this about Yolŋu, their light-hearted humour. I can learn from them.

'Mary, Mary, you Mary?' One of the girls wades through the water and hooks her thin arm around my waist. Her finger goes straight to my nose ring; it's very popular here on Yurrwi Island. She leans over and looks up my nose to see what's there.

Affection is another quality so easily shared here. '*Yow*, I am Mary.' I return the hug.

Water is up to my shins, drowning my long skirt.

'Where's your mummy?' She pulls at my hair, sliding her fingers down the length of it tightly to drain the water out of it.

Two other boys squeal and splash around, entangled in a water fight. I point to the sky. 'She is in heaven.'

I leave her standing with a bewildered look. I don't really know why I said that. I don't think Mum is in the sky, she is with me in my heart, always.

Anyway, I mutter to myself, I'm on a mission for cyclone supplies. I reach down wring out my skirt and empty my heavy boots of water, slide them back onto my saturated socks and scurry on.

I arrive back home with a Cherry Ripe, long-life milk and olive oil to bake vegies in and to use to massage my feet occasionally. I place the choccy on the top of the fridge, not in the fridge because I like melted chocolate. I drink a tall glass of water and sit on my yoga mat. The wind is starting to pick up now but I don't feel perturbed by it. I close my eyes and breathe deeply. I am calm and I feel safe.

'Cause I'm hearing rain beating on my tin roof, splashing on my windowpane,' I sing as I chop up pumpkin, parsnip and spuds, sprinkle mixed herbs on top and pop them on a baking tray in the oven.

Dogs bark outside. I take a deep breath. There is a rawness about life here that I already love: I can feel it in my bones. I put some rice on the boil and get on my mat for a while. I emerge out of Balasana, sit in a comfortable cross-legged position and practise Nadi Shodana, alternate nostril breathing. It balances the left and right hemispheres of the brain, nourishes the nervous system and is deeply calming. I noticed its effect immediately when I was a first-year-out teacher with a challenging class of Year Two students. I often practised alternate nostril breathing in the staffroom bathroom of the primary school I was teaching at. Even only five minutes of practice calmed me down and perked up my confidence to face the kids again. I need it now so I focus on a quiet smooth breath, using the gesture with my right hand to regulate the breath through the nostrils. After some minutes I lie in Shavasana and rest.

Smells of baked vegies permeate the air. I roll over onto my side, come up and sit for a moment with my hands on the floor. In the kitchen, I pop a spud into my mouth and arrange vegies, rice, a dollop of tahini, garnish of parsley on top and finally a sprinkle of sesame seeds.

With my back to the wall, I sit on the floor, a cushion at the edge of my spine, enjoying my dinner. My body feels relaxed but niggling thoughts begin to disturb my equanimity. What exactly am I meant to do when this cyclone hits? I am unsure. There is no one I can ask.

Geckos scurry along the skirting boards at a faster pace than usual. Perhaps they know what is going on; and the dogs haven't stopped yelping outside.

Niko is in the house on my left and Stuart is in the house on my right but the rain is beating down and I can't bring myself to go out in it. The phone line is down so I cannot even contact my family or friends down south. I wash up my dinner plate and put the leftovers in a bowl with a saucer on top. I exhale, look around and push the wooden table into the wall, then move some cups and a pot into the cupboards. I find three lime-green floating candles and some matches in the third drawer. I didn't think to buy more candles when I was in the shop.

A belly full of Cherry Ripe, I lie on my side on the bed reading an article on ESL on my computer. What I am discovering is that English is not really a second language here on Yurrwi Island but a third or even fourth language. Some of the kids speak more than one other Yolŋu language.

The whistling wild wind is starting to distract me now so I put my computer away in the wardrobe and sit up with my spine straight and focus on my breath and the palms of my hands. I intend for us all to be safe. I keep bringing my attention back to the sensations in my palms. They grow warmer.

After about thirty minutes, I lie down, fall asleep and doze in and out. Fleeting faces appear in my dream state. Mum. Dad.

Around one in the morning, a cracking thud on the roof, perhaps a tree branch, wakes me into an upright position. It's pitch black. The light I had left on is out. There is no power. I must get myself a bedside lamp or a decent torch. I fumble for the phone. It's still dead.

Quivering in the dark, I can barely hear the howling dogs now for the rain hammering on the roof. The moan of the wind grows loud. It fills me with dread. Soon it gets louder, whipping and roaring a haunting drone. I don't know what it will do. The house shudders. Branches scrape against the windows.

A light flashes through the window, slicing the darkness. I jump up, wondering if it's the troopie coming to evacuate me, but no. Momentarily I give in to my mind's terror. Will the roof be ripped off? What the hell am I doing here? My life was so calm before here. I can't believe I've only been here nine days and I'm in a cyclone. Yes, I wanted change but I don't think I really expected to be thrown into the unknown so deeply.

Barely breathing, I shakily light a lime-green candle but it blows out. I force myself to deepen my breath and begin to repeat a Sanskrit chant.

'Ommmm,' I start and then the familiar words and tone are immediately soothing. This simple mantra helps me to connect to Surya, the sun, and its life-giving qualities. By connecting the words, sound and feeling of the mantra on the light of the sun in my heart, it starts to settle my fear and calm my mind. I have always used chanting as a way to steady my mind and body. And I loved to chant it on the beach at sunrise as I walked barefoot to Broken Head headland. That life seems so far away now.

I repeat the mantra for courage really and to stop my mind running wild. I wonder what the Yolŋu are doing? Probably all snuggled together and having a laugh. They know how to do that. I wonder too if there is an ancient story about cyclones and what their significance may be for Yolŋu. I'm sure there must be one and I'd like to hear it.

A calm presence embraces me and Mum comes to mind. I cannot see her but smell a whiff of gardenia (her favourite flower, or one of them) and am held in her warm presence.

'You'll be okay, love,' she says. 'Go and sit in the bathroom. There'll be one more.'

'One more what?' I gasp.

I am reminded of times I spent during earthquakes in Japan. I was always told that the bathroom is the safest place in an earthquake.

I follow Mum's instructions and creep through the hallway in the dark, clutching my candles, matches and a woollen shawl I got in Ireland, even though it's not cold. I huddle in the bathroom but then decide I feel the toilet could be a safer bet so I crouch in the corner and light my candles. The wind roars outside but it's quiet in here. The flame's flickering shadows on the wall are comforting. I crunch on an apple and feel better. I don't know what is in apples but they always bring me calm. I keep watching my breath. Threads of the mantra hum in my mind.

The wild woolly wind perseveres, banging and clattering away, threatening to claim the roof. I remain hunched against the wall, dipping in and out of sleep until dawn. Relieved at the light of day and the roof still on, I slink back to bed and sleep for another hour. I'd love a cup of tea but there is no power to boil the kettle.

Standing outside the secondary classroom the next morning, Stuart and another teacher Jenny approach.

'How were you in the cyclone?' he asks.

'Fine. I meditated,' I answer, then burst into tears.

'It would be good to have a meeting about this,' says Jenny comfortingly.

Stuart reaches out his hand and lightly touches my shoulder, giving me the space to feel.

'I just didn't know what that wind was capable of and where it was heading,' I say. I appreciate his compassion.

Marilyn comes to see how I am doing today too. Everyone is kind, actually.

I enjoy the shrill of the phone ringing again and the boiling of the kettle in the house now that the lines are working. Aunt Margot is relieved to speak with me, as she had been trying to call and was worried. I ring the girls in Byron and they are off for a cocktail at Dish. Oh, for the life of Byron. Stuart rang to see if I was okay.

I survived the cyclone. It actually wasn't such a bad one apparently. I don't even know what category it was but those gusty winds did peak and that was scary enough for me. A few trees landed on rooves, causing some damage, but everyone is okay, or as far as I know they are. In my moments of terror last night, in my disorientated state I lumped all my fears together and decided that the choices I had made in life regarding work, relationships and, well, everything were wrong. I realise my harsh self-judgement came out of fear. Fear and panic can lie to you. I'm much clearer today. Thanks be for yoga and Mum.

Within the structure of the eight limbs of yoga are the *Yamas* and *Niyamas* They provide a guide for us to explore our behaviour and align it with harmony, a healthy body, a steady mind and our own internal strength, growing confidence in ourselves and our creations. This exploration helps me see myself clearly in daily life, to become aware of my attitudes, my response to my environment, to myself and to others. My new life here is giving me so many opportunities to be a witness and to grow.

# 5

# New friends

*Dhakal wäŋa ŋarraku*
Island home this [is] mine
Home of the Saltwater people

Cyclone week is over. It's Friday night, my first night out socially on Milingimbi Island. I'm at Stuart's yellow pole home. It's several metres away from my place. There is a mango tree between our houses. His son Mitch is here, Jenny, who is a teacher from school, and Maureen, a nurse from the clinic.

Before they arrived, Stuart and I sat and talked about our lives before Milingimbi. I admire Stuart's courage and his ability to communicate so clearly. He is very expressive and into creating authentic friendships. I find his openness as a man refreshing.

Jenny and Maureen soon arrive. Jenny has been working here for several years. She is tall with a beautiful face, high cheekbones, and seems very committed to her work and knowledgeable about the community. I assume I appear most ignorant to her and starry-eyed. Well, I am, I just got off the plane, but I hope to both contribute and learn something. I'm sure I can learn a lot from Jenny. Jon the music teacher at school and his wife Trish have talked about going out on their catamaran with Jenny too, which would be amazing.

Maureen has worked here for a while too, I think. Stuart's house has an identical layout to mine and he has some local art around the place and loads of great books like *The Native Born*, a selection of art and stories about artists from Arnhem Land. He is pottering around the kitchen making leek and potato soup and a rice dish with nuts and snow peas.

Mitch is making green jelly. I feel very comfortable here at Stu's place. It has a funky arty feel, like him.

After a lovely dinner and wild green jelly, we chat over a cup of tea. Stuart and Jenny are talking about all the bushwalks here on the island. I'm keen to do the one out past the airstrip to the billabong. Apparently, though, when there is sacred business, some of the tracks can be closed for months. I am intrigued by the thought of sacred business.

This humid Saturday morning, I mop the floors of the lounge room and kitchen, clean the bathroom, hang out some washing, plan some activities for the next week of school and relax. I really want to find balance within work, home, relationships, the environment and myself. Right now, though, I feel a lot of tension growing in my head. It reminds me of the time I met Mayrparr, the initiated man from the Katherine region, in Sydney in June 2002. 'Will you say yes to the spirit?' he had kept asking me. I had a very physical reaction to the experience.

Stuart comes over in the afternoon with two maps and two aerial photographs of Milingimbi Island. We spread the A3-sized laminated sheets on the wooden table in the lounge room and examine them.

Stuart's glasses rest on his chest, the cord holding them loops around his neck. 'Perhaps these pics will give you a perspective of where you are on the earth. The island is seven kilometres by eleven. Here we are.' He dons his glasses and points to a round yellow sticker on a section of houses and trees. *'Gätni* Camp and there's *Ḍarawundhu* or Bottom Camp where I was adopted,' he says.

'Oh, right on the beach?' I say.

'Yes, and there's *Ḍamuyani* or Top Camp and then *Ḍiltjiŋu*r or Bush Camp and *Mewa* or Army Camp – five camps with different yet interconnected clan groups. Yolŋu live here in Milingimbi, Yirrkala, Galiwin'ku, Ramingining, and speak several languages. The population here's around a thousand. There's the Arafura Sea and we're about two hundred kilometres west of Nhulunbuy. That's not far from Yirrkala where you first visited the Arnhem Land.'

'Thank you so much, Stu. Much clearer,' I say, running my finger along the map of red dusty roads shrouded with green scrub and corrugated-iron houses. I remember loving looking down on all this scenery from the charter plane the day I flew here.

Across the road from my place lives a large family. Jo lives there, a tall lean minister with plump cheeks and grey curly hair. Jo has the role of council chairperson.

I look at Milingimbi on another map. It is a tiny dot, one of a string of the Crocodile Islands floating off the top of Australia. I read the top right corner of the map out loud.

A remote and largely inaccessible region of exquisite beauty and surprising contrasts, Arnhem land covers almost 97 000 square kilometres. It is bounded to the East by the Gulf of Carpentaria, to the North by the Arafura Sea, by Roper River to the south and Kakadu National Park to the west. Access is strictly controlled by a permit system administered by the North(ern) Land Council.

'Wow! How did I end up here?' I laugh, still amazed by the radical shift.

'Well, let's go here,' Stuart says, pointing to Damuyani. 'Well, actually further than here, to Rocky Point.'

'I'm ready for my first walk on Milingimbi Island,' I smile, grabbing my hat and water bottle and pulling on my Blundstone boots.

Witney, Stuart's adopted dog, walks with us. She is black with a tan face and gentle eyes and I think she just began to hang out with Stuart and go for walks with him. I would love a dog too.

We are at Rocky Point, but I am sure it must have an Indigenous name. A cluster of brown rocks leads to a vast expanse of ocean; green mangroves grow along the edge of the sea. I take a deep breath and enjoy the salty smell. I just want to jump in, though. Thoughts of crocodiles and stingers squash my desire.

'It's an interesting relationship you grow with the sea when you don't swim in it,' says Stuart.

My skin prickles and my heart sinks somewhat. I love my relationship with the sea just as it is; I love the rejuvenation of a jump in the ocean. I spot a group of Yolŋu fishing on their tin boat. I need to soften and open to new ideas but I can feel myself holding on to the way life has been.

'This place is very calming and healing,' says Stuart.

I close my eyes, breathe out and tune in to what Stuart is referring to. A calm quiet does exist here and my body feels grounded yet serene.

We amble through the Christian cemetery. Brightly coloured plastic flowers adorn the graves. We stop at two sandy river mouths with clear water.

'These are good fishing spots,' says Stuart, taking a swig from his water bottle.

Jon the music teacher's lone catamaran docks out further in the sea in the other direction.

I pull off my Blundstones and we soak our feet in the warm water. Stuart informs me about the millions of sand flies here and the huge welts that some people experience as a result of their bites. I am not looking forward to them at all and hope when the time comes they are allergic to me. I take a deep breath and enjoy the sight of the lush grass and magnificent trees around us. The huge tamarind tree that impressed me on my arrival here at Milingimbi is further up the road, close to the sea.

Dogs snarl and rush out of the corrugated-iron houses onto the road before us. Witney remains unperturbed by them.

'The dogs here are territorial and you need to be assertive with them, Mary.'

'*Sha*!' He yells at them. 'Say *Sha*,' directs Stuart, stepping closer to protect me.

'*Sha*,' I yell. I hope I learn this quickly. With a snarling dog before me, I seem to go a bit numb.

As we arrive back at Stuart's house and walk up the stairs into his kitchen, I am aware of a strange headachy feeling. Again, Stuart brings out some great books about Milingimbi and Ramingining art and culture. I am excited about the living culture here.

'Did you settle in quickly here?' I ask Stuart.

'Yes,' he says with a smile on his face. 'After all I'd been through, I felt loved and embraced. I was adopted after only three days of being here. I knew my soul was in the right place.' Tears came to his eyes in gratitude for his experience.

'The day before Milingimbi rang me, I had asked my soul what it wanted,' I confide. 'Now I'm here, I know my soul wants to be here but I have some great resistance and sometimes feel sick but I don't know why…fear of the unknown?'

'Mary,' Stuart holds my gaze intently, 'you've travelled to this remote island alone, and you must honour the courage it's taken you to be here now.'

'I don't feel very courageous.' I bite my lip.

'We must be as authentic as we can with what we feel.'

I nod in appreciation.

He reaches over and puts the kettle on. 'The next thing to do is to take you down to Bottom Camp to meet the women and they'll take you hunting.'

'Yes, I agree.' I perk up.

'They don't bother about niceties, they'll just get on with it and expect you to as well.' He plonks the tea bags into two blue cups.

'No, I bet they won't,' I smile.

Jonathan rings. 'How are you doing? Hey, there are about ten of us over here in Yirrkala who'd love to do yoga. Why don't you come on over and teach some?' he suggests.

'I'd love to,' I say and get off the phone inspired to go to Yirrkala one weekend, but also want to start classes here at Milingimbi.

More people are coming into my life now. After my Saturday afternoon with Stuart, I go down to the beach with some of the teachers. There are Yolŋu people here holding candles for world peace. We sit on the shore, staring at the moon, almost full, shimmering across the water. The candles flicker and I wish I had my camera with me. Apparently, this peace vigil started in New Zealand and is happening in all parts of the world and here we are on remote Yurrwi Island, being a part of it.

Down by the ocean as I breathe in the salty air, some of the Yolŋu women talk to me about how their elders grew up here on the mission that was established here in approximately 1923. Until this day, I have never known anything much about this history. I certainly wasn't taught about it at school. I am intrigued to learn that in fact some Yolŋu were living in the Milingimbi region before the mission. Some of the older men's ancestors lived on Ḏipirri, a place a boat ride away from Milingimbi, and some others retreated to the bush on Milingimbi when the mission came.

Warmbirrirr walks me home and I flick through Stuart's copy of the book *The Native Born*. I've ordered a copy for myself and it's on its way. I find the words of Tom Djawa, born in 1905, a senior of the Gupapuyŋu clan in Milingimbi. In an interview by Michael Christie in the 1970s, he shared,

> You and I, we really are strangers, we belong to a faraway place. I think the mission brought us here and we stayed here, and had children and we want to go back to our places but seem unable to do so because we would go and then long to come back to Milingimbi. This is because we would think, 'that is the place where we were born and had our children'.

I take a deep breath and sigh it out at the complexities that exist for Yolŋu.

I met Pipa, a nurse, down by the ocean at the peace ceremony last night. I had a quiet morning this Sunday morning, filled with cups of tea and a couple of hours of school planning. Pipa and I met again this afternoon. Tall with white-blonde short hair, she wears funky clothes and knows Jonathan in Yirrkala. Adopted by some Yolŋu women, she excitedly describes to me how they took her hunting mud crab. We had a great talk about our similar cyclone experiences and she is very interested in healing too. Sitting in the shade of the back deck of her blue corrugated-iron house, the nurse's house, we munch on a great salad with lettuce, carrots, tomato and pawpaw for lunch – yum. We had hoped we'd go hunting but ended up going to the football at the oval with some of her Yolŋu family.

As I stroll back to my place, the words 'When it's time, my family will come and they will be the right family for me' are in my head. I take a deep breath in, exhale and surrender to the unknown. Right now I'm so glad to be alive.

# 6

# Adoption

We lived travelled and hunted together, attended many ceremonies and finally he adopted me as his elder brother.

— Donald Thompson

It's Sunday, 23 March 2003. I stand in my Arnhem kitchen leaning into the mottled, dreary bench, staring through the mist of steam rising up from the plastic kettle. My legs are still clammy from the brisk walk I've just had through the bush with Stuart. As I left for my walk today, I discovered one of my sandals at the bottom of the stairs chewed to bits by a mangy dog. Beads of sweat form on my forehead. I am sipping hot tea from my blue cup with the yellow daisy on the side. 'Hot tea will always cool you down,' my mum used to say.

I gaze through the wire mesh window at the green leaves on the tree outside. I love looking at trees, the moment of stillness and stability they offer, and I love my big red corrugated pole house, despite how difficult it is to keep the dust at bay.

My mind wanders to school. I've been here about three weeks now. I smile as I think of Friday when our whole class walked down to the beach to collect shellfish. The students held my hands and excitedly showed me different types of shells containing food. I came alive in the presence of their dynamic spirit and zest in the world beyond the classroom.

I reach into the fridge and pull out my latest cooling system, a spray pump bottle with water and a few drops of the essential oil of lavender added to it. I've written the words 'stay cool' on a piece of masking tape and stuck it around the purple bottle. I close my eyes and revel in the coolness of lavender spray on my hot cheeks.

'Mary. *Yapa* Mary.' A voice meets my ears.

I head over and push open the ripped wire door and step onto the wooden veranda. The planks sink under my feet and I wonder how much longer they will hold. I look down the stairs but I can't see anyone.

'Where are you?'

'Down here.' Jessie Murarrgirarrgi, a teacher from school, is squatting on the brown earth, hauling a long green vine from among the tufts of grass. Swirls of blue white and orange on her dress flash against the green of the lawn and her black skin.

'*Yapa*,' she calls me.

Yapa means sister. I have heard that yapa is at times used as a generic term until we know our kinship name. The day I met Jessie in the school office, she stopped, looked at me and sang, 'I am sixteen going on seventeen'. I didn't really know why she sang it, but instantly I discovered how cheeky and playful she is.

'What are you doing, Jessie?'

'Visiting you and picking these yams.' She plucks a plump orange potato out of the ground and follows the line of the green vine, tugging until she finds another.

'Yams? I didn't know I had yams.'

'I'll cook them on the fire later and eat them for tea.' She has a big smile, her hair falls down in thick black curls, her cheeks are round and a glint shines in her big dark eyes.

'Come and sit with me, *Yapa*.' Jessie tilts her head and pouts her lips to the side. This is a Yolŋu facial expression, a way of pointing that I have noticed these last weeks.

We nestle into the grass on my front lawn, right on the edge of the tar road. Frangipani blossoms perfume the air, as the white and yellow flowers fall silently to the ground.

An ochre-coloured jeep pulls up with the school librarian, Susan, at the wheel. Jessie stands and opens the creaking back door. Two women sit on the ripped black seat on the left side of the jeep as I clamber in. At their feet a bunch of long-speared grass is neatly tied into bundles. I step around this pandanus and sit opposite the women and Jessie climbs in, closing the door, and sits next to me.

'We've been out in the bush, *Yapa*, collecting pandanus,' says Jessie. 'Come to our home by the sea.'

The two old women, wearing bright floral dresses, sit comfortably in their fleshy bodies and hold me in their gaze. I relax in their presence, their ease. A wave of stillness washes over me. Momentarily, I link in with the fabric of their natural connectedness to the earth, spirit and each other.

'This is Elizabeth Yibi Yibi and Muwalkmuwuy. We are all *yapa*s,' says Jessie with her arm resting around my shoulder.

Yibi Yibi has strong shoulders and full lips. Muwalkmuwuy is the older of the two. Her wispy hair is snow white.

'Oh, my mother's name was Elizabeth and it's my middle name,' I say, thinking of my mother for a second. I wonder how she would have felt about me finally living in a remote community at the top of Australia. But for now, there is nothing more to say. No need to fill the air with words.

'*Yow, Yapa,*' the women say.

The jeep stops by a large *djambaŋ* tree. With its thick trunk and wide branches, it casts generous shade that breaks the incessant heat. We climb out and subtle currents of breeze come up from the blue-green sea and puff lightly on my skin, cooling me. A large cloth is spread in the shade of the tree.

Susan takes a purple cabbage out of her bag and starts chopping it up to make purple dye. Jessie collects twigs and sticks and builds a fire. She blows on a tiny flame and throws on more twigs. I watch the flames grow high; the heat from them is strong on my face. Then I look up at the big black crows squawking in the tree.

Muwalkmuwuy has smooth skin and a plump face with round cheeks like Jessie's. She looks me in the eye and points up to a sleek black bird. '*Wäk*, crow! That's my mother looking down on us.'

Muwalkmuwuy divides the pandanus spears into two bundles and tucks one under her pink and blue skirt. Gently, she selects a long spear and using her fingernail, slices away each side of it, leaving a fine strip for weaving.

'It's time to weave baskets,' Jessie announces.

This old lady Muwalkmuwuy is not saying much in English and I am glad. I wish I could speak with her in Yolŋu language. Her smile is generous and encouraging.

Elizabeth Yibi Yibi sits. I am slightly intimidated by her. I hope I never cross her. A thin line of grey smoke curls up from her Winfield Red cigarette and swirls around her strong featured face. Her brow is deeply furrowed and grey wavy hair is pulled back high off her forehead. She stares at me for what seems like a long time. My skin prickles in response to her steady intent look.

'Where's your husband?' She takes a long drag of her cigarette.

'I'm divorced.' The words come out more easily these days.

'Where your parents live?' She stubs the cigarette out on the ground.

'They are dead.' I look away for a second at Muwalkmuwuy stripping pandanus.

'*Djamarrkuḻi*'?'

I know this word from school. 'No,' I answer.

'*Yuwalk? Bäyŋu?*' She raises an eyebrow.

'*Bäyŋu*,' I repeat. I no longer react to these questions.

The women are eyeing me and speaking in a low tone with each other in Yolŋu *matha*.

I sit still, watching the old woman's fingers on the pandanus. For once, I have no desire to seek elaborate conversation. I have no interest in giving my life story, no need to explain what has brought me here to this remote island. I am at ease in this silence. I am relieved by it.

'Elizabeth Yibi Yibi wants to adopt you,' pipes up Jessie, her cheeks round as she flashes another smile. 'You will be our *yapa*.'

'Wow, how amazing! What should I say?' I look at Elizabeth Yibi Yibi, who is smiling at me now.

'*Manymak*,' says Jessie.

'*Manymak*,' I repeat.

'She has a name for you, *Yapa*. She will share her own name with you. You are our sister: Elizabeth's and mine. Muwalkmuwuy is our elder sister,' she confirms again, pointing to the weaver.

Was this all planned, I wonder? 'Okay, wow, *manymak*,' I say, sensations stirring in my heart.

'*Yow, Yapa*, I call you Yibi Yibi part two, *ŋarra* (I) Yibi Yibi part one,' says Elizabeth.

'Yibi Yibi. What does that mean?'

'Long-neck turtle, *Yapa*.'

'*Manymak, manymak* very much.' I say, smiling.

Jessie begins to sing. She has a melodic voice.

Elizabeth Yibi Yibi looks at me, aligning her arm with mine and she says, 'Same skin.'

My arm is so white next to her black one, yet she says we have the same skin.

In this moment, I am welcomed into the Gupapuyŋu tribe. My moiety is Yirritja, my *mälk* Baŋaditjan. My *waŋarr*: *Gurrutjutju*, *Wurrpan*, *Gapu*, *Guku*, *D̪errk*, *Men̪d̪uŋ* and *Marrŋu*.

I look out past Yibi's yellow house on the shoreline. A lone tin boat is bobbing up and down on the bright blue-green ocean.

'*Yow, ŋändi*.' I'm realising *yow* can mean hello or yes, and *manymak* can be used as good or thank you.

I take my eyes off the boat and see a young woman smiling at me, her cheeks round like my sister's.

She says, 'I call you *ŋändi*. You call me *waku*.'

Several more *waku*, all women, walk over from surrounding houses and come to me, shaking my hand, touching my shoulder. One *waku* is Yibi Yibi's daughter Vanessa. An old man steps toward me. He is tall with white hair, a weathered face, white beard, baseball cap and checked shirt. He reaches his hand out and looks into my eyes.

'This is Jo Djembaŋu. Call him *wäwa*,' Elizabeth Yibi Yibi says proudly of her brother.

'Hello, *wäwa*.'

*Wäwa* takes my hand. His eyes smile into mine. Unexpected tears spring up in my eyes.

'I've adopted you into a *yindi'* family,' says Elizabeth Yibi Yibi.

*'Yow, yindi', Yapa, manymak,'* I say with a smile.

Susan offers me a ride home but I decide to walk.

'Jo is an important elder,' she says. 'It's quite a family you've been adopted into.'

'Thank you,' I say, feeling excited about going hunting and weaving with my family.

I walk home slowly, dazed yet renewed. The feeling I experienced out in the community today was very different to the feeling at school. Sitting with Yolŋu, I feel unaffected by time. I pass the old mud-brick church, and a few palm trees. Yolŋu sit outside the shop chatting and smoking cigarettes.

Kids laugh and eat ice cream. 'Mary, Mary,' they call as I pass by.

Something in me has shifted deeply. There is a profound sense of relief. At last, at last, at last are the words in my head, though I'm not exactly sure why.

Where is your husband? Yibi's words ring in my head, taking me back in time once more to a bar I worked at in Sydney while I was dancing away my days. The minute Shaun had stood at the bar asking me about my Claddagh ring, 'Mary, here is your Irish husband' were the words in my head. We fell in love. It seemed natural to be with an Irish man. My own roots are Irish. I did Irish dancing for eight years as a child and we all spoke to each other in Irish accents at home on a regular basis, though none of us had ever been to Ireland. St Patrick's Day was a very special day in our lives every year. Not the correct components to make me Irish, I guess, but I always felt in my soul that I was.

Shaun was a great gift in my life after the losses I had experienced. We shared some wonderful years together but apparently we were not meant for forever. Once again, my life would radically change. Despite our fiery clashes at times, our adventurous spirits and joy united us and emanated through our lives together. I dwelled in the ethereal realms and Shaun was my rock, solid, grounded in the earth, practical yet intuitive as well. In the beginning, our differences didn't matter. In fact, I was happy we could be different and be together. But then the divide took over and we could no longer live within it.

# 7

# Walkabout

What you see when you stand in the Australian bush depends on who you are.

– James Vance Marshall

A whole day has passed since my adoption into the Gupapuyŋu tribe. This evening is cooler than lunchtime and I'm sitting at the top of the concrete stairs that go down into my large backyard with its tragic clothesline. I'm content now to open the door with the three steel bolts and be outside. In fact, a tradesman will come soon and remove those bolts. Yes! That feels right. No bolts required. I'm happy to have a lock on the door, but three bolts? No. My meagre garden is in the white polystyrene box next to me. Sprigs of parsley and tiny tufts of rocket push up through the soil.

I scoop mouthfuls of red split-pea dhal into my mouth and look out beyond my backyard into the darkness. Not far from the frangipani tree, the light from a street lamp shines on the tar road, creating a glow where the Yolŋu sit and play cards. A white ute pulls up next to the circle and a man with grey hair leans out the window to talk. Shouts of laughter ring out into the night.

I look up to a sky sprinkled with glistening stars. I like being outside and watching Yolŋu people go by, kids playing, mangy dogs skulking around. So far this evening, I have not been bitten by sand flies or mozzies. One of the women on the road looks up and gives me a quick wave. I wave back. We are slowly becoming familiar with each other.

I recall the words that ran through my head after my adoption: 'At last, at last, at last,' and I remember myself as a teenager, on the blue and green cradle swing. Dad had erected a swing set in the shade of the two thick-trunked liquidambar trees in our backyard in Sydney. I see myself curled on my side, knees bent into my chest, reading *Walkabout* yet again. The book compelled me. I was completely still as I read, and soon I was unaware of the trees. It was as if they disappeared and the swing dissolved beneath me. I was transported to the red earth and what was taking place there. Two children scrambling like ants on the massive sand dunes, dry-lipped and windblown, trying to find their way across the desert to their uncle's place in Adelaide.

*Walkabout* is a book about two children lost in the Australian desert after their father tried to murder them. They escape and then the father shoots himself in the head and the girl takes her younger brother away from the scene and they become lost.

I loved that the character's name is Mary. It could be me. I imagined myself a white girl who meets the Aboriginal boy in the Australian bush. But the Mary in the book is unable to be at ease with the bush boy as her young brother is and as I read the words I wanted to be more like him.

'Arkooloola,' the bush boy grinned.

Together, the black boy and the white girl pushed through the tangle of fern until they came to a tiny pear-shaped basin carved out of a solid rock by the ceaseless drip of water. Beside the basin Peter was flat on his face, his head, almost up to his ears, dunked in the clear translucent pool. In a second Mary was flat out beside him. Both children drank and drank and drank.

The bush boy drank only a little. Soon he got to his feet, climbed a short way up the cairn, and settled himself on a ledge of rock. Warm in the rays of the setting sun, he watched the strangers with growing curiosity. Not only, he decided, were they freakish in appearance and clumsy in movement, they were also amazingly helpless: untaught: unskilled, utterly incapable of fending for themselves: perhaps the last survivors of some peculiarly backward tribe. Unless he looked after them, they would die. That was certain. He looked at the children critically, but there was in his appraisal no suggestion of scorn.

It was his people's way to accept individuals as they were, to help, not to criticize, the sick, the blind and the maimed.

I had stared up at the quivering lime-green liquidambar leaves and wanted to know more about that bush boy. I wanted to know what he knew.

The bush boy broke off the yam; then, following another skein of underground foliage, he tracked down a second. Fascinated, Peter watched. He got the idea quickly. Soon he too had sought out and pulled up a third *worwora*.

A 'shaboobili' (the nickname we gave the spikey round green seed pod from the liquidambar tree as children) fell from the tree and hit me on the head. I was back on my swing in the suburbs of Sydney, rocking slightly in the breeze. I remember back then as a teenager wondering if *Walkabout* was a true story or not. I was barely given an education about Australia's Aboriginal people at school. There were parts of the book I did not understand. I didn't know if the story was respectful or even if the language used was correct.

I was moved by the way the boy walked in the steps of the old people and became one with the land, or at least that's how I interpreted it. What the book did trigger in me was a desire to connect with the original people of the land I was born in. I became determined that one day I would go to live with the Aboriginal people and spend time with them in their world hunting and learning some of their ways. I had no idea where they were or how I would go to them. But I knew I would.

I also watched the movie that was based on the book. The most important inspiration for me was the sense of mystery and deep culture that I got from the boy and the land. Something of deep stillness and ritual awoke in me. I knew the vast country I was born into held something so strong but I didn't know what. When I read the book, I understood that it was the Aboriginal people who knew the land and held this knowledge.

My desire to spend time with the original people and my love of children was strong enough for me to study to become a schoolteacher. In addition, I dreamed of the experience of being able to communicate without words, to dwell in a timeless way of life that originates from nature.

I now sit motionless on my Yurrwi Island doorstep, drawing the night air deep into my lungs. For a long time, this desire to live with Aboriginal people was some forgotten dream buried deep down. But here I am all these years later, living with the Yolŋu people. I am transformed by this experience. How powerful our dreams are, even when we lose sight of them. The events that brought me here have not unfolded in a linear or logical fashion. I followed the synchronistic cues. This life has been dwelling inside me all along, year after year, simply waiting to unfold; waiting for me to say 'yes' to it.

# 8

# Mayrparr

> Tribal Voice
> Within each of us there is a voice of truth. Call it intuition, insight, knowing.
> As a child, mine was loud and scary. It spoke things I didn't want to hear.
> It speaks to me daily.
> I have a choice. Do I listen? Or do I ignore?
> In the Yolŋu world, I witness a strong tribal voice.
> Yolŋu hear it, they listen, they know it.
> And they live from it.

And speaking of saying 'yes', I am reminded of the day I met Mayrparr in Sydney, after my first visit to Yirrkala in 2001.

Soft waves rippled onto the wooden boat ramp where I waited at my friend Fiona's house in Bayview. Annabelle anchored her tinny and extended her hand to aid me onto the gently rocking boat. We cruised over to her home on Scotland Island. Flowers and gum trees dotted the coastline. It was hard to believe it was the city of Sydney, as I felt I was in the middle of the bush. There were plenty of trees, but there were spaces filled with yachts and houses along the way too, then clumps of native greens.

The woody scent of my childhood reassured me. I was calm and at ease, whizzing along in the tinny and taking pleasure in the light wind and water spray on my face. Annabelle pointed to specific Aboriginal sites, and their power drew me in. I drank in her words, hungry for knowledge. A well-known sensation stirred in my belly, that feeling that something important was about to happen. We climbed the stone stairs through native bushland and entered her island home.

We were barely in the door when she said, 'This is Mayrparr, an Aboriginal man from up north.'

My skin jumped at the sight of him.

'Yes, I look different from the people you would have seen up north because I'm from the Katherine region,' he explained.

'No, I jumped because I've seen you in my dreams,' I replied.

'Excuse me, I'm impatient, we must talk.' Mayrparr began to fire questions at me about my first time in Arnhem Land. His face was round, his skin black and smooth and head thick with black curls. 'So, you know something?' his gaze seared through me, testing me.

I shrugged and scratched my neck, feeling somewhat under scrutiny in the conversation.

'Why did you leave? You shouldn't have left. You have to go there.'

'I can't just walk in there.' I remember hearing the words escape my mouth.

'It's your land,' he had said.

The familiar sensation I had on the boat began to coil in my belly again.

'Now go there and spend time there, go to the women. I've been initiated,' he urged.

I knew what he was saying was true. I was in the presence of an extremely intuitive man, a traditional man, an initiated man no less.

A serious look crossed his face. 'Did you receive healing up there?'

'Well, I found it a very healing experience!'

'No! What you had was a spiritual experience, not a healing.'

'Isn't a spiritual experience healing?' I dared ask.

'Have I offended you?' he asked.

'No, I'm just interested to understand the distinction you make between healing and spirituality.'

Our conversation was food for my soul. There it was yet again, the pull to Arnhem.

'I'm sorry to say this, but you will be very accepted by the Aboriginal people,' he continued.

Why be sorry, I am thinking. What a privilege.

'You left Arnhem too soon, you were about to come into your full power, you must go back.'

'I went with an open heart, tried to expect nothing. I didn't want to push.'

'Good, you went with an open heart and had a spiritual experience.' He stood very still and held my attention in his gaze.

'I had a dream when I was sleeping on the beach some distance from Yirrkala,' I told Mayrparr. 'Perhaps it wasn't even a dream but anyway a large serpent appeared above me, it stared into me then it slid into my belly.'

I remember that night so vividly, snuggled in my sleeping bag on the sand, nourished by warm crackling flames under billions of shining stars. Soothed by the sound of gentle waves splashing on the shore, I wanted to keep gazing up into the night's beauty, wishing on the stars that were shooting out of the sky but I just couldn't keep my eyes open. I fell asleep and lulled into a vivid lucid dream state. A giant, thick-bodied serpent permeated the sky, its skin covered with a multitude of designs, dots, ablaze with vibrant colours. Reds, browns, ochres, white. The one eye I could see was closed. Tingles of fear ran through my blood, my eyes fixed on the snake. Then its eye sprang open and peered intently into me and slowly it slithered: coiling out of the sky it slinked down into my belly, where it curled up and lay to rest. 'Hah!' A strange jolt of shock burst from low in my throat. I could not move. Awake, asleep, awake, what was I? My skin and blood buzzed, spirited, alive. I found my breath within the pounding of my heart and encouraged it to deepen. I lay locked in this experience, every cell pulsing. Finally, dawn woke. My eyes widened to a magnificent pink horizon. The huge burning orange ball of sun rose out of the salt water. I remained motionless, in a trance-like state, a deep space of equanimity.

'That was spirit trying to contact you,' said Mayrparr. 'That was a point of contact. There are several. Did you know that?'

'No,' I had replied, feeling light-headed.

'That was a very significant dream. You must spend time with the people and they will open to you.'

An air of relief rushed through me as though some long yearning had been met and understood.

'One day of sun is equal to eleven years. I know that you had a relationship for at least eleven years and it delayed your spiritual growth and spirit wants to know if you are ready to accept them. Are you ready to accept them? Will you say yes to the spirit?' Mayrparr was referring to my marriage with Shaun that had just ended. For me, my marriage had been an important sharing as it reconnected me with my Irish roots and was, for a large part of it, a time of love and sharing.

'Will you say yes to the spirit?' Mayrparr repeated sternly.

'Yes,' I found myself saying. 'Yes.'

'I hope you don't mind me telling you these things. I've been initiated.'

Hearing Mayrparr's words again hit me deep in my core.

'Thank you, I am honoured that you share, Mayrparr,' I said despite my growing angst.

'The women with children will teach you many things,' he added.

'The women and children were very healing on my last trip,' I replied.

Mayrparr spoke of Kakadu and the healing waters. He said that if I went there I would be taught about the reproductive organs.

'One woman I know who went there could not conceive. Then she swam there and conceived a child.'

I had told Mayrparr nothing of my life, but he knew me already.

'You must go back and receive your totem, then you will be in your full power and then you can come back,' he added.

Mayrparr went on to explain some of the other experiences I'd had in Arnhem Land. He was blunt and quite urgent in his delivery.

'You people think these kinds of situations are coincidences but it's simply the spirit guiding us.'

Then Mayrparr's manner softened and he looked at me and said, 'Wanjina will guide you, Wanjina, face with ears, eyes, but no mouth because Aboriginal people listen but do not always need to speak. Find a picture of Wanjina and you must connect with the female spirit of Wanjina.' Once again, Mayrparr held my gaze and asked, 'Will you say yes to the spirit?'

'Yes.' I looked back to him. I felt breathless, dizzy, and knew I needed to leave in order to digest the conversation.

After joining Annabelle in a healing circle for a woman in need, I crossed the water back to Fiona's house and crawled into bed, shaking with a mixture of sensations; relief, uncertainty, gratitude and sheer terror churned inside me.

What have I said 'yes' to? This question scratched out of my voice, waking me up in a hot sweat.

Since Scotty had introduced me to Arnhem Land in the first place, I called him to tell him about the day. 'What have I said yes to, Scotty?'

'Some pretty heavy shit, Mary, some pretty heavy shit!'

On my return to Byron Bay, I shared this story with my friend Leanne as we sat on her beautiful veranda, looking out to Lennox Head, drinking a cup of tea.

She jumped up, ran to her bookshelf and plucked off a book with a picture of Wanjina in it. 'This is Wanjina,' she said.

I read the words:

There was a time when this earth – he made earth and sea and everything. This is Wanjina – he made people. Wanjina is Wanjina. He gave Man to live in this earth, for this world, the Tribal country. He put the Wanjina in the cave for him to remember this Wandjina, to follow his Laws,to go about the right ways.

Wanjina he said,You must believe Wanjina. If you won't believe in Wanjina you won't live. This is because Wanjina gave us that Law to follow. And then he says, I give you this land and you must keep your Tribal land. You can't touch somebody's Land because it is your body, and your body is right here, and the Aborigines believe his body is his own Tribal land.

– Albert Barunga, Mawajum, *Australian Dreaming: 40,000 Years of Aboriginal History,* Jennifer Isaacs

Through my connection with Wanjina, I was led to the book *Wandjuk*

*Marika*, nestled between books on Quinkins (spirit people) in a second-hand bookshop in Byron Bay.

Before my dear Kiwi friend Jacqueline passed away in Sydney, I had asked her, 'How will I know when you're with me after you've gone?'

'The Quinkins,' she whispered on her deathbed, 'You'll see the Quinkins and the Willy Wagtail.'

In that time after my first trip to Arnhem, I was restless; something needed to change in my life. Certainly a lot of radical change had occurred already in those last few years. I had gone from a marriage break-up and infertility, from the loss of my home and business in Sydney to an intensive nine-month yoga teacher training in Byron Bay. It was the best place for me to grow through the hurt and cultivate new friends in the yoga world. I loved teaching yoga and was still seeing clients in Sydney, but a profound change was evolving deep within me. Meeting Mayrparr had brought back that incredible depth of connection I had had in my brief time in Yirrkala.

I reflected on memories of travelling through the Arnhem bush. I could almost still smell the scent of smouldering charcoal from campfires as it permeated the air. I thought of a conversation I'd had with a Yolŋu woman as we bumped along the red earth road in the troopie. How strong I felt her spirit was. One child slept with her head on my shoulder, the other curled up in my lap. This had melted my heart open after the grief I had been through back in New South Wales and it felt so familiar, as if I had come home. After only a few experiences of collecting honey with the elder's wife, cooking fat yams and oysters in a crackling fire on the beach and melting in the hot afternoons, I knew I must return.

I'm thankful for the synchronistic meetings with Scotty and Jonathan. Engaging in these events gives me a sense of a bigger picture unfolding, one that I cannot imagine, and now Mayrparr has been totally direct about what is coming up next.

I still have that picture of Wanjina dear Leanne gave me. Now it's on the back of my bedroom door here at Milingimbi. I stare at the picture of Wanjina, at the round head, big eyes, no mouth. It's true, the Yolŋu don't have any need to fill the air with unnecessary chatter. I gaze again at the photo. Ancient: familiar yet unfamiliar. With respect, I ask permission to call in the feminine essence of Wanjina. I ask her to guide me. A visceral surge of life force always flushes through my cells as I ponder Wanjina.

I wonder what's next.

# 9

# Magic Yapa

> The privilege of a life time is being who you are.
> – Joseph Campbell

I amble along the black tar road this afternoon, sun shining in a cloudless sky, camera slung over my shoulder. Photography was my major work in art when I studied to become a teacher. I dreamed of being a photographer back then and now this passion for taking pictures has unexpectedly reignited here in Arnhem Land. I edge my way into a shallow pond just off the road; the water is soft and warm on my ankles. This pond nestled close to the paperbarks forms during the wet season. It is starting to disappear now, though, as *Dharratharramirr* season (May–August) unfolds. It's still hot, but the nights are getting cooler and there are more snakes around. Soon, parts of the bush will be burned to the ground. There are still some purple waterlilies growing, though, and dragonflies dance on lime-green lily pads. I lean forward to photograph the pale lilac petals. In times gone by, the Yolŋu ate the roots of these plants.

I walk a few minutes further along the road to the island's one and only brick building, the shop, and run into Pipa outside the health clinic. We stroll together along the sand by the sea. It's pretty. The water is so clear. Green mangroves steeped in grey mud cluster along the edge of the blue-green water.

Down at the *djambaŋ* tree, old *Yapa* Muwalkmuwuy sits quietly on the earth, wispy white hair lightly touching her smooth-skinned face, round eyes focused as her long fingers delicately manoeuvre the curved needle, threading brown, yellow and natural coloured strips of pandanus together. She seems unaffected by the heat and the incessant squawking of crows fighting over some morsel nearby. Her full attention is on interlacing each string perfectly, so that the basket will be strong and won't fall apart. Pipa sits down next to her and I wander over to Jessie's and find her in her garden. In the last week while I was in Darwin for a holiday, she has planted lots of flowers and palms.

It feels like I just got here really, so I wasn't planning to go anywhere until June, but Stuart and Mitch encouraged me to come away for a break and so I did. In Darwin, I bought Jessie a little journal. I have written Jessie's journal on the cover and stuck on a photograph of us together at sunset.

'What are you doing here?' The sharp tone of Jessie's voice shocks me.

'Visiting,' I reply.

'Do you like my garden?' She beams a big smile now and I relax.

'*Yow*, it's beautiful. You've been so busy while I was in Darwin. Here.'

I hand her the present. 'You can make a book. I think you have so many stories, *Yapa*.'

'*Latju*,' she says. 'Write the date on this photo of us.'

'Okay, we can take more photos and write next to them.

'*Yow*,' she said. 'Photos of my garden. What about Yibi Yibi?'

'Always thinking of the tribe. I have something for her too.' I smile.

'Come and see Yibi, then meet more family.' She pulls me by the arm.

Yibi Yibi stands on the edge of the wooden veranda of her yellow seaside home. Hair pulled back tightly in a bun, her thick lips form a large welcoming smile as she hands me a long string of brown and cream shells she collected herself from the sandy shore and laced together on fishing line to make a *manimani*. The shells spill over the side of a small, tightly woven, chocolate-coloured basket.

'Welcome to our family, *Yapa*.' She hands me the basket and necklace.

'How beautiful! *Manymak, Yapa*.'

'You made these for me? What a wonderful welcome.'

'*Ma, marrtji*,' Yibi says.

I am still adjusting to how blunt people seem, but really, Yolŋu don't stand there raving on about nothing or saying hello, how are you or goodbye a hundred times and it is quite refreshing.

Jessie grabs me by the arm again and guides me to the edge of the headland.

'What about crocs?' I have an uneasy feeling as I look across the stretch of blue-green sea, a bunch of tangled mangroves in the distance.

Bill, the principal, had announced at our induction meeting after school one day, 'Don't tread the same path around the island when you go for your daily walk.'

Paula, a Yolŋu teacher from school, was also at the meeting. She nodded to affirm Bill's words and also mentioned to be careful of the dogs.

'*Manymak, yapa*, don't worry,' Jessie responds softly in my ear. She threads her arm under mine and pulls me closer to her.

'Yibi Yibi part two,' women call from their homes as we pass. '*Yow, Yibi.*'

'*Yow,*' I smile back, enjoying the sound of my Yolŋu name.

Jessie takes me to a cluster of *djambaŋ* trees on the edge of the translucent blue ocean where women and children have gathered. Years ago, Yolŋu people traded with the Macassans. They came to Milingimbi to collect *buṉapi'*, a type of sea slug. Tamarind trees came with the Macassans. They are not native to Australia. These large, tangy fruit-producing trees dot the island and cluster around the old well in Bush Camp and along the beach here.

Water laps on the shore, a smouldering fire crackles and naked babies run around after each other. Women roll dough to make damper, their hands covered in white flour. Lirrinyin, a woman with short-cropped hair and big lips, is my *waku*, takes a stick and smooths out the layer of sand on the hot coals. After rolling the large round white dough out several times, she carefully places it in the fire and covers it with more sand. A red tin of white flour, a plastic bottle of golden syrup and a tub of margarine sit close by. Tea boils in a huge tin on the other half of the fire. We eat the dates and oranges I have brought with me to share.

I lie down on the large black and red checked blanket, eyes half closed. Old *Yapa*, Muwalkmuwuy, appears with the basket she has been working on. I look up in surprise at the warm smile on her face as she presents me with her work of art.

I scoop the round basket up into my arms and press it to my heart. 'For me? *Dhapirrk! Maaannnymak, Yapa.* Are there any magic spells in the basket?' I ask, touching it lightly and juggling a chubby baby that's just been plonked on me.

'Magic, *Yapa*? No!' Jessie responds curtly.

I am growing used to her gruff manner that usually melts into affection. 'Oh, I think there might be. Well, if not spells, then there must be sacred stories woven in there, I reckon.' I put the basket and baby down and reach down and grab Jessie's sandy feet, casually pressing with my fingers into them.

'No, no my neck.' She pulls my hands up around her neck.

Tension spots crop up under my fingers and I stare out to the blue-green ocean, still not quite believing where I am in the world.

'*Wäy*! I can feel your hands can see inside my body. Magic *Yapa*!' Jessie shouts out loud. '*Manymak, Yapa.* Now you can do my *yapa*.' She drags my hands onto a large woman's back, another sister I haven't met before.

'Can you teach me Yolŋu ways of healing please?' I ask, digging my knuckles into the large woman's shoulder blade.

No one responds to my request. Currents of energy pulse through my veins and my face and hands are filled with heat. Excitement tingles through my skin. What will I say now? I know I'm ready for new knowledge. This is where I want to be.

'Here, do this one.' Jessie leads my hands onto another sister's large back.

'*Yä, latju, Yapa*,' the woman murmurs as I work into her back.

I take a deep breath. And here we go again on the healing journey, I think.

I have always aspired to create a balance between the seen and unseen forces in my life, between the academic world and the subtle realms. I enjoy both worlds. The energy of spirit has been alive in my life ever since I can remember, streaming through me, a silent knowing guiding me, but way too weird and intangible for my family and friends, or so I perceived from their reactions when I was a child. Very simply, in some of the work I do, I hold my hands above different parts of the body – areas in pain or that feel unbalanced. Sometimes I hold the feet or the head, or place my hands on the heart. I always encourage the person to connect with their breath in their heart area. At times, my hands are still or moving slowly around the body.

    I started this in my teens on my friends. I experienced energy pulsing through my hands. I didn't know where it came from, but I was urged to let it move through my hands and witnessed it help people: physically, mentally and emotionally. There were times when I did not touch anyone, just sat quietly, and I would feel that pulse flowing through me and move to the other person. This simple form was enough in itself really, but for some years, I let myself get swallowed up by the need to be qualified in all kinds of ways. And yes, I was intrigued by alternative therapies, especially after seeing some of my closest loved ones ill and unable to be helped by Western medicine.

    Over the years, I've used a variety of modalities to support people of all ages, ailments of mind and body and backgrounds. The work is interactive. The person and I talk together and an opportunity for understanding occurs so they can witness something clearly about themselves or their life that they would like to change. It is then possible for them to see things in a new light and have the courage to let go of grief, trauma and negativity, shift current perspectives and activate their own ability to heal and be open to change. Using my intuition became a career for me, but despite working with hundreds of people over the years, I'm not sure that the term 'healer' is suitable. I don't think I heal anyone. Together, we create a space wherein a person can realise something that perhaps had never occurred to them before. I think the body has a tremendous capacity to heal itself. Sometimes it can be as simple as sitting with the person and creating a space together where we both connect with our breath and our hearts and cultivate feelings of calm and peace. This allows a person to relax with whatever is going on in their body, mind or emotional state. When we slow our breath down it is a signal to the body that we are now safe. It gives them permission to feel exactly what they are feeling and allow it to run its course and bring new understanding. It can release pain and shift patterns that have limited our potential for years. I prefer to see myself as a support to cultivate tools that will help them heal themselves and increase their well-being. The subtle realms are involved and deep trauma can be cleared.

I do think there are powerful healing energies that exist and can be instrumental in bringing someone back to a state of health, sometimes without explanation and within a short moment of time. We are capable of sustaining focus on our attention in order to receive information. This could be to do with physical healing – accessing insight, creativity, understanding emotions or making life decisions – and as a result it is possible for change to occur instantly. I aspire to this. What I have learned is that there are many tools that can be beneficial on the well-being journey, including talking about something that we may be going through. However, it is when we shift our energy that we change our life.

I've still remained slightly awkward about it all, mainly due to my own conditioning and mindset about it. I've been relaxed about my own connection to spirit but not so confident about exposing it in a world where it can be so easily misunderstood.

As a child, or even as a young adult growing into my intuitive nature, I was not scientific about mysticism or healing. Nature, death and spirit were my teachers. It was through my tangible experience with each of them that I learned about energy. Today, though, science has proven the existence of a field of energy around each of us and all life forms. This field connects us to each other and all. The Earth's magnetic field, our heart and physics are all interconnected. The effects of meditation on the brain can now be measured and explained. Studies show that we are more than our physical existence and that when we become conscious of this energy, we are able to affect our mind, body, life and relationships in beneficial ways.

Indigenous cultures hold knowledge about healing. Here on Yurrwi with the Yolŋu, I don't feel awkward at all. In fact, due to the Yolŋus' natural connection and ease with spirit, and with the obvious language barrier, there is no need to speak at great length; and actually, the less said, sometimes the better. Here the work is interactive on a more subtle level. When I think of the term 'healing' now, I think of it as a return to wholeness: a way to transform and transcend what is no longer required or what is not working. An opportunity presents itself for us to connect honestly with ourselves through our heart and spirit. Healing is then the natural outcome, allowing us to move freely into our own natural way of being in the world and live from there.

Rich gold and red streaks spill across the sky as the sun goes down, and the light is a soothing balm on my face.

'Walk. Walk, Mary,' says Jessie, pulling me up off the ground and in close to her. '*Latju, Yapa,* I'm feeling really *manymak* now,' she smiles. 'Walk. Walk is what we do at sunset.'

Pipa joins us in our walk.

'What about Yirrkala, what about the elders I met at Yirrkala, how are we related?' I ask Jessie.

'*Dhuwal miyalk* is my *gutharra*,' says Jessie.

'But she is older than you,' I say.

'Long way down the line,' Jessie explains, reaching her arms out wide.

'I have no clue,' I say, hands in the air.

'But we are all sisters,' Jessie states, drawing Pipa and me together. 'Because Pipa's sister is my *yapa*, so we are all sisters,' says Jessie.

We giggle and squeeze each other's arms. I let go and link arms with Yibi Yibi.

We pass her house onto the road in the direction of the shop. Daylight disappears and dusk falls. Yolŋu are strolling along the road too.

'What happened to *nhuŋu* husband? Where is he?' asks Yibi Yibi.

'It didn't work out. He is in Ireland.'

'*Wanha? Barrku wäŋa?*'

'Sorry, *Yapa.*' I shake my head. I don't understand the words.

'Where is he? Long way away?' Jessie intervenes.

'*Yow, barrku wäŋa.*' I attempt the words.

Oh God, how hard I had tried with Shaun. I knew in the end it was right that we both start new lives but I certainly resisted it at the time. I had intended to be married for life as my parents were. And hell, how could I help so many other people resolve issues in their relationships in the work I do and yet fail so miserably at my own? And did our separation need to be so abrupt?

The words I share with Yibi Yibi now barely touch on Shaun walking out that Friday morning. I've hardly seen him since, just a few times to sell our house and sign the divorce papers. The words barely touch on the almost thirteen years we spent together, the complexities in our relationship and the beauty of it. They scarcely reveal the sudden loss of long-term companionship, affection, a home, a business and potential motherhood. Shaun was my Irish soulmate, my best friend and love. I wanted to be the mother of his children and I know it got rough but never thought I'd be without him.

'I had three daughters. Two passed away and my husband passed away too, in an accident,' says Yibi Yibi.

'Oh,' I say. Wow, I murmur under my breath.

But Yibi Yibi looks right at me then whispers in my ear. 'I am free, *Yapa*, and you are free too.'

'Free?' I have fluctuated between periods of knowing my marriage ending is a great gift and other times of mooning over it as another painful loss and a failure. Perhaps life is right in any case. Perhaps Shaun followed his heart back to his homeland, Ireland, and I followed mine to come here and live with the Yolŋu people.

At the old red, mud-brick church, Yibi Yibi says goodnight. Jessie walks a little further with me and we arrive at my favourite waterlily pond.

'I love this pond, *Yapa*,' I say. 'Look at that purple waterlily.'

Jessie tugs at my arm. '*Dhulumburrk dhuwal, Yirritja dhuwal.* You and I must call this *Manyi*, because it means grandmother to us.'

'*Manyi*, wow, how beautiful. Thank you, *Yapa*.'

We hug goodbye.

'Now *bondi* get home,' she says, giving me a light push.

Black silhouettes of tall thin palm trees loom against the light pink and blue sky as I walk the last metres home, feeling a wave of timelessness wash through me again, thrilled to know that the waterlily is our *manyi* and excited at the possibility of learning Yolŋu ways of healing. Then again, Jessie agreed to nothing.

As a child, I grew a desire to help others. I used to crouch under the silky oak tree in the backyard, not far from my wooden tap-dancing platform behind the garage. The pine needles provided a soft floor to sit on as I bled green, blue, yellow and red ink from Texta colours into old glass Tutti-Frutti bottles filled with water. To me, they were magic potions with healing powers for all kinds of ailments. I would get lost in that world for hours on end. Once a year, with pocket money in hand, I combed the gemstone fair in our local community for the right stones. Certain ones seemed to jump out at me and I kept them in an old shoebox lined with white cotton wool. I rolled blue sodalite, orange carnelian, green agate or tourmaline and many other stones around in my hands, nestled them on different points of my body, and slept with smooth gems under my pillow.

I never really knew why. My family were steeped in religion, so there was certainly no one in my life who showed me these ways or even engaged in such matters. To me, the stones were alive and pulsing, each with their own vibrations and qualities. They were my secret source of spiritual experimentation as I grew up, along with precognitive dreams and spirits visiting me frequently. I wonder if there are stones with power on this island. Being here, with the most ancient culture on the planet, is a natural progression really. I just need to be patient and let things unfold the way they already are.

Boyukarrpi sits in a circle with the children on the floor as they say the Yolŋu *matha* alphabet. Maṯay's face scrunches up.

'*Nhä dhuwal*?' She points to the large rip in my dress, casting her eyes suspiciously at Boyukarrpi then at me.

'Mary, what happened?' she asks me.

'*Dhuŋa ŋarra*. I think it just melted in the heat.' I look down at my torn blue dress. A couple of little girls run up and run their tiny fingers along the rip with crinkled foreheads of concern.

Matay grabs the nearest stapler. '*Gu*,' she commands, then drags the flimsy worn bits of material together and staples them.

'*Yow, manymak,* but go home at lunchtime and change,' she scolds.

'*Yow*, Matay, *manymak.*'

'Mary's a magic *yapa*,' a voice at the door announces. I spiral around to see Jessie entering the room.

Wide eyes and bobbing curls, Jessie divulges other information I can't understand because it is spoken in Yolŋu *matha* with the word 'Mary' laced several times in between. The children clamber all over Boyukarrpi and Matay as they sit very still, listening intently.

'What are you saying?' I grin at Jessie's animated way of story-telling. Arms flying, then grabbing me and massaging her fingertips into my shoulders, forming soothing movements with her palms across my brow. I start to relax.

'*Manymak yapa, ŋayi.*'

I am nervous. What is she going to do? I'm at school now. I can't talk about this. I am, however, inquisitive and I feel quite happy to work with some people in need if that's what she is talking about. I can do sessions on the weekend. I'll set up my table in the spare room at home. It will be different here because Yolŋu people are deeply connected with their spiritual essence. They are living energy. They already know this is what I do; no need to prove myself or explain anything. What a relief. What I would really like, though, is to know who the Yolŋu healers are – I want to meet one.

Jessie leaves the room. Boyukarrpi and Matay are studying me even more closely now and talking together quietly with their eyes fixed on me as I gather the students to read *The Very Hungry Caterpillar*. Perhaps now is my chance, I am thinking. Where are the Yolŋu healers – can I meet one? But within a moment I become absorbed with the children.

It's ten o'clock in the evening. I am in bed when I hear a loud horn beep beneath my bedroom window and the lights blare through the window slats.

'*Yapa, Yapa!*' It's Jessie in a car packed with family. '*Yapa, Yapa*, I was worried about your dress. I have another one here for you.'

Jessie clambers out of the car full of Yolŋu laughing and chatting away. Local Yolŋu music blares. Her shadow moves across the bright headlights and she climbs the stairs. I run to open the door for her.

'*Dayi*,' she says. smiling at me.

'*Manymak, Yapa.*' I take the long blue dress and give her a hug. 'I'll wear it tomorrow.' I am touched by her sisterly care.

I'm awake with excitement. So much is happening this month. Astonishingly enough, I've been adopted into the Gupapuyŋu tribe! In addition to all this new connection with Yolŋu and healing, I am feeling slightly more comfortable as a schoolteacher again and I attended a ceremony where people's faces were painted in red and white ochre and some carried spears and leaves. The power was incredible. The ground sung and a tribal vibration rose through the atmosphere. It was haunting. I was ensconced in the ancient world independent of time.

More Yolŋu people are talking to me. I'm sure I'm still being observed but feel less conspicuous, though sometimes I feel *baba'mirr*. I love that word *baba'mirr*, ha ha. And I started teaching my first yoga class on Thursday evening at five-thirty for an hour and a half. There were five people, including Stuart and Jenny. Marilyn thinks a yoga class is a great idea and a support for teachers, and so I can teach the class in the library. I have invited everyone from everywhere to come but this first class contained non-Indigenous teachers. Before yoga, I spied the book *Sorcerers and Healing Spirits* by Janice Reid on a shelf in the library and borrowed it. I had it years ago.

It appears things are happening when they are ready to happen or, more truthfully perhaps, exactly when I'm ready.

# 10

# Yolŋu essence

Losing my religion

'The lord is my shepherd, I'll not want,' Jessie croons as we sit on the lawn in the shade of the trees at school during morning teatime. All the Yolŋu teachers come and sit here in their breaks and I like to sit with them. Beyond the spot where we sit is a large grassy field with a few trees dotted on it. A worn track leads onto the mudflats where kids play footy and ends down at the beach at Lapuluŋ's house at Top Camp. Lapuluŋ is a teacher, strong community member and musician.

In 1923, the Methodist mission established on Elcho Island was reconstructed at Milingimbi. I am fascinated yet challenged by the influence of religion here. I lived and breathed Catholicism throughout my school years. Even my teacher training was in a Catholic university. But I've spent years *losing* my religion, shedding the blind faith and the guilt entrenched in my cells. I have, however, great respect for Christ and I know there is something greater than myself that I am a part of, but it is not in the form of religious punishment or religion as a means of superiority or power over others. Disdain emerges in my throat at any fire and brimstone attitude. I wonder if the introduction of religion into Indigenous communities is a corruption of Yolŋu natural essence.

But the words of the hymn flow out of my lips in unison with Jessie, in an automatic response from years on bended knee in a chapel with nuns.

'Hymns make me sad, Mary *Yapa*. I don't understand why that woman got sick and died last week. She was a health worker. Why did she get sick, Mary?'

I can't think of an answer. I shrug wordlessly in response as I dig a hole in the ground with a broken stick.

Jessie continues her diatribe with eyes closed, her face in the direction of heaven, smooth round cheeks glowing, and a wrinkled frown on her brow. 'Anyway, she had a beautiful singing voice, and when I sing that's her voice coming through on the second verse, not my voice, Mary, *Yapa*. She was very good at harmonies. I will sing at her funeral and I want everyone to sing at mine.'

It's Sunday morning. I wake up to the sounds of *bilma* resonating from a house a short distance away. I lie in bed and allow the rhythm of tapping wood to travel through my bones. My heart skips for a second as I take in the joy of what unfolds organically around me.

It is the beginning of the funeral for the woman Jessie was talking about.

Screeching microphone noise reverberates through the trees as I swig my fresh carrot and ginger juice. I have an urge to attend the ceremony, partly to respect this woman I have heard about and also, I want to experience and understand this culture more. I rinse my glass and walk under Stuart's pole house next door to the other side of the road into *Mewa* Camp.

I stand at the edge of the driveway where the ceremony is, waiting respectfully, then *Waku*'s white hair and waving hand come into view. I first saw this strong woman at school. I remember noticing her walking along the path by the staffroom. I walked on and then stopped and looked at her again. An ethereal quality emanated from her. I want to meet that woman and learn from her, I said to myself.

Her name is Judy Munymuny and she is a prominent elder and religious figure in the community. High cheekbones, white hair pulled back in a blue scrunchy, long smooth limbs, she is my *waku*. *Waku* radiates strength, yet there is softness about her.

I walk over and sit down next to her. Sand has been laid on the earth for people to sit and dance on. The body of the deceased woman lies under a tall four-pole *gurrugurru*. *Gurrugurru* is the general term for a shelter but different names are used for different tribes. The poles are made from brown branches and the roof is a thick blanket of leaves. It creates a sacred space. A small fire of burning leaves smoulders at the entrance to 'smoke' the area.

Small groups of women, men and children sit in the shade cast by trees in close proximity to the shelter. Some chat, some are quiet. Small campfires burn close to the groups. Smoke swirls up to the sky. I now enjoy the familiarity of the woody smell. There is a large space in front of the shelter for dance and ceremony. A group of men play *yiḏaki* and *biḻma* and chant for the woman who has passed away.

A group of women rise up and begin to sing, dressed in crisp white shirts, some wearing black skirts and some an array of brightly coloured skirts, bare feet rooted in the brown earth, blue skies laced with puffs of white clouds above. A naked child clings to the skirt of one woman. As I sit on the earth, I experience myself sinking into a deeper state of calm.

'You can get up and join in for the opening,' suggests a grey-haired woman wearing a bright blue and red floral dress.

I stand between Munymuny and Nancy Djämbutj. Their hands feel cool in mine. We stand in a line with other women and sway gently, our bare feet pressed into the earth.

Bäpa Jo stands gallantly, engaging the crowd with his presence. He is my adopted father but due to being a minister others also call him *Bäpa*. He and his big family, live in the red house opposite mine. *Bäpa* wears smart, freshly pressed black pants, shiny black shoes, a dark blue shirt and dark sunglasses. Clean-shaven with grey curls nestling around his ears, he stands under the shade of a tree holding a large thick red Bible. He sings in Yolŋu *matha* and English.

Once again, my past negative memories create resistance to this religious practice but at the same time I want to be respectful, and actually the tone of this environment is very calming.

The women's exquisite island voices illuminate the space. They sing in perfect harmony, their hands stretched out open to receive.

'We are standing on holy ground in the presence of the Lord,' exclaims *Bäpa* Jo. 'Angels watching on holy ground,' he continues. 'Angels around us in all four corners,' and he opens his long lean arms, rotating his body in all directions. 'Here there are angels and they walk with us.'

A lukewarm feeling rises from my gut up into my heart and tears come into my eyes. A vigorous pulse moves in my veins, running through my arms and legs. A strange lifting pulling sensation occurs in my skin. I am in my body and above, watching it at the same time. Tears stream. I can't stop this pulse. My God, my legs have given way. I am falling, falling, and yet at the same time lifting, floating higher and higher. All I can see are the women's bare feet on the swirls of sand. The hands holding mine become arms circling my waist, propping up my weight as I plummet toward the ground. What's happening? I float high, looking down at the women holding my limp body.

Time has stopped. I can't hear anything at all. There is silence.

I manage to catch *Waku's* soft face for a second, wet with tears too.

Entrenched in moments without boundaries, I experience oneness, pulsation, and peace. I am not my body any more but hundreds and thousands of molecules and atoms vibrating very quickly.

Fragments of faces, slithers of green leaves, portions of blue sky, flashes of treetops, pass quickly across my vision and yet I have a sense of being connected to everything and everyone and a deep sense of peace about this connection.

Slowly I awaken to my body once more, slumped in the arms of the Yolŋu women in the heat and white glare of the sun. More women circle me.

Having no clue of time, I find my limbs again, alert to the weight of my shaky body gluing itself back onto my bones; feet sinking into the earth, my eyes open to the beauty of the women's faces around me. Their smiles reach into my heart and comfort me. I am ushered onto a sandy spot in the shade.

'*Nhe manymak?*' the women ask.

'*Yow, manymak,*' I muster.

'God loves us in every moment, we must pray. Pray for courage and read his words.' I can hear *Bäpa* Jo again now.

I sit fuzzy-eyed for a time and then look over to see his thin, silver-framed glasses hanging on the tip of his nose. Jo reads from his Bible and speaks in Yolŋu *matha* about the woman who has passed from this world. I cannot understand his language but the women share bits with me.

'She was a wonderful woman, a health worker, strong Yolŋu *miyalk*,' *Waku* translates.

'Only God can help us through this painful loss of our loved one. We must turn to God.' The minister speaks English with earnest face.

The women rise up and fill the air with their island voices once again. My limbs are light and heavy at the same time, the skin around my eyes puffed and there's still a slight trembling through my veins, but there is freedom in my heart.

Funny, I gave up religion a long time ago and here I am having a mind-blowing mystical experience in the Christian part of this traditional ceremony.

Legs still like jelly, I gently sway in unison with the women, a chubby smiling baby in my arms. I am nourished by the gentle compassion of these woman and their knowing glances.

'*Ḏarra marrtji*,' I whisper. I decide it's time to go home, digest the experience and do my weekly muffin-making ritual.

I return silently to the trees where I left my swanky new beaded Balinese sandals. I experience *Waku's* long piercing gaze and gentle smile.

We don't say anything.

'*Wäy*! Where are my shoes?' I am brought to earth with a thud.

'*Mak* on their way to Galiwin'ku by now *mak bay*,' a voice utters from a group of Yolŋu sitting beyond the trees.

'Someone must have borrowed them,' I shrug.

My bare feet walk me home. I am worn to the bone but incredibly calm. This wholeness, this connection to all I have experienced came unannounced; there was no ritual, meditation, visualisation or invocation by me to instigate it. I certainly wasn't looking for it when I woke up this morning. An outpouring of spirit, my own and that of the infinite cosmos, instigated through the heart and spirit of the Yolŋu and mother earth. I am still in this tranquil state now. Once again, I experience the truth that spirit is alive here in this Indigenous community. Religion or no religion, Yolŋu essence shines through.

What was that altered state I encountered? Was it actually my true state of being that I feel so separate from at times? I delve further into the event with myself as I whip the wooden spoon around the bowl of dates, raspberries and muffin mixture. Waves still oscillate through me. My body is light, emotions balanced, mind free. Yes, it was the Christian part of a Yolŋu funeral but maybe it was the deep interconnectedness of the Yolŋu that I contacted; an expression of wholeness, undivided by bones, body, mind or action. I feel connected with a divine presence. I'm intrigued but also have no real urgency about working anything out right now.

I walk over to the wooden bookshelf adorned with ESL texts, yoga books, Aboriginal art, feathers and bits of nature I have picked up on my walks. I close my eyes, and hold thoughts of the morning's occurrence strong in my mind. I run my fingers along the line of books, choose one and randomly open it.

My eyes fall on an abstract from A.H. Almaas. It fits perfectly.

The essence.
The mother.
To find the soul, one must step back from the surface, withdraw deep within and enter, enter, go down, far down into a very deep hole, silent, still; and down there, is something warm, tranquil, rich in contents, and very still and very full, like a sweetness – this is the soul.

# 11

# Gutharra

*Märi-gutharra* [is] the link between an entity (a person, clan group, song, totem, piece of land etc) and its mother's mother. The *märi* are the mother's mother and her brother, and her *mala* group, land, histories and totems. The reciprocal (opposite) of *märi* is *gutharra*. If I am your *märi*, you are my *gutharra*. *Märi-gutharra* can be understood as two yothu-yindi joined together.

– Michael Christie, *Yolŋu Languages and Culture: Gupapuyŋu*

'I heard about your experience yesterday,' whispers Elizabeth Ganygulpa, embracing me in her strong arms as we stand outside the school office near a tall gangly palm tree at morning teatime. Dancing eyes and a heartfelt smile, this is a woman of great strength and spiritual depth. She speaks fluently in English and is strong in Yolŋu and *balanda* worlds.

Ganygulpa shows a genuine interest in sharing stories with me and encourages me to be a part of Yolŋu life. I see her often in the school office but I first witnessed her dynamic enthusiasm at a 'petrol sniffing' meeting I attended with Stuart one Thursday evening. It seems that there are cycles of petrol sniffing, mostly by young men in the community. Ganygulpa's large eyes widened as she spoke passionately, saying that when she was a child the family sat in a circle telling stories and that the stories were passed down from generation to generation, but she feels that is not happening so much any more. Also, perhaps some of the young men are bored. They have finished school but there are not enough jobs. The support group aims to help families become aware of the risks of petrol sniffing and the damage it can cause to the brain and emotional behaviour. Skills training and recreation strategies to reduce petrol sniffing were also discussed. In general in Arnhem Land, the community clinics and the school develop the health education programmes. I felt sad about the sniffing and went quiet as the nurse drove us home in the ambulance.

'News travels fast in his community.' Ganygulpa engages my eyes in hers, lips curling up in a big smile. Her motivation and zest for life are infectious.

I call her *Gutharra*; she calls me *Märi*. Apparently *mari* and *gutharra* have a lot in common and we can have a fun relationship. Every day since the day of my adoption, I discover the relationships I have with Yolŋu. To understand this, I can learn the different relationship terms and the responsibilities those relationships hold towards each other. Usually, as soon as I meet someone, we work out how we are related. The fact that Yibi adopted me as her *yapa* means that everyone can work out where I am in the system. It is important for Yolŋu to be able to place everyone within the intricate *gurruṯu*.

Maria, another schoolteacher, and I are on one of our walks. Maria has Italian blood and is the only person on Milingimbi Island with a cappuccino machine. The delicious aroma of coffee wafting from her place makes me wish I drank it. Shadows from the clouds mark shapes on the road and the scent of the dry crackly leaves and bush clears my head. Black cockatoos squawk as they wing their way across the sky. We try to walk to 'Hell' and back at least three mornings a week before school. 'Hell' is the word written in white chalk on the black tar road out near the airstrip. Today we walk along a track off the main road to the airstrip and see three *weṯi*, *djanda* and *bäpi* tracks.

'Mary!' Maria's big brown eyes grow wide. 'What happened?' She pulls her long dark plait that falls down her back and places it on her heart. 'The women are talking about you. We were sewing together last night and all I could hear was *Mary Mary Mary*. I wish I could understand more Yolŋu *matha*.'

'Really! How's the sewing going?' I ask, taking the conversation in a new direction.

'Great. I think we'll have a fashion parade with all the pieces we're making, but listen,' Maria came back to the healing topic, 'I told them about you being a healer, and you know what a sceptic I am.'

'Yes, I do.' I look down at our Blundstone boots treading the earth.

'Anyway, they said tell that Mary she can give us healing any time, we want healing *djäma*. It's amazing, Mary,' Maria smiles.

Even though this is great news, I have resistance. 'Oh, I don't know, Maria, I left that world. I like this new one, I love the kids. I enjoy being back in the classroom again.'

'Well, Yolŋu people talk with their feet, Mary, and they're walking right up to your doorstep.' Maria's eyes were big and round again.

'Well, I guess you know, Maria. You've spent quite a few years here after all.'

It's dark by the time we emerge out of the bush to Army Camp. The *buŋgul* for the health worker is in full flight. A Yolŋu woman waves to us to approach, so we quietly walk to the outer edge of the ceremony. Fires are glowing and there is a smell of burning leaves. Just outside the shelter where the body lies, men are playing clap sticks and *yidaki*. They form a circle, and a Yolŋu woman tells us they are doing the octopus dance. Perhaps it was her *waŋarr*. Men, women and little children dance, and their silhouettes grow in the dark, creating a powerful presence. 'What a privilege to see and feel,' is all I can say.

The next evening, after teaching yoga, I stroll home through the mini jungle made up of long, thin, dark yellow bamboo in my neighbour's backyard, dry leaves crunching under my feet. I am thinking about a conversation I had with a Yolŋu woman I met outside the shop after school. I had asked her about traditional healers and she told me they are called *marrŋgitj*.

'I must meet one,' were my words to her.

As I arrive in my backyard, I find six women sitting in a circle on the grass, cigarette smoke swirling up to the sky. Faces smile as I approach.

'*Yow*, Mary, we heard about what happened to you at the funeral.'

It seems everyone knows. I accept what happened and I've certainly felt energised and clear after the experience.

'Mary, what's this yoga *djäma* and healing *djäma* that you do?' they ask excitedly.

We adjourn to the lounge room and sit drinking tea, sharing stories of spirit.

'*Yow*, so that *miyalk* knew that her mother was going to pass away before it happened.'

'*Yuwalk?*' I say.

'There are many spirits here on Yurrwi, Mary.'

'*Yaka*, I want to know can that healing *ga* yoga *djäma* help us lose fat, Mary?' A woman grabs her stomach and we all crack up laughing.

'Healing *djäma dhiyaŋ bala?*' asks a slim woman with long black hair, visiting from Darwin.

I am excited by their enthusiasm but I want to learn about Yolŋu healing.

I usher her into the spare room where the dark blue massage table is set up. Somehow I can never remove the thick red dust that collects on the window slats and green lino floor. The built-in cupboards are royal blue and often mouldy, especially when the rain pelts down. I barely want to put anything in the dusty old room let alone turn it into a healing space.

I place my hands at her feet, run them above her body and hold them close to her head, cupping her ears. I encourage her to gently breathe in and slowly breathe out stress and pain.

'*Manymak?*' I ask. It feels good to let the energy flow through my hands again.

'*Latju*. Warm hands. You should make a business for the whole community,' she says, opening her eyes to me for a moment.

'Set up a clinic? I ask

'*Yow*, we need this here on Yurrwi.'

I hear laughter from the women in the lounge room but then they lower their voices to whisper.

I return to hold my hands close to her feet again, not touching though. I concentrate on the energy coming through into her feet.

'*Yow*, my headache is going now, *manymak*.'

'How do you say headache?' I ask.

'*Liya rathala*.'

'*Liya rathala*,' I repeat.

The young woman sits up and sighs. '*Yow, manymak* now.'

The next day, I am in my pokey little office preparing classes for the students. It used to be the first-aid room at the school. I spend the mornings with Boyukarrpi and Maṯay working together with the whole class and then I bring small groups of students to this office for oral language. I am creating some pictures to go with a story about a campfire. The students will build vocabulary and sequence the story orally with the pictures.

'*Yapa djäma dhiyaŋ bala*.' A woman sticks her head in the door of my office. Her hand clasps her paining back.

'So sorry: *yalala*. I can't do it here. I'm a schoolteacher now.'

I jump up and peep out the door to find three more people waiting. Shit! I am thinking, God, I don't think this work will go down too well with the principal. Lucky there are no students with me right now. What a shame. I would love to do this now but I can't.

'*Yalala, ŋarraku wäŋaŋur*,' I say to them all, looking around a bit sheepishly to see if anyone can see what's going on, but it seems okay.

More and more people are coming to see me. I like the balance in my life now. I enjoy being in the academic world with the children at school and then being part of the Yolŋu spiritual world, attending ceremonies, being out bush with the women and now also through people coming for help.

I could easily fill every day with sessions. Thoughts of setting up a clinic grow strong in my mind. Once again, I've done nothing to instigate these opportunities, just followed the synchronicity cues as they've presented themselves. Sure, I've questions and what ifs but I stayed open to what was occurring in the moment.

Gradually, *Yapa* Jessie and others begin to come over and take me to people who are very sick and cannot come to my house. I start to work with people under a tree, outside their homes, on verandas of homes, inside homes. The massage table in my room seems ludicrous after a while in this rich organic environment and yet in my own world in New South Wales the ambience of a workspace seems to be such an important part of the whole process. Here, people simply love lying on the single mattress or yoga mat in my lounge room with the door wide open and the breeze flowing through.

'Knock knock, *märi*.' My *gutharra* Ganygulpa is standing at the wire door.

'*Yow, räli gu.*'

I guide her into the lounge room and she lies on the massage table I have moved to the lounge room. Her hair is wet after a shower and she is wearing a yellow and red floral skirt and loose blue T-shirt. Her eyes smile when she talks.

'*Dhuwal ga dhuwal*,' she points to the pain in her body from a car accident. *Yow*, this hip is really hurting and I have a sore neck and a tight chest. It's hard to breathe, *ga balanya*. *Märi*, Yolŋu people believe in spirit and they believe in the healing power of touch and energy.'

'I see that, *gutharra*, and I appreciate it.'

*Gutharra* has an air of confidence when she speaks, and mischievous deep eyes that seem to expand when they look at me and grow bigger.

I lay my hands just above her swollen tender hip, allowing the heat to permeate the pain and soothe it.

'Your hands remind me of a Yolŋu woman I know who does this. You must meet her,' she says as I move my hands to hold her neck.

'Yes, please, I would love to meet her. I would love to learn from her about Yolŋu healing.'

Once again, there was no further discussion. I do wonder why no one is saying anything when I ask. I wonder if I should be asking but I can't help it. Perhaps I am overstepping a line. I hope not. I have great respect for the Yolŋu and want to learn from them too.

My yoga classes in the AV room at school on Thursday afternoons are going well. It's rather a strange room where all our assemblies are held, a dark space with grimy carpet, dusty narrow windows, noisy air con sticking out of the back wall and about six wide stairs on which everyone is doing yoga postures. Still, I'm very appreciative that I have a space at all. Yoga can be done anywhere and at any time. We are thinking of doing a sunrise practice out near the Telstra towers one morning. The class is growing bigger every week, mostly with teachers and nurses. I have invited everyone in the community. Boyukarrpi and Maṯay say they want to come yet they are never there.

'Why don't you and the Yolŋu *mala* come?' I ask after school one day.

'*Gora*,' says Boyuparrpi, looking down at her desk.

'*Gora*? You are shy? Well, you know you're very welcome, don't you?'

'*Yow*,' she says.

'Would you like me to start a class just for you all?'

'*Yow, manymak*,' she says.

Jon the music teacher invites Stu, Maree, Jenny and me around for breakfast. Trish, his wife, is holding sweet Bella their baby daughter in one arm and eases a tray of croissants into the warm oven with her other hand. Wow! I never even think of croissants any more. I step into the kitchen space to help, rummage around finding cups and make a pot of tea. Jenny plonks on the table a fresh banana cake she'd baked.

'Mmmm, that smells great, Jenny.' I sniff in the cake fumes.

And these people are remote chefs extraordinaire. Trish works in the classroom as a tutor and Bella comes to school too. Sometimes we are in the secondary classroom at the same time. Trish loves yoga. The Yolŋu kids adore Bella and pass her around the classroom cuddling her and pinching her soft white cheeks while Trish works one to one with the students. I love the community spirit.

I look around Trish and Jon's place enjoying the local paintings and grass weavings they have. They were both born in England.

'Yeah, we met in England and went out for a while, then I travelled to Australia, ended up here on Milingimbi Island teaching music and sport,' Jon says, tucking strands of his straight brown hair behind an ear. 'Then one day I went back to England to find Trish again.' He smiles at Trish, and Bella in her arms.

'Yeah, Jon came all the way home to get me and bring me back to Milingimbi.' Trish's big brown eyes squint a little and she giggles, her smooth English skin aglow.

It must be nice to be here with your partner. I sigh.

A snapshot of Jon and his family remains clear in my mind as I walk home. They represent what I had hoped for in my own life. I've always loved having a partner, someone I can share with, a space where we can express ourselves or aspire to. I still think of the affection my parents shared with each other. I see it with my brothers and their wives. Life seems unnatural without it.

Five naked kids are screeching with laughter, looping arms as they take turns to dance on two old rusty tins. 'Mary Mary,' they scream. Their smiles of delight never fail to bring one to my own lips.

Jenny, Stu, Mitch and Maree came for dinner last night. Cooking Indian food is a love of mine. The kitchen filled with delicious smells as I chopped garlic and ginger then tossed it in some oil in the pan, adding turmeric, cumin and some Patak's curry paste – my favourite. Spice permeated the room. I stirred the paste with a wooden spoon as it sizzled in the pan, then I tossed in a cup of chickpeas, some green beans, eggplant and some tomatoes. A saucepan of basmati rice bubbled away on the stove and I leaned down to turn on the gas grill and threw some papadums in there. Stuart was chopping cucumber and Maree had brought a cake.

'Yes, my mother is in Ballarat,' said Stu.

'I live in Ballarat with Mum,' said Mitch as he collected some plates and forks and popped them on the table.

'Where are your parents, Mary?' asked Maree.

'They're dead.' I snatched the hot pappadums out from under the grill before they burn. I didn't mean to sound so dramatic. The words just popped out that way.

No one said anything and then the conversation changed direction. With change, past sorrows tend to surface for review and here they are.

# 12

# Ṉilatjirriwa gul̲un

Waterhole
Silken water
Ancient trees
Place of power

It's Saturday morning and I'm at Stuart's place. 'We'll walk to the billabong out near the airport,' says Stuart. He and I go for a lot of walks and share tea and meals sometimes. We enjoy deep conversations about the growth of human potential and read poetry out loud, especially Mary Oliver and Rainer Maria Rilke. We both like to spend a lot of time outside school in the community. Stuart is my non-Indigenous kindred spirit.

Mitch, Stuart's son, walks with us as we hike at a strong pace through lush palms, pandanus grass and red earth ant mounds. I am surprised not to feel fitter, though it is very hot.

I begin to feel that old familiar strange energy in my head. The feeling I get when I am intuiting something or important change is occurring or when I feel a strong presence of spirit. I am uncertain about this place where we are heading. I am still very new here on Milingimbi Island and I wonder, is it right for me to go to the billabong? Isn't it a sacred place? Is this resistance telling me I should not go there?

We walk solidly for an hour through the bush and come to an expansive hole of still water. Tiny birds flit in and out, skimming across the top of the billabong. It feels unbearable not to go into the water.

For the last ten minutes of our walk, Mitch has been telling stories about women being dragged away by crocodiles.

'*Yew*,' I shiver in response.

Mitch has clear eyes and brown wavy hair. He is in my secondary class in the afternoon and right now he is successfully scaring me with his wide eyes and looks of horror.

'Are there crocodiles in the billabong?' I ask, wondering if that's what I am picking up on.

'Some say there are, some say there aren't,' says Stuart.

I shudder.

The *gulun* lies surrounded by ancient rainforest. Long chunky vines weave a canopy over the thick green scrub and one rare, tall, thin-limbed tree climbs its way to the sky, a clump of leaves at its peak.

I gasp at the beauty of the *gulun*. Perfectly round in shape, plump with green-brown silky water, lush foliage spilling around its edges, the billabong radiates tranquillity. I stop and allow its peace to sink into my veins. As I stand here, I realise this sanctuary is calm yet strong, powerful and alive with the presence of spirit. I am quite in awe of its olden allure. It must hold so many stories. Ripples flow across the surface and fish fly up and then plop back into the water. Pungent bush smells greet my nostrils but still my headache is growing stronger.

Sweat streams down our faces and limbs, mosquitoes abound. We decide to venture in.

I can't get used to being totally surrounded by stunning water and unable to swim in it because of crocodiles and box jellyfish. I take a swig from my waterbottle and consider the idea of going in.

'Do you think we'll be okay to go in?' I ask, hesitating.

'Absolutely!' says Stuart enthusiastically.

My long flowing clothes are cumbersome after wearing next to nothing in Byron Bay. I just want to strip off and luxuriate in the water naked.

Long thin reeds grow out of the waterhole. Fully clothed, we slink into the dark hole. I stick close to the edge.

The water, soft and warm, seeps through my clothes and envelops my body. I'm relieved but wary of what may be lurking below my dangling feet. Stuart and Mitch swim out a bit further, smiling and laughing, not the least bit in fear of predators. Sun shines on Stuart's face as he glides his hands over wet hair. Mitch disappears under the water for a moment then leaps up out of the hole in mock crocodile pose.

I clamber out onto the grassy banks, clothes stuck to my skin. Even after this brief immersion, I'm feeling better. I always feel totally refreshed after a swim. Despite the fear and my questioning mind, I am lighter but I still hold a strange feeling in my head.

As we tread through the greenery on our way back home, I grow more and more uncomfortable, bones aching, head pounding.

We arrive back to the airstrip hot, sticky and waterlogged. Beside a windmill stands a large tank on steel poles. I've been here before on walks to the Telstra towers, where *damala* nest, though I haven't seen any of them yet. The windmill scene looks like something out of the movie *Bagdad Café*. I wish I had my camera.

A waterfall tumbles down from the windmill, forming a tiny pool. Stuart and I stand under the shower, welcoming the feeling of cool water on our skin and gulping down splashes of water. I let the water flush my eyes and welcome its pressure on my face. Sometimes the dogs drink from this puddle and not far from here a flurry of cockatoos congregate in the clump of trees. I'm not sure why. There are lots of feathers to be found on the leafy earth here. Once, when I was walking with Maria, we came across white feathers with a yellow tinge and plain black ones. I found a black cockatoo feather with an orange circle on the end. It reminds me of a burnt sunset.

We walk on and my strange headache appears again as we cut across the oval to avoid the snapping hounds.

It's still light when I arrive home. I clamber up the stairs with tired legs. The headache looms like a brick on my crown and, despite all the exercise, I have lost my appetite. I shower, make a cup of peppermint tea, crawl into bed and sink into a deep dream state. I dream about a large craggy-skinned crocodile lurking in the long grass. Terror shoots through my bones, waking me in a sweat, the tea by my bed untouched.

I stare at the glowing stars on the ceiling. It's about one a.m. now.

Goosebumps ripple through my skin as I reflect on our visit to the billabong. I don't understand it. I don't understand a lot of things, but the Yolŋu will help me understand their world. I must be patient.

*Gutharra* Ganygulpa speaks to me so freely that I decide to share my experience with her the next time she comes over. We sit on the floor in the lounge room sipping cool water.

'We call this *gul̲un*, billabong, *N̲ilatjirriwa, märi*.'

'Thank you, *Gutharra*, I felt that place commanded reverence and I didn't know if I should go in there or not,' I said to *Gutharra*, a frown growing across my brow.

She is looking intently at me. Her eyebrows lift and she nods. '*Yow*, it could have been that you were menstruating and your blood disturbed the spirits,' she smiles. *Gutharra* is very expressive, using her hands as she speaks and her eyes too; they grow wide and her round cheeks glow.

I nod.

'Some places are very sacred and we do not wish to disturb the spirits. In women's business, we understand our body is sacred and our female cycles are sacred. At this time, we don't eat big animals – *mala, miyapunu, buliki*. The sacredness of it keeps us really private about it and we are careful about where we go at that time.' Her eyes shine as she speaks. 'And sometimes we feel the spirits of our ancestors watching over us,' she says.

I love her clear direct communication and that she wants to share her knowledge with me.

*Gutharra* has left now. My mind is at the *gul̲un*, the thought of its allure takes my breath away and a shiver glides over my skin. The lake back home in Suffolk Park with its soft silky water, tanned from the tea trees that surround it, enters my awareness. The lake was so close to the backyard of my studio at Suffolk Park. I loved that backyard. It was full of trees that stood with sleek bare limbs. The ocean was virtually next to me and I often lay looking out at those trees, their trunks smooth and naked, shimmering in the moonlight, the ocean's roar and smell of salt water soothing my soul.

The tea tree lake was directly through those trees and I've heard that the local Indigenous people call it a sacred women's place, a birthing place. I couldn't help feeling that my time post-infertility spent so close to a women's place, no less, was deeply healing and nourishing. To then travel from there to here in Arnhem Land has been an unexpected natural progression.

I walk over to the bookshelf and pick up the book *The Native Born*. I take a breath, release a slow exhalation and flick through the pages. I pause at the photograph of the spectacular waterhole at Ramingining. It doesn't look completely dissimilar to Nilatjirriwa.

I read,

*GULUNBUY*
From the waterholes
Before my birth my spirit was left in the totemic waterhole
Where the ancestral spirit of my forefathers has always been
The dhuwa spirit of the shark and the yirritja spirit of brown rock kangaroo
My mother's spirit came together and put my spirit into a human body...
– Jack Mirritji, *My People's Life*

I put the book down on the corner of the lounge for a moment, get up and stare out the window through the trees onto the street near *Bäpa* Jo's house. A naked child is pushing a pram with a baby in it. His mother stands chatting to another woman holding a baby not far behind. 'Children everywhere,' I say out loud.

I take a sip of water and go back to the photograph of the billabong. I flick through the pages again, stopping at the photo of the stunning Ramingining billabong. It makes me reflect once more on my reaction after swimming in our billabong.

I read on.

The Djambarrpuyŋu word *gulun*, used for billabongs, waterholes, pools, lagoons and fresh water swamps, literally means 'stomach' but more importantly 'womb.' The adjective gulunbuy means 'of the belly' and is synonymous with the mother-child relationship. Waterholes are full of life and are thought to include the souls of unborn and deceased people. New-born catfish are thought to be the souls of unborn people.

*The Native Born*, Museum of Contemporary Art

I hear children's laughter outside and smile. I had been unable to conceive a child and here I was, dipping in the womb of creation. No wonder I had headaches and strange feelings in my gut. I don't like the thought that I disturbed the spirit. I certainly did not intend to. I'm yet again transformed by new understandings of my own spiritual nature and the pieces of my life that fit together now with more understanding.

# 13

# Hunting nyoka

*Yä nyoka, latju ŋatha marrkapmirr.*
(Oh crab, beautiful food...beloved food).
– Nancy Djämbutj

It's Saturday morning and I'm baking date muffins in the kitchen. A horn beeps and someone yells out from a car outside, '*Limurr (u) ga marrtji huntinglil.*'

'*Yow,*' I yell excitedly, grateful the baking is just done. Everything happens in the moment and now is the hunting moment. Over time, I think I have gotten better at being in these spontaneous moments. When I first came to Milingimbi, I couldn't wait to go hunting and everyone was always inviting me and telling me we were going but then it just never happened. Initially, I'd get quite disappointed about the falling through of plans. Yolŋu time demands I let go of control and get into the flow. Our Western culture in general is not comfortable in uncertainty. We are programmed that, on demand, everything must fall into place so that we are 'secure' in our plans unfolding in a certain way and by a certain time. Now I am learning, ah well, it will happen when it happens. Or not. This is not to say at all that there is no planning within Yolŋu culture. On the contrary, there is a depth of organisation that I have not yet grasped and may never. This is so different to what I have grown up with and provides an opportunity for understanding and growth.

The pandanus is starting to fruit and it's turtle season now. The mangroves are flat, so it's the perfect time for hunting *nyoka*.

I race around and grab fruit, muffins, water, sunscreen, a large hat and camera. I run out and jump in the back of the troopie. There are several women seated on the long seats in the back of the four-wheel drive but by the time we've stopped at lots of homes, there are about six kids too. All these women are my *waku* yet some of them are older than me. Being my child does not necessarily make someone younger than me in Yolŋu culture. I love this.

It is nice to be outside the classroom with Maṯay. She has velvet-smooth black skin, and a fit body. I'm told her husband is my poison cousin, though I've no idea what that means as yet, despite the explanation Maṯay gave me after school one day. Apparently, we can call each other *gudi*, a short way of saying *gurruŋ*, because we are in an avoidance relationship and do not call each other directly by our names. When we do talk to each other, we hold one elbow and point our arm toward each other. This breaks direct contact between us. There is extensive sign language in Yolŋu culture.

I've so much to learn and understand. Maṯay has long wavy hair but I've rarely seen it out. It's mostly up in a tight bun on the top of her head with a red scrunchy. Her smile lights up her whole face. Maṯay is very passionate about the children and about her culture. Old *Yapa* Muwalkmuwuy is her mother. Gwen Warmbirrirr is a tall, pretty woman who also teaches at the school. She is gentle, kind. Warmbirrir likes to hold meetings for the woman of the community and helps me learn new Yolŋu words. She is well travelled in Australia and comfortable in two worlds. Esther Rarrinya also works at the school. She and Maṯay are very close and they are always together.

Gamuti and her husband George Milay work at the school too. He is my *wäwa*.

I adore these days cramped in the troopie, going out bush, laughing, sticks flying in the window, sweating in the heat, hugged endlessly by children, looking out for *djanda*.

Bumping along the dark brown earth through the bush, over the saltpans, we arrive at the edge of the mangroves. I gaze across the stretch of dry cracked grey mud: leaves stuck in various spots create a mosaic effect on the earth. A bunch of other women arrives in another truck and disappear off into the mangroves.

My *waku* lead me into a lightly sprinkled mangrove area where the earth is wet. Everyone grabs a *dharpa* and starts to dig for *rägudha*. Maṯay shows me a crack in the earth, 'That's how we know they are here.' She digs deep and pulls out a mussel.

I do the same with my stick too and pluck one out. Its shell is black and smooth and I feel very satisfied at learning to feed myself in the bush.

'*Marrtji*, Mary,' calls Maṯay. 'Leave your bag here.'

I pull my black rubber booties out of my bag and slip them on my feet, grab some water, my camera, and leave the bag nestled in a clump of leafy shrubs.

Maṯay is very caring. In fact, all the women are constantly teaching me and caring for me.

We walk out into the open. The clear blue sky is huge and the ṉinydjiya dry, crusty and hot beneath our feet. Ahead are deeper darker mangroves. Off we venture into the thick bush, where trees have thin white trunks and light green leaves. ṉonḏa, mud creepers that have a long spiral shape and are relatively easy to pick up off the ground as they reside on the ground among the shrubs. I lengthen the strap on my camera and sling it over my shoulder, across my body, so my hands are free. Gradually, the earth thickens. Gnarled grey roots like flying buttresses wriggle up from the thick salty mud below, their limbs entwined. I look out at a forest of entangled grey roots.

The deeper we go, the darker and danker this habitat of mixed plants gets. Mozzies and sand flies buzz in my hair and ears and bite my flesh through my heavy clothes. Spindly strips of sunshine rush into the dark, creating patterns on the mangrove branches. This cool place holds a unique sanctity of its own and is alive with all sorts of creatures. My skin ripples as I feel I'm being watched from all angles by earth and spirit. Dark mud cakes around my ankles and bits harden in my hair and on my face and fingers.

I perch on a thin root, careful about where to place my foot next in case I snap a branch. I'm wondering if these booties are such a good idea, as I can't really grasp as well as I can when barefoot. I am a barefoot girl but have heard there are lots of bits of sharp shell in the deep mud here that can cut severely. Some of these mangroves look flimsy but I realise now that they are incredibly sturdy, thriving here where land and water meet. After all, they consistently bear the brunt of saltwater oceans, storms and frequent tidal changes

With lightness and ease, the women are nimble in their movement, almost tiptoeing from branch to branch. Pools of mud get thicker and deeper. My legs are sucked down, thick grey mush over my knees, which I can barely lift up out of the depths. I fluctuate between feeling clumsy and like a nimble fairy, but I stay with my breath, which helps me absorb the great serenity of this place. Actually, my breath is fluid here. There must be a good dose of oxygen releasing from this complex ecosystem. My legs sink deeper and deeper and become heavier. I swing between experiencing a great lightness of being and a heavy bound ball of flesh like a fly frantically trying to get out of a spider's web. I fall behind the women.

'*Nhe manymak?*' *Waku* Maṯay continuously calls.

'*Manymak*,' I reply.

For a while, I sit propped on a root, absorbing the light air, gazing at thin roots that stick up like snorkels, listening intently to the popping of the mud crabs. I refocus and stare hard into the mud, desiring to glimpse one. There is a buzz of life here and yet a vast stillness that holds me in a strong nurturing embrace. The women are so present and in tune with the earth here. I appreciate these moments of depth and stillness. Then once again I wade through the thick black mud and scramble over the twisted knotted roots of the mangrove forest. The sting of mosquitoes hits the bare skin of my neck. Thank goodness for long sleeves. Minutes later Rarrinya appears holding a *nyoka* by its razor-sharp claws.

'*Yä manymak, Waku*,' I yell.

Deeper into the grove we continue, my rubber booties finally sucked off my feet, toe rings gone, top ripped and chocolate-coloured with mud. I am having the time of my life. Again lightness eases me through the root systems, my hat seized from my head and whisked away.

'The mangroves took your hat, ŋändi,' Warmbirrirr deduces.

'*Yow, yuwalk, Waku.*'

Warmbirrirr is very intuitive and we love to talk about spirits together. She is also very religious.

I stare down at my naked feet, mud-laden, scratched yet well earthed, satisfied by this adventure that is just another normal day in the life of Yolŋu. We walk on. Warmbirrirr moves further ahead.

Light cracks the darkness ahead and I finally make it out into the open again. My eyes squint in the light and at the expansiveness of the ocean. Fresh salty air floods my lungs. Ahead, the parched cracked saltpans come into view. I am drawn to observe the many footprints carved in the dry grey mud, ancient footprints of people who have walked with the spirit of the land for so long. I turn and head back into the dark muddy groves. Quickly my legs sink in deep over my knees once again. The women don't seem to sink like me, I mumble under my breath, doubts rising.

Rarrinya, a natural born hunter yet very shy, appears and encourages me. We start to dig for other kinds of shellfish. We spy a hole and then dig deep into it. It's fun trying.

'*Nyoka, nyoka,*' Rarrinya calls. 'These are the tracks.' She points to a wave carved into the thick grey earth.

Finally, the crab becomes visible to my eyes. I reach for my camera and snap photographs. Rarrinya leans down and simply scoops up the stunned crab. We venture back into the heart of it all again. Blood pours from a fresh cut on Rarrinya's ankle.

Back in the heart of the grove, we creep across a thin tree lying over a mesh of roots. Vibrant currents wildly wash through me, shaking me to the core. In a small pool of water ahead, Rarrinya washes all the mud off her. I am dying to jump in the sea but that isn't going to happen with all these *bäru* around. Everyone tells me there are *dharrwa* crocodiles and I believe them but I haven't seen any, except a baby one down on the barge ramp and I've seen a couple of dogs with chewed ears. My *yapas* told me the bites came from crocodiles. The Yolŋu seem very good at avoiding them. I marvel at the women once more, so strong, yet so graceful and feminine, rising up out of the mangroves with nothing less than dinner. I soak in another pool, washing caked mud off my face and hands. We sit together around the campfire enjoying the freshness of the evening meal. My clothes are shredded but I am alive and full of joy.

'When *nhuŋu yapa* adopted you as her sister, you came into the Yirritja moiety,' says my *waku* Maṯay as we dry off by the fire and eat the catch.

'You are Yirritja, your father is Yirritja and his father is Yirritja. *Wäwa* Jo is Yirritja. *Nhuŋu ŋä<u>ndi</u>* is Dhuwa and her mother is Dhuwa. I am your *waku* and I am Dhuwa.'

I look at Maṯay's finely chiselled face. Every strand of hair is perfectly pulled back and her skin radiant. I know I am Yirritja, I know Yibi adopted me into the Gupapuyŋu tribe but I had no idea on that day in 2003 how complex this kinship system would be. It's all been a fog and I don't know if I will ever get it. Occasionally, a fragment becomes clear and the more I slowly understand, the more I realise what a rich and important system this is and what a privilege it is to be part of it. There is something effortless and comforting about being a part of this system and I appreciate this.

I chomp on a piece of mud crab and stare into the orange flames of the fire. For a moment I'm transported back in time to New Year's Eve at the Woodford Folk Festival in northern New South Wales in 1998. Shaun, my sister-in-law Alanna and I were dancing wildly to the band Yothu Yindi outside under the brilliant stars. I was so happy. We all were. Alanna had come all the way from Ireland to visit us and it was her first time in Australia. At midnight, the lead singer of Yothu Yindi brought out a very old man, an elder I presumed. He sang an ancient *manikay*. My arms prickled with goosebumps. There I was dancing with my Irish family and though I did not know it yet, I was in the presence of Yolŋu family too.

Back then I didn't know that the essence of *yothu–yindi* is a system whereby people of opposite moieties cultivate relationships, plan ceremonies, hunt, trade and learn to respect and work with each other. I didn't know that everyone, everything (totems, songs, *buŋguls*), every part of the land has a *ŋändi* as a care giver and a *waku* to support with that care, or about *Märi–gutharra* or *yapa–waku*. I didn't know about the intricate web of creation expressed through Yolŋu *gurruṯu* and these much deeper connections between Yolŋu and land, animals, songs, dances, clans and tribes. Nor did I yet know that the lead singer of Yothu Yindi was my *gutharra*. I certainly touched on something beyond my knowing that night but I also just thought Yothu Yindi was the name of an Indigenous band I loved to dance so wildly to.

I breathe out and look back at my *waku* Maṯay.

*'Märrma mala,'* she continues taking a crab claw from Rarrinya, her *yapa*. 'Dhuwa and Yirritja are the two groups that talk about our relationships. *Warrakan'*, *ga wäŋa, ga gapu, ga matha* are Dhuwa and Yirritja too. And Yirritja marries Dhuwa, *yaka rrambaŋi mälk, wiripu mälk marry, nhe marŋgi?'*

I nod. *'Yow, Waku,* thank you.' Even after a day out hunting in the depths of the mud, she is still teaching me.

## 14

# Gunga – Part 1

It's all out there in the bush for us, *ŋä<u>nd</u>i*. Everything, *gunga*, *miny'tji* to make *bathi* baskets, mats, *ŋatha* to eat *ga dharrwa <u>d</u>iltjipuy mirritjin'* for when we get sick. It's all here on the land, in the sea and in us, our spirit is in us.

– Judy Munymuny

'Bring some *ŋatha* and something to drink,' *Waku* Munymuny advises from under the *djambaŋ* tree. 'We will be gone all day.'

High cheekbones, thick lips and feminine in body, a soft air of grace always emanates from Judy Munymuny. Book in one hand, she peers up and over her the rim of her glasses. *Waku* is always reading, and generally books of a religious nature. She sits on the large cloth on the ground in her pink skirt with white flowers, holding an unlit cigarette in the other hand.

'What shall I bring? Muffins?' I start thinking about my weekly ritual of mixing dates, seeds and raspberries in a bowl.

'*Yow, babalamirri*, just something you would like to eat and water. Bring cold water. We will bring tea, milk and sugar.' Her large brown eyes wander over to *wäwa* Clancy.

Hair curly white and cheeks round, *wäwa* Clancy lies totally relaxed with his head propped up on an old pillow and one leg crossed over the other bent knee. His belly falls down over his grey shorts. Inhaling smoke through his nostrils, he beams a smile. '*Yow*, bring some of those muffins, *Yapa*. *Latju*, you should make *dharrwa* and sell them all over the community, *Yapa*.'

'*Yuwalk, wäwa*?'

He is married to Munguli, also my *waku*, a large strong woman with thick lips, a wide nose and wavy white hair. She emanates queen bee energy of a high order. Grandchildren clamber over her as she sits, pen in hand, doing the weekly crossword puzzle. The dogs sleep, whiskers shivering, eyes twitching as they dream. Children swing on the branches of the trees, giggling, their eyes dancing.

'Wäy, yupthurru,' the women yell out to the kids dangling one-armed from the tree.

Weekend after weekend, we sit under the *djambaŋ* tree. Gentle breezes waft over us. There are two big trees that cast shade outside Munguli's yellow corrugated-iron house. One is a *djambaŋ* tree. These trees are not native to the top end. The Macassans who came from Indonesia to fish for trepang brought them. Long brown pod-like tamarind fruit grows and we scoop them up off the ground as they fall. Their flesh is rich and tart and I've been told the leaves are good to put on a toothache. I don't know what the other tree is, but its green leaves splash out from a thick-bodied trunk and it exudes stability. Children shriek, run after each other and play under those trees and a narrow pathway has been trodden into the grass to the school.

There is a nurse's house across the road, the blue corrugated-iron one with a breezy back veranda and views of the ocean. The principal used to live there. It's been empty for a while now but I hear the new special education teacher will move in there. It is at the end of this street that the patch under the paperbark trees turns into a waterlily pond.

As the weeks roll on, more and more of my time is spent between my *yapa*s down at *Ḏarawunduh*, and the *Djambaŋ miyalk mala*. Sometimes I go for walks with one of the nurses I meet and some of the teachers from school. My friendships with non-Indigenous people are valuable. As we grow together, there is a unique understanding that can only come from living so remotely and sharing a life within an ancient culture. I like to spend as much time as I can with the Yolŋu, though. This is why I am here living on a remote island, by myself, far from the life I knew. I see how often I fluctuate between staying here and going, though. I am never sure how long to stay and I miss my other world too.

Stuart also spends a lot of time with Yolŋu people outside school hours. Non-Indigenous people have their own particular journey here in Arnhem Land. I work hard at school and take work home, but I don't have a boyfriend or a TV, so I figure this leaves me with the opportunity to be more fully immersed in the culture.

'There used to be mango trees growing all along this street, *ŋändi* . It was called Mango Lane,' says Nimanydja, lifting sweeping strands of hair out of my eyes. She often does this.

For years, Nimanydja, Dorothy, Djämbutj, Munguli and her family have sat under the shade of this tree, *djamarrkuḻi* ' playing, sharing stories, playing poker, weaving baskets, living through family dramas. Week after week, the women wait patiently for *Wäwa* Clancy to drive us in the white Land Rover out to the bush. Why doesn't he just get up off the rug and take us, I sometimes think, never as patient as the women.

'I'm going to sit with the *Djambaŋ* girls now,' I often say to Stuart after one of our many cups of tea on his veranda on a Saturday morning.

Contentment settles into my bones. A lackadaisical feeling envelops me when I am with the women. I feel at times this will never change. But nothing is permanent.

Finally, *Wäwa* Clancy rises off the ground and clambers into the Land Rover, cigarette hanging from his mouth. '*Ma! Gu!*'

We pile into the car bundled with empty buckets, fishing lines, assorted sticks, muffins and large tin teacups, and we head out to the old airstrip.

A tiny hand softly directs my face to look out the dusty window at the fire ripping through the grass on the side of the road. *'Nhäŋu*, Mary, *nhäŋu djanda*,' says Joshua Bungalkthun glued to my lap.

I look out the window at the smoke billowing black against the blue sky but I can't see a goanna.

Smiles radiate from every face. I'm calm. My heart is happy and peaceful. In these moments, I always experience a rush of gratitude at where I am, what I am doing and who I am in the company of. I am not even sure why I am so delighted by these experiences, but I often put it down to the spirit of Yolŋu and their ease of being out on the land with kin. Life is less complex in this situation for me. I'm less in my head and more in the moment, present and alive with the sights, the sounds and smells of nature and relaxed in the fabric of Yolŋu kinship.

Red dirt anthills dot the landscape. '*Gun̲dirr, ŋän̲di,*' points Munymuny. 'Sometimes we burn them to keep away the mosquitoes or add coals in the fire, *ŋän̲di.*'

We stop at a patch of trees near the old airstrip.

'*Dhumumu'*. We use these leaves to make black dye,' reveals Munymuny.

I reach up and pull a branch of leaves off the narrow trunk.

'Don't pick the really tiny ones, they are too young,' says Nimanydja, smiling through the thick bunch of leaves she has just pulled off the tree. The sunlight adds a golden glow to her warm smile. She hands the branches to Buŋgalkthun, her grandson, and he puts them in the back of the truck.

Nimanydja is quite tall with fuzzy, silver-grey hair that like most of the women is usually pulled up off her face. She loves lying under a tree in the shade with the kids combing through her hair. Nimanydja is married to *Bäpa* Jo. I call him *mori'*. They are a big family and live across the road from me. Often, church is held there. I love listening to them singing and trying to work out what they are saying in Yolŋu language. Sometimes, though, it feels like the loudspeakers are in my lounge room. *Bäpa* and Nimanydja have six daughters, one adopted son and several grandkids. Three of the daughters, Nunydjulu, Bambaniwuy and Melissa Natuyŋa, work at school. Nunydjulu works in the library, Bambaniwuy in the literacy production centre and Melissa Natuyŋa works in the canteen. They are my lovely *yapas*. Buŋgalkthun is Nunydjulu's son and in my class at school. Nimanydja is always patiently sharing knowledge and welcoming me to join them. I find her sense of humour very nourishing. They frequently bring people over the road to me for healing.

I examine the leaves to make sure they are not too tiny then grab handfuls off the bush and stuff them into the back of the truck too. The leaves are green but once boiled they will produce black dye.

'*Nhäŋu*, Mary, *biḻayn*!' Buŋgalkthun is standing on the edge of the back of the truck; he touches my shoulder and points up in the sky.

The drone of the low-flying plane calls me to look up. This is the difference between living on a remote island and in a city or even a small country town. Even the arrival of a five-seater is an event.

We don't stop long here.

*Wäwa* Clancy is in the driver's seat, arm slung out the window. '*Räli marrtji*,' he instructs, eager to get out hunting.

Everyone is chatting away but as yet I have no clue what is being said really except for a few isolated words like *manymak* and *nhäma*.

We clamber back into the truck, bunches of leaves filling the space between the long seats and *wäwa* drives us to another area. Entering a bit deeper into thicker bush, sweat immediately drips down my arms and off my face, mosquitoes buzz loudly in our ears and swarm in droves around us. I scramble around, collecting sticks and twigs for the fire Munguli is lighting. Nimanydja throws a bunch of leaves into the blaze of orange flames. A mixture of smoke, sweat and the woody smells fills my nostrils.

'We burn these to keep away all those mosquitoes,' says Nimanydja.

Thick smoke billows through the air, dispersing the wretched creatures. My long thick skirt and long-sleeved top are cumbersome but they are modest and protect me from the mozzies and sunburn. The women's colourful floral dresses are long but the fabric is light and thin; their black skin is less tormented by the sun. They are used to this heat.

The sky and the sun are hidden from view in this bushy grove; it's a world away from the saltpans, paperbark swamps, mangroves, grasslands and Milingimbi town right now.

*Wäwa* Clancy is on the outskirts still waiting in the truck.

The children chase each other between trees covered with lush green vines as we dig. Munguli has a long steel rod that she digs the soil away with. I furrow around and find a thick sharp stick to use.

'*Manymak?*' I hold up my stick for Munguli's approval.

'*Yow, manymak*,' she grunts. She is a woman of few words at times.

Nancy Djämbutj and Nimanydja use kitchen knives to dig under separate trees. Djämbutj, also my *waku*, is slim with a moon face and wide mouth. Her eyes dance and sometimes she has a look of surprise on her face. Other times she looks quite serious and a frown grows on her forehead. She often makes jokes and makes me laugh.

I sit close to Munguli, stop and swallow almost half my water but she keeps digging silently for *guṉinyi* roots. Faces light up with joy as the rich bulky roots surface up from the deep red-brown earth. These roots produce lots of rich yellow colour for weaving. I scratch deeply beneath the surface and haul up more chunky roots, eagerly pulling the mud off them, my fingernails cracked and filled with dirt, my heart full of glee.

'*Yä, manymak,*' Nimanydja yells over when she sees the root I have dug up.

Munguli is still digging and digging calmly until she pulls up a huge thick root from deep in the ground. '*Djamarrkuḻi*',' she yells to the kids.

Buŋgalkthun scampers around, finding a large piece of brown feathery bark. He puts it down and runs off to chase the child that has just tagged him. Munguli places the dirt-coloured roots down on the bark. Inside the root is bright yellow. We all lay our findings down on the bark.

Though parts of the bush are lush green, crackly dry leaves, bits of sticks and roots make up the earth floor.

A long decaying skin lies among the leaves.

'Snake,' says Munguli. 'King brown.'

'*Bäpi, bäpi,*' shouts another one of my *waku*. He is tiny yet strong as he hurls a handmade spear into the bush.

'*Nhäŋu*!' says Nimanydja, holding out her hand covered in tiny red seeds.

'Beautiful,' I say. I look down to find more seeds.

'We call these *Yiriŋaniŋ* and we can make jewellery with them,' smiles Nimanydja, 'but now we will collect *gunga*.'

'*Manymak,*' I say.

*Wäwa* Clancy, asleep over the wheel, wakes up, lights a cigarette and drives us deeper into the vicinity of a pandanus region and then leaves us for the day to do our *miyalk gunga djäma*.

'*Ḏarra ga marrtji huntinglil,*' he says with a wave.

*Gunga djäma* is women's business, after all; he wants to be off in the wild with the men catching food.

'*Yow, manymak, Wäwa.*' I reach into my bag pull out a muffin and hand it to him.

'*Yow, ma!*' he laughs, puts the muffin on the dashboard and drives off. The car leaves a trail of red dust as he goes off into the distance.

The women have already dispersed and are collecting pandanus. I can't see the children either.

I look at Munymuny and wonder what she is spying for.

She leans down, picks up a long stick, and pulls off a few leaves and thin branches. She leaves one short branch at the top of the stick that makes a natural hook.

'*Nhä dhuwal*?' I try some Yolŋu *matha.*

'*Dharpa.* We use this to reach up high on those *yindi* 'pandanus trees and drag out the leaves.'

I watch her reach the stick up high and hook the pandanus and pull it out. She makes it look easy. I have been out quite a few times with the women before but I haven't pulled much pandanus on my own; well, a few times with Muwalkmuwuy and Jessie.

'We pull out the centre of the plant.'

I look at the bunch of long streamlined spears nestled firmly together.

'*Birrka'yun,*' says Munymuny.

My hands are soft and it's quite a painful task. In fact, in my past efforts it hurt like hell. I pull and tug and haul and still the centre remains in the plant. My hands are red and torn by the spikes. The women step and reach up and it seems they barely tug and out slides the central stalk easily and effortlessly.

'*Bitjan,*' they say in unison, calmly. '*Bitjan nhe dhu djäma!*'

'*Ma*',' I respond.

I am impatient and grunt in frustration, but finally I get the central stalk out and throw it on the growing pile of pandanus. I realise that with less effort the pandanus will just slide out. I notice the women each have a pillowcase to put their pile of pandanus into.

With plenty collected, we settle in one place for the rest of the day. This spot is a clear space on the red sandy earth with fewer trees. The dirt road here leads back to town, another flows deeper into the bush and out to the billabong. The airstrip is beside us. I can see the sky again now with its large vertical clouds hanging high against the blue.

I help collect sticks and twigs for the fire that is beginning to crackle. Munymuny uses narrow pointed tweezers to draw the *dimitimirr* from her slender hands. I use my dirt-filled fingernails to prise the pointed spikes out from under the skin on my shredded fingers and wrists. As the weeks pass, I am always the one with the most spike-ridden hands.

'*Dharrwa, dharrwa,*' laughs Munymuny.

'*Yow, dharrwa, Waku.*'

We gather more wood and build up the fire. A large tin for boiling water for copious cups of tea is immediately placed on to boil. A bag of tea bags, sugar and tin of powdered milk lie next to the fire. Old powdered milk tins, lemonade cans or whatever we can find are used for cups when there aren't enough real ones.

# 15

# Uluru

Welcome to Aboriginal Land

'You are as big tea drinkers as the Irish,' I say to the *Djambaŋ miyalk mala* as we sit around watching the tea brew in the big tin pot.

I stare into the flames and remember my ex-husband Shaun. We drank a lot of tea. I recall a moment some years ago when we sat sipping the hot liquid, our shivering skin warmed by a crackling orange fire on our Uluru journey, the one that changed everything forever.

My mind takes me back to that time and place now. I am back in the desert, back in the campervan with Shaun, driving along the Stuart Highway heading for Uluru, grey and pink galahs wheeling across the sky. It was getting late and we were keen to make the most of the seven days we had up there. I wound down the window and gazed at the expansive red earth.

> Blood red earth and a mind as blank
> As a cloudless sky, hey I know why…
> I'm thoughtless
> My mind is in peace
> I've fallen for this outback land
> that takes my hand and drives me out along this highway
> Take ancient culture with their stories so strong
> After thousands of years you still hear and feel their song
> You'll find it along…this highway
> Add a little taste from every culture in this world
> Mold it together with our tears and our bloodied earth
> You'll find it along…this highway

The words of my brother Johnnie Mac's song 'Highway' poured through my lips.

I breathed in the spaciousness and rugged beauty. I smelt the heat. The bare open flatness before my eyes was liberating, the colours and earthy scent of the land welcome on my senses. Mulga shrubs and desert oak trees dotted the dry landscape. The air was warm, but not too hot. It was winter and so good to be on the road again. Shaun and I were gypsies at heart. He loved to drive and I loved to sit with my feet up on the dash, singing, my hair flying in the wind as I leaned out the window.

At dusk, we pulled up at a rest stop with wooden tables, chairs and fireplaces, and parked among the gum trees. The stark burning sunlight softened as the sun went down. Shaun and I were immediately at home in our mobile house. We collected sticks and wood, built a fire, and set up our steel-framed camping chairs and table. I sat on the chair but ended up as usual sitting on the earth close to the fire, digging a hole in the dirt with a stick just as I did in my suburban backyard when I was a kid. I spread the red plastic tablecloth out and laid out snacks for us to enjoy. The local blowflies were hungry too, but apparently they were even worse and impossible to shake off at the hottest time of year. As night fell, the temperature dropped quickly and we began to shiver.

I looked at Shaun and felt I was seeing him for the first time in ages. His face was relaxed and the shadows around his eyes had faded in only a day or two. The pressure of the world, I was thinking, is too much to bear in a big city but at least we lived in the beach suburbs now.

Shaun took my hand and we both looked up at the same moment and shouted 'Wow!' at the sight of the Milky Way, a liquid stream of milk floating in the dark night sky, sparkling with masses of stars.

The temperature dropped even more. Shaun poured a pot of water on the fire and the flames sizzled out spreading smoke through the dark. Quickly we packed up, brushed our teeth under a tree and scrambled into bed in the van. I pulled blankets up over us. We peered out through the back window, whispering to each other about our perfect view of the stars above.

'Shooting star, shooting stars,' I squealed as I watched two burning gold stars plummet out of the sky. I closed my eyes tight and made two wishes. I wished we could be like this all the time, content within ourselves and with each other and inspired by life. I wished we could make a baby together right there on the wild red earth. After all we had been through that year with me not being able to conceive, home renovations and Shaun's dad being unwell, this was a moment of calm content relief and it brought new hope to me for our future together.

It was 26 June 1998 and I woke up quickly and instantly refreshed. Morning birdcalls greeted my ears and the sense of expansiveness of the outback was most inspiring. I jumped out of bed just in time to witness the huge ball of the sun ascend beyond mother earth. I was speechless for a second and shivering with cold. Our outdoor table was covered in ice, but my eyes were pulled back to the sunrise and I reached my arms up and out and breathed its bright yellow rays onto my face and received its warmth into my body. The sky was a vivid blue and the day beautiful.

'Shaun, Shaun, you have to see this,' I called.

In seconds, he leaped out of the van and started jumping up and down. It felt good to see him so happy. We used to be such a playful pair and for now, in this new environment, we were feeling a little this way again. We made tea and toast on the camping stove and headed off for Uluru.

Finally, we came to our vision, the icon, the magnetic red rock Uluru. A wedge-tailed eagle soared across the sky above us and a large sign stood with these words:

*Puku Ngalaya Yanama*
*Ananguku Ngurakutu*
*Pukulpa Pitjama Ananguku*
*Ngurakutu*
Welcome to Aboriginal Land

I attempted to read the sign. The welcome messages were written in Yankunytjatjara and Pitjantjara, the two main dialects spoken by the park's traditional owners.

'Pretty amazing, isn't it?' said Shaun as we walked towards the rock.

'Totally.' I could barely speak; my feet were stuck to the ground. We stood before the massive red rock. People were climbing it. We did not. Sweat formed on my skin and tears spilled down my face as we walked around it. In addition to grief, I also experienced the strength of Mother Earth. Her power is alluring. I am like an ant in her presence, so tiny yet enshrouded in this depth. The power is Uluru and the energy of its ancient people, the original people who lived on this land now named Australia. My feet sank deeper into the earth there, grounding me. An incredible energy emanated from the giant rock, a mixture of calm, spaciousness, yet haunting stillness. I was captivated in its sphere under the vast blue sky. The birds, trees, shrubs, every stone and rock pulsated with life and the power of the hearts of the people who have dwelled in this area for so long.

I was abruptly urged to respect this place, aware of the privilege to be there yet somehow I recognised it and felt at home. I was transfixed in a lucid mystical web. My body softened and loosened, permitting the earth's strong hold, and received the invitation into the stillness of the moment. At the same time, I had some trepidation of the enormity of what I was experiencing. Deep in me, I was aware that the event was life changing, that nothing would ever be the same once I left there. I struggled to put the feeling into words.

'This place is so different, isn't it, Shaun?'

'What do you mean?' he asked.

'I feel strong: earthed here, held in something larger than me. It's like another world.'

'Oh yeah, it's eerie all right.'

He was quiet. I knew something was different for him there too. We were both more relaxed and calm in the majesty of our surroundings.

I continued to walk with my own thoughts. It was strange and wonderful. Contentment settled in my cells but I was afraid of what it would do to my life as it was then, to my life with Shaun. This moment reeked of an opportunity at the price of deep loss. A knowing grew in me that part of me wanted nothing but to remain in ignorance. But that would not be possible. I am a woman who claims to want truth and if I wanted that, I was going to have to be strong and possibly even alone at times. Perhaps my tears of sorrow were for the atrocities on Indigenous culture, and also for the pending loss of my life, as I knew it then. I have always experienced grief before it occurs in tangible form.

My dreams leading up to that trip to the desert had been memorably vivid. It was as if I was going through a deep learning curve and a confronting preparation for change was taking place.

In the evening, I lay under a tree, scrawling down my thoughts in a recycled paper journal I had brought with me. I took my new black-ink pen and drew a kangaroo, echidna, snake and a goanna. I added various dots and lines to the outlines of the animals and then I drew some clap sticks and a boomerang. I was totally absorbed as I drew; something was waking up in me, some knowing. I sighed. What the hell am I thinking? I know nothing. But it all seemed so familiar and an excitement was building in my heart, something new was opening in me with the influx of all this knowledge.

Sinewy trees. Alluring land. Magnificent stars. Peace at last. Thank you.
Spirit dwells here in this land and it pours through my cells like liquid gold.
I will be on Aboriginal land again one day soon.

These were the last words I scrawled down in my journal that day before I snuggled up with Shaun for another cosy night in the chilly wilderness.

The sun went down after our big day at Kata Tjuta and a spectacular show of colours began to form. We stared speechless, in awe of the brilliant hot pink, blue, purple and vivid gold that tinted the sky. That day, I had walked alone through the craggy rock valley. I was a bit jumpy at times. Spirit was so tangible, walking with me, lightly touching my face with its breeze. 'Mary, who are you? Who are you?' The wind had whispered in my ears and stopped me in my tracks on the solid earth. Yes. Good questions. 'Who am I and where does my true strength lie?' I inquired.

We sat quietly, both deep in thought about the energy of where we were and, for me, about life beyond this magic. What will it be like? How will we be? Can we make it? But we said nothing.

Darkness quickly dissolved the residue of daylight as we drove off the road and quickly found a spot and started up a fire to cook some red kidney beans. The white crescent moon glowed, orange flames crackled, breaking our silence. Held by the depth of the desert, I was deeply soothed and my heart expanded, open.

We nestled into each other, keeping warm in our campervan bed. In the night, I woke up crying from a very lucid dream. In the dream, my gold and emerald Irish wedding ring flew off my finger, snatched by a whirlwind of red dust, and was blown wildly into the arms of Mother Earth. My face was wet with tears. My body shook. I lay shivering in the icy cold desert air, clasping for my wedding ring to make sure it was still on my finger.

'Mary, it's just a dream.' Shaun hugged me close, comforting me as I shared with him.

'No, no, that wasn't just a dream at all,' I said weakly.

It was a call from the red earth, I whispered to myself. This is the red earth's claim.

Some sixteen months later, my marriage with Shaun ended. It was not too long after a trip we had made together back to Ireland. While there, we celebrated our marriage again and had our wedding bands blessed by an Irish priest in the local church where Shaun grew up.

Back in Australia, the tension between us was now insurmountable, the divide between us great. Shaun and I were different in our habits. I had liked this and appreciated the fact we were two individuals yet shared a great deal as well. It did not seem to matter for years. Now it did. There were lots of pressures. But perhaps it was none of those influences, perhaps it was just time for each of us to move on. My intentions of harmony just eluded me. Why? Expectations? Karma? Trying hard to make something work when it just doesn't? The expiry date had arrived but I didn't want to know about it. I was tired of trying to figure out why.

Back in my healing room at our home in Mona Vale, I pulled myself up off the floor into a meditation position with my spine straight, shoulders relaxed, face soft. I closed my eyes and brought my attention to my breath. I opened my eyes again and flicked the lighter, creating a strong flame to burn some more white sage. The smoke was thick and rich in scent. I wanted the truth. That was my intention for the ritual. My life could not go on as it was. I sliced the air around my energy field with the eagle feather and called in spirit for help. Smoke is purifying. It clears the way forward. I allowed the sage to continue to waft in its ceramic pot.

I have always found this ritual perfectly natural and essential for well-being and for moments of transition. As a child, I burned eucalyptus leaves as I sat on the pine needles under the trees in our suburban backyard. As the smoke curled and wafted around me, I was soothed by its scent. I knew nothing of smoking ceremonies back then. I cannot claim to know another culture's way with smoking ceremonies but I am certainly interested in such practices and love learning about them. I've always been intrigued by other cultures. After seeing an advertisement in the *Sydney Morning Herald*, I was compelled to attend the Festival of the Dreaming. I am still moved by the memory of the Smoking of Sydney Harbour at Bennelong Point on 14 September 1997. With traditional dance, song and didgeridoos, the land was cleansed and the spirits awakened. As I let the smoke billow over me and through my cells, I believed I was cleansed too and that something awoke in me. That night on the steps of the Sydney Opera House, under the stars blurred by a white smoke-filled sky, I intended for change, for our original people and for me too.

I placed the backs of my hands onto my knees and focused on my third eye, the space between my eyebrows and the centre of my palms. I listened to my breath and tried to be still. My mind was so busy and my emotions turbulent but I kept returning to my breath and the sensations in my body. I held Shaun's image in my mind's eye and I spoke to him.

'I don't know what to do any more, Shaun. I don't even know you. I know it's been very hard but all of a sudden I have no way of reaching you. I want us to be together forever but I just don't know how to make it happen.'

Heat burnt through the centre of my palms, tears rolled down my cheeks yet I remained still, quiet and listening.

Then I heard his voice in my head: 'I love you Mary, but I can't go with you. I can't go where you are going.'

'Where am I going?' I asked out loud.

I was perplexed but accepted his words. 'Okay.'

I often talk to people during a meditation. I find there is a clear link between us that way. Of course, talking face to face is ideal but when the power struggle is on, it helps get the truth out simply and freely. After all, we are made up of molecules and atoms and intrinsically linked to each other, so it makes sense we can communicate without being in the same room, or the same country for that matter. I cannot control anyone through this ritual but I can speak my own truth and offer an opportunity for another person to share theirs for the good of us all.

My body slumped with the grief at this reality. I curled up on the floor once more and cried.

Half an hour passed and Shaun edged his way in through the heavy door of our healing room. Large shadows circled his eyes, his face pale. He stood before me. 'Mary, I have to go. I'll go tomorrow. I have to go.'

Shaun was gone, and two days later wanted a divorce and our house, and my business on the market. I knew so well it was coming. My dreams and walks along the beach were screaming at me but I admit my resistance. It was happening so fast. He might as well have been dead, because after living so closely for so long I didn't even know where he had gone. I just came home to find empty wardrobes and spaces where things of 'his' had been. I was feeling physically severed, gut-wrenched, and there was a wide gaping hole in my heart where he had dwelled. In truth, though, we vacated each other well before that day. Under my shock and pain there was a sea of calm, the feeling that it was absolutely right, but I was conflicted between that knowing and my resistance.

On one of the first mornings I had woken up alone in years, I walked into the kitchen to find the kettle boiling. Thanks, Mum. Yes, I was traumatised and could have been hallucinating, but I knew better and I know spirit exists and family who have passed over can be close at times. And Mum was there for me.

I stopped doing healings after Shaun left but I kept one or two of my classes going. Some of my students had been coming to classes with me for years and were a great support. I smoked the whole house and said out loud, 'If it's time to leave, then I'll leave. Clear the way and sell this house!'

'Have you sold your house yet, Mary?' asked Marg, one of my long-term students, after our meditation class the Tuesday night after my smoking ritual.

And that was it. The house was sold, quickly and simply, thanks to my acceptance of change, spirit, timing and Marg.

I left the healing space, my Sydney home and marriage to embark on my own journey of restoration. With a mixture of sadness and excitement, I decided to head north. That night Banjo, my nephew, was born in a pool on the lounge room floor in the forest of Northern New South Wales.

# 16

# Gunga – Part 2

When we weave, *ŋän̲di*, we know that everything is okay. As we thread each colour in and out, in and out and as our basket grows bigger, and strong, it must be strong, there is peace in this quiet time and we enjoy each other and we enjoy being out here on the land.

– Stephanie Nimanydja

My mind returns from the past and my eyes to Munguli, Nimanydja, Munymuny, Gamuti, Djämbutj and Ganyawu. We each have a pile of pandanus grass neatly stacked beside us. We begin to strip the grass using our fingernails to split it. This process is called *giyalaram*. We discard the part not needed and keep the best piece for weaving. The strips are laid to dry and kept as natural colour, or a bunch added to one of the tins of water with roots boiling on the fire. *Gun̲inyi* roots for yellow colour, green leaves for black colour and reddish brown roots for brown dye.

*Waku* Munymuny appears from the bush, a grey-coloured branch named *guŋurru'* in the crook of her arm. She dips it into the fire and takes a sip of her large silver camping mug of tea. She waits patiently for the branch to burn to the ground. Flayed by the fire, its bark cracks and burns into a mound of light grey ash. *Waku* scoops up the ash with a tin cup and mixes it with the yellow dye, producing a stunning red purplish colour.

I plonk some firewood down, watching *Waku* intently. In this moment, the depth of her knowledge profoundly moves me and I realise that there is so much we don't know, not only about how connected our first nations people are to this land, but we know so little about how sustainably they have worked with this land for thousands of years.

'See that *dharpa*,' points Munymuny, 'it is used to make red dye. In the wet season, this area will be swamp and we won't be able to collect *gunga* then,' she declares.

The stripping back of pandanus spears requires patience and learning. Some days I just give up in frustration. The women are always so patient. Tea continues to boil on the hot fire amongst tin cans of yellow, brown and black dyes simmering away, performing their alchemy.

Nimanydja hands me a small round green fruit. I bite into it and its taste is tart yet sweet.

'*Mmmm manymak, nhä dhuwal?*' I ask.

'*Munydjutj,*' smiles Nimanydja.

We snack on bush fruit and home-baked date muffins with our tea.

The troopie pulls up with two lean young Yolŋu men hanging off the back and *wäwa* driving.

'*Manymak ŋatha,*' says *wäwa* as he throws some freshly caught trevally fish on the fire.

One of the young men puts down a brown paper parcel next to Munguli.

'Mmmm, *gurrumaṯtji,*' says Ganyawu (Munguli's daughter, my *gäthu*, eyeing the brown paper parcel. She gets up and pulls some green leaves off a nearby bush to make plates to put the food on.

The men vanish.

'Has *wäwa* had some *gurrumaṯtji* to eat, Gäthu?'

'*Yo bili, mukul.*'

Gäthu Ganyawu puts some leaves down before me and places a piece of magpie goose on the leaves. '*Ḏayi,*' she says. Wavy shoulder-length hair, plump shape, her face is the same round shape as her mother's, Munguli, and she's very warm-hearted and affectionate. Ganyawu teaches me a lot about everything but is constantly helping me understand how I'm related to whomever I meet. Gäthu works in administration in the school office.

The men had cooked the bird as soon as they caught it.

'*Manymak ŋatha,*' says *gäthu*.

Everyone is smiling and encouraging me to eat the catch. I hesitate for a moment. It's been twenty years or more since I last ate chicken or red meat, but I decided when I came up here that if I was out bush with the Yolŋu, I would be part of the community and eat whatever was offered to me. This way of life is Yolŋu tradition and I want to be a part of it. I shyly take a bite. Its flesh is soft, warm and salty.

After lunch, we get back to work. More tea is put on the boil. I have lots of questions brewing in me, one about the billabong.

A small plane flies over; its drone calls our attention. There is great discussion about who may be on the plane and where they are going. Everyone is linked to everyone and everything going on at this island Yurrrwi. We are positioned at the edge of the airstrip facing the bush.

'When you go up in the plane, we will wave up at you and be crying, *Ḏä<u>nd</u>i*,' smiles Djämbutj.

'*Yä marrkap*,' I smile at Djämbutj.

'What is special about *<u>N</u>ilatjirriwa*, our billabong, *Waku* Nimanydja?' I finally ask.

'It's *manymak*, a creation *wäŋa*, a strong spiritual *wäŋa*. It has a sacred *dharpa* growing under it and it's your old *Yapa* Muwalkmuwuy's *waŋarr*,' says *Waku* Nimanydja. 'That means it is your totem too.'

'Wow, I like that. *Manymak*,' I say, tingles running down my arms.

'Munguli has started a new *bathi* for you,' says Ganyawu. She hands me a small sphere of tightly woven brown pandanus. 'Weave, Mary.'

*Yapa* Muwalkmuwuy was the first one who did this for me down at Ḏarawundhuh.

I focus hard on moving the long thin silver needle in the right direction.

'You got it back to front, Mary,' Nimanydja smiles.

'*Bäydhi*,' Muwalkmuwuy said to me when I sat with her. She patiently pulled apart my efforts and helped me start all over again.

Finally, my skin eases as the day cools down and dusk emerges. Tinges of pink and purple spread across the sky. A tremendous stillness melts all my tension away; the silence draws me into deep peace. A bird's song brings my wandering mind back to the moment in a beautiful way. I love these days so much and marvel as I watch these women of such grace working away, their warmth and laughter with each other. They are like strong trees deeply rooted into their land, culture and language. I receive their strength and their grace.

I lie down on the earth and allow my body to soften. After a few breaths, I feel the earth holding me and I relax and receive its natural energy. My limbs unwind and pain and tension melt away. I lie very still, gazing up to an expansive blue sky, absorbing the vibration of the soft lull of Yolŋu language. A welcome breeze washes over me, the sting of the bright sun now gone. I hear a stream of Yolŋu words in my ear, not only from the women but also through the whispering wind as if from the ancient past.

'*Walu, Ḏändi.*'

'*Waku.*' Munymuny's voice brings me back from my drowsy state.

I sit up and scrounge around for my pen.

'*Ḏalindi.*'

I repeat the words and write them down on my post-it notepad.

The meditative state I feel when basket weaving calls me to reflect on and accept my past and move through it. Fertility is about the creation of a child in one's womb but it is also the power held within each of us to create in many ways, in life-giving, joyous ways. And the question I quietly reflect on is, how can we best use this creative force in sustainable ways that are supportive in community? Now that I'm not a mother in the traditional sense of the word, how can I use the creation energy that lies within me in a way that is beneficial? At times I have equated not birthing a child with my worth in the world or lack of it, but actually I do hold the same power as a mother, and so how shall I express this power now? I rest my hands on my chest and feel my breath moving in my heart and lungs. I imbue this thought with the life force: this thought that I am worthy despite my perceived failings. I acknowledge my true feelings as they arise and then breathe the power of acceptance into the cells of my body and mind.

The energy of potent sacred spiritual creation is alive in each and every stage of the weaving process. To be truly present, one must slow down and be fully focused on the weaving journey, thorough in every action to produce strong, stable baskets. Dilly bags, ceremonial armbands, mats and teapot stands, hats and even bras are created from the simple, strong pandanus fibre. To start with, the women choose a colour and begin to weave a tiny ring of pandanus. They can weave with their fingers or use a thick shiny silver needle to weave in and out, threading colours together. Each ring is created with thought and calm. Each thread is weaved tightly with care and grace to create a structure that is strong, resilient and can endure time: strong enough to hold a baby if need be. Baskets can be used to collect bush food or medicine and these days used as handbags. Traditionally, though, and still at times today, armbands and *bathis* are used for sacred ceremonies. Weaving is done with great care so that as each unique creation emerges, it contains the energy of shared time together, whispers of the breeze like ancient tongue speaking, the language, the ancestors, the spaciousness of silence, the stories, the harmony, the joy, the listening of the women, the laughter of children and the experience of life as timeless and culture as strong. The pandanus mats, baskets and unique creations hold the strength, the rich knowledge, the wisdom, the calm, the feminine power and presence of Yolŋu women and their ancestors. These creations hold the stories of past and present. The women pass these stories on to the children for future generations.

I liken these processes to meditations I have experienced. All kinds of thoughts, feelings arise during each process and no matter how far I wander or allow my insecurities to try and take over, I must return to what I am doing, digging up roots, pulling pandanus spears or weaving a basket. Over time, the basket grows and reveals itself more fully. As I grow into it, it is possible to let go of doubts, fears, desires and dreams that have surfaced during its creation. The women are completely at ease in this unfolding beauty, centred in this production of magnificent pandanus creations.

Out there in the bush with the women, I know they are so happy to be doing exactly what they are doing and not wishing for more or different, and that is also how I feel with my Yolŋu family, content and blessed to be alive. In yoga, we call this state *Santosha*. Out here for a period of time, I am removed from the predictable stream of thought and allow deep stillness in the moment.

The day I finish making my first basket, I believe I have achieved a new level as a woman. I have rekindled my female power. No, I have not birthed children, but the energy of creation is alive in me, potent and wanting to be expressed in whatever I feel called to do and share. Right now, my maternal instinct is expressed in the classroom and this community with Yolŋu children.

I admit that I've had some help. In fact, all the women have done a little work on my basket at one time or another. I'm happy that my *bathi* is infused with the power of Yolŋu women. The reason being that often, as soon as I settle into my weaving out here in the bush, a truck pulls up next to us with someone who is in need of healing or I'm picked up and whisked off to someone who is unwell. Yolŋu always know where to find me.

'*Djirripuma*: healing *djäma, Dändi*. This one wants *djirripuma* healing *djäma*.'

Something new is evolving for me in my practice here. The more healing work I do on Milingimbi, the more I notice my hands begin to move about and flick energy in ways they never have before.

'*Marrŋgitj*,' the children whisper as they giggle and wave their hands around in the air, mimicking me.

# 17

# Old Yapa

She was elder *miyalk*. We called her Ḏerrk.
She was wise because she was close to *wäwa* mob. They used to talk to her about everything, small or big, any matter. She was strong in the community. *Yapa* used to give support to the family. She was a culture woman *ŋayi*, and she used to teach the young people how to hunt and gather and she encouraged the young mothers. She would say 'strong women, strong culture, strong babies.'

She would dance at any *buŋgul*, *waku buŋgul*, *bäpa buŋgul*, Gupapuyŋu, Djambarrpuyŋu, she used to dance.

Ḏerrk, Yibi Yibi and Mawukuwuy, are the women the *wäwa*s go to. *Wäwa* respect those *miyalk*. They work together in the community.

– Jessie Murarrgirarrgi

The welcome breeze of *Mayaltha* season caresses the skin on my face. Waves of heat still press against my skin, though. It's blistering and some rain would be nice. It will come.

Time has rolled on and now it's February 2004. By the end of last year, I was in conflict about whether to return or not. I'm learning so much, I love my reunion with school teaching, the kids and the culture but I tend to go overboard with schoolwork and helping out in the community with healing work. My fair skin suffers in the heat; it itches, and rashes and bites plague me at times, and sometimes I worry about not getting the right food. Perhaps, though, it is my belief system that is holding me back. Maybe if I didn't worry about food and my skin so much it would be okay.

I had a special Christmas here. Jessie turned up on the doorstep with a huge turkey for the family for later. She stuck it in the oven and pulled me by my arm and walked me down to *Ḏarawundhu*, where Yibi and two of my *waku* formed a circle around me. They hugged me tightly and began to wail. Within the tightness of their embrace and resonance of their throaty wail, I started sobbing.

'These are tears for you, because you are not with your other family, and tears for your family because you are not with them, and tears of happiness for us because we are here together,' said Yibi Yibi.

A week later, I flew down to New South Wales to see everyone. Now, I'm happy to be back here, excited even and I'm thinking I will probably leave in June at the end of term two but I really don't know. What I do know is that once I'm immersed in life again here, I'll become absorbed once more in the ripple of Yolŋu time, where everything is in the moment and the moment changes, and so whether or when I come and go doesn't really matter.

White cockatoos screech, wings flap and span wide as they flip themselves around the branches in circles on the trees some distance away. '*Ḏerrk, litjalaŋ waŋarr*,' explains my white-haired old *Yapa* Muwalkmuwuy.

She is always making reference to spirit in some form other than human; in fact, so are most of the women. In Yolŋu culture, land, earth and spirit are one. The two realms meet and are inseparable. Spirit is not some far-off topic to be discovered, realised, remembered or discussed when the time is right. Spirit is experienced in everything all the time.

Discussions on spiritual healing and premonitions are frequent in our times together.

'I always know when someone has gone.' Old *Yapa* whisks her hand up and raises her eyes to the clear blue. 'I pray for the sick,' she says. *Yapa* points to an old man not far away. '*Bun'kumu rerri ŋayi*.'

A tall thin woman with straggly hair approaches. 'Hello, *Yapa*,' she says. 'Can you help me? I have lung cancer, my arms ache and *Djawaryun ŋarra*, I'm tired.'

Muwalkmuwuy ushers her to sit down. I use an old blanket to prop her back up and gently encourage her to become aware of her breathing. I hold her head and feel her body relax.

After a while, she says, 'I'm *manymak* now, *Yapa*.' She rolls over onto her side and slowly comes up and walks off.

'*Ḏarra dhiyaŋu bala*,' says old *Yapa* Muwalkmuwuy. She lies down on her back and takes my hand and places it on her chest.

'*Ḏarra ga djawaryun. Rirrikthun ŋarra*. Asthma, *Yapa, ga mel*. We are healers, you *ga* me. We can help the sick. Now you can help me.'

I encourage her to sit and bunch pillows so she is upright for more freedom in the airways, and rest my hands on her smooth skin.

'*Wäy, marrkap*.' A smile lights up her face. She begins to pray in Yolŋu matha. The sounds of her gentle voice and language permeate the air.

I connect with my breathing and help *Yapa* to slowly deepen her breathing too. I look down and notice a tear trickle down *Yapa*'s face.

I run my fingertips lightly over her forehead and hold my hands just over her eyes.

'*Latju*,' she murmurs.

Her hair white as snow, face round, gentle eyes, she is motherly and generous with her time, warmth and knowledge. Old *Yapa* can speak English but she speaks mostly in Yolŋu. This inspires me to attempt to learn some Yolŋu language. Old *Yapa* works at the clinic with the Strong Women's group and sings hymns at the old, red, mud-brick church.

*Yapa* falls asleep. Most people do after I work with them.

I sit for a moment and focus on my breath. I remember the frustration I felt one day as I spoke to Jessie.

'When am I going to learn your ways of healing, *Yapa*?'

Jessie stopped and lightly touched my face, holding me in her gaze. 'We learn by doing, *Yapa*.'

And it hit me: all these sessions I am giving are also my education and something is changing in the way I work with my hands.

I jiggle the noisy gearstick in my hand. Spluttering sounds echo out from this old ochre Jeep I am driving for old *Yapa* Muwalkmuwuy. She bought it from the teacher-librarian who was leaving the community. Our *waku* drives her around often but lately I am the designated driver for our trips out to collect pandanus. *Yapa*, in her white dress with orange flowers, sits quietly next to me, holding a large blanket my dear friend Kim from Sydney sent up as a gift for her.

We are heading back to *Ḏarawundhu* after a day in the bush. My hands are covered in thorns from the spiky leaves but I don't care. Today the whole of the camp is closed off due to sacred business. This means no *balanda* can enter the area. A woman is very sick, so *Yapa* is taking me to her to give some healing.

'*Dhunupa*,' she points, directing me forwards.

'What about sacred business?' I ask nervously.

'*Manymak, Yapa*,' she responds.

The Jeep door creaks loudly as I open it and step onto the ground.

A group of men sit under a tree outside the blue, brick house. They play *yiḏaki* and sing for the sick woman.

*Yapa* ushers me into a dimly lit room. There is no furniture. I am blanketed by heat.

A thin woman lies on a simple mattress inside. Her bones protrude. Women and children lie and sit around her, some speaking in low voices. Their hands gently stroke her long limbs. Her fine hair whispers against her thin, gaunt face, her eyes blink rapidly.

'*Yow,*' the women greet me as I enter the space.

The dying woman's floral skirt sits above her breast line and falls down around her frail body. Her arms writhe and wave in restless turmoil. A steady stream of sweat pours down her arms and legs. For now, she cannot find comfort. Her face harrowed, tears spring in my eyes. Women massage their strong hands into her feet and hands.

Everything in my life is diminished into this moment. Nothing else exists. In fact, when old *Yapa* asked me, I was more than happy to give support, but I wasn't expecting this. It is an abrupt awakening.

I look over at old *Yapa*, sitting against the wall. The *biḻma* beat hard and loud outside, the men's chanting intensifies. Old *Yapa's* shoulders curl over and large tears tumble down her cheeks. I am sitting behind the women immediately surrounding the dying woman.

'*Gapu, gapu.*'

The woman's cry brings my eyes back on her.

A woman brings a plastic cup of water to her parched lips and pours some over her sweat-drenched body.

Women and children wander in and out of the room in the blue house, weeping, wailing and showing their love and care for her.

Momentarily she is still, then she sits right up and looks me straight in the eye. Waving a finger, she yelps, 'Help me, *Yapa*, help me.'

I want to help but I can't understand why I am even allowed in such an intimate space. Suddenly my thoughts are loud in my head. It feels weird, wrong even, that I am here. I don't know her except that a few times she came and lay under the tree for healing with me. I find myself squirming uncomfortably.

Her breath clatters in her chest; she must be close to death now. I have seen this before in other people and heard it referred to as the 'death rattle.' What touches me is the time and concern this woman is receiving on her deathbed from her family and in fact the whole community. This is the first intimate involvement I have had with death on Yolŋu land, and something tells me it won't be the last. I have experienced plenty in my own life but there are generally not swarms of people around a dying person in the world I come from.

'Okay, *Yapa*, do your *djäma*,' a woman behind me softly utters, as if hearing my conflicting thoughts. She touches my back to edge me closer.

I exhale deeply and get out of my head. I join the beauty of the woman's presence in the room and go to work to help relieve her suffering. I kneel close to the woman and place my hands just above her chest. I close my eyes and encourage a space of peace for her so that she can have a calm, smooth, death transition if that is true for her now. My hands wave over her chest and sweep up through the crown of her head. Her body becomes limp as she relaxes and allows peace to prevail.

I relax too at the sight of the change in her. Her face softens and her body rests in a limp state.

A dense mood of sorrow, tears and heat penetrates the room. The space is held sacred for her by the sounds of the men chanting and playing *yidaki* outside.

I sit back down on my heels with my hands in my lap and glance over at old *Yapa* Muwalkmuwuy again. She moves her mouth towards the door, signalling to move outside the room.

We sit quietly together around a glowing campfire.

'When Yolŋu *rirrikthun*, those *dirramu mala* sing the old songs to help them feel *manymak* and get their strength back,' old *Yapa* explains, using some words in English as she pokes the fire with a long stick.

She cooks two white fish on the hot coals then drags them to the edge of the fire. When it's a little cooler, she extends her hand to offer a piece to me. Several young men stand close to us. They caught the fish earlier today. One is holding a baby kangaroo.

'Those men are singing songs of her clan and calling spirit and helping her go at the right time'.

'*Manymak*,' I say, the flesh of the white fish hitting my taste buds.

I walk home briskly, reflecting on my reaction to being in such an intimate ceremony.Unlike the culture I grew up in where death is so private ,Yolŋu welcomed me wholehearted into the space and invited me to contribute.

The next morning, Matay tells me the woman passed away not long after my talk with *Yapa*. A hearing ceremony is held to let everyone in the community know of her death.

'Hearings are short. Everyone gathers to learn about the death. We don't say the person's name. We say who is related to that person. The deceased is so and so's oldest brother or youngest daughter, *ga balanya*. And if there is someone in the community who shares the same name, then they change their name,' Warmbirrirr, my *waku*, tells me at school. 'The men, they are chanting for that *miyalk*, *ga miyalk mala* are wailing for her. Then *bilin*, everyone goes quickly when they know who is gone. And soon there will be a smoking ceremony too. We burn leaves where that person was to cleanse their home. If someone who works at the school passes away, we burn those leaves,

Maypiny leaves *muka*, and cleanse the school. D̲ad̲a'yun, we call that ceremony and we have them at the funerals too. They will help the spirit of that person move on to where they need to go, back to their ancestral land.'

I often dream about the death on the eve of one here on Milingimbi. The air is so vibrant and alive that currents like electricity pulse through my blood. The dreams I have are not always clear descriptive dreams. At times, I fluctuate between dreaming and lying wide awake, but the next morning I wake up knowing someone has died, or I will be walking through the bamboo to school and the words someone has died pop into my head. I always tell the Yolŋu and usually that day, or sometimes days later, they let me know of a death.

'*Dhäkay ŋäma*, Mary?'

I don't necessarily know who it is but I know the tangible feeling that blankets my body with heaviness at these times. Often, I dream images or cry in sorrow for no reason. This is not new for me. I have experienced this many times since childhood. This sensitivity is what allowed me to work with people who have been traumatised by grief and loss. Here, with so much death occurring, it is much more frequent and sometimes I am confused and weighed down by it.

How do the Yolŋu deal with so much recurrent pain and loss? Is it by connecting so closely with spirit through the rituals they express at the time of death? They certainly celebrate death. Or have loss and grief become 'normal' because there is so much of it in Yolŋu communities?

# 18

# Dharpa Buŋgul

> I'm the tree you are me
> with the land and the sea
> we are one life not three
> in the essence of life
> we are one.
> – Kevin Gilbert, 'Unity', *Black from the Edge*

It's April. *Midawarr* season has come around again. Much to everyone's delight, an abundance of food will be here again soon. I've been on my island home just over a year. Here I am on a dark night, Yolŋu everywhere.

*Yapa* Jessie appears in the crowd and takes my hand. The *buŋgul* begins.

A group of old grey-haired women sit outside *Yapa* Muwalkmuwuy's house and Jessie says, 'Mary *Yapa*, they are our *ŋändi*.'

I smile and wave at my mothers. My heart pounds as I am seized by an incredible, vibrant force. Men swarm around a long thick branch that represents the *dharpa*. It is painted ochre and brown and adorned with feathers.

'*Manymak* to take a picture or *bäyŋu*?' I ask.

Jessie doesn't reply.

'*Yow, manymak,*' comes a woman's voice through the crowd.

The air is electric. Spirit is here. Strong, mesmerising. Varying degrees of rhythm and tempo resound through *bilma*. Chanting fills the ethers and the women dance. Splashes of bright colours flash from the swirling of their skirts, arms held high, leaves shake in their hands. I am awestruck

There is a sharp thump in my back as Jessie's push thrusts me into a throng of men painted in white clay, carrying the *dharpa*. An odour of sweat and woody charcoal permeates. Lightning-shaped flames from campfires flash in the darkness. Unseen forces are at work here amidst men dancing, the *dharpa* moving wildly, children clutching their mother's dresses and teenagers dancing.

Jessie pulls me in close to her now as we join the long line of Yolŋu and move to the old *djambaŋ* tree by the sea, the tree I laid eyes on on the day of my arrival here. Water laps the shore. Hundreds of stars light up the sky. I breathe in this indescribable moment: earth and spirit together expressed through the heart of the Yolŋu. Our trail leads to homes where we have been to funerals before, where Yolŋu have passed over.

'People will cry because they feel the ancestors with us tonight, *Yapa*. We remember them, those that went before us,' Jessie says, her voice quivering.

Over the last few weeks, Maṯay has promised she would see to it I wouldn't miss the *Waṯu* men dance at the *Mandayala bungul*, the final part of the ceremony. Everyone has been talking excitedly about it throughout the community. *Mandayala* is a sacred men's ceremony but here at Milingimbi not all but large parts of the ceremony are public, hence the crowds. It is an initiation for boys of both Dhuwa and Yirritja moiety, but this is a Yirritja ceremony.

And now on this Friday afternoon, here we sit down at *Ḏarawundhu* as the Yolŋu and visitors gather for this sacred *buŋgul*.

A row of boys and their mothers sleep together under colourful sheets. For the most part, the boys are not in our view. This is the last time the mother and child share together and signifies the four boys' transition into manhood. Two of the boys are from Milingimbi and two are from Ramingining across the water. Their skin is covered in a thin film of red ochre. Tufts of cottonwool balls reach from one side of their face to another in two lines, crossing at the nose. Honey is used to stick the cotton balls on the skin along their upper arms and torsos. The women and older men are also painted in red ochre called *miku*. One boy has small circles of white clay on his body and ochre dots across his nose.

*Wäwa* Trevor is wearing a red lap-lap. He beats two *ga<u>l</u>iga<u>l</u>i* together as he leads a group of men dancing. The men's bent knees rise and fall in repetition, their bare feet thud the earth as they move like a swarm of bees, humming in unison as if they are one.

A bit further away, another group of young men gathers in two lines, forming a gateway to the women and boys. Their faces are lathered with *miku* and skin dotted in cottonwool balls too. Several of them beat woomeras together as they stare ahead with a trance-like gaze. About fifty metres across the road dance the two *Wa<u>t</u>u* men. Their lower legs are covered in white clay and bodies smeared with a mixture of white and red ochre. Thick clumps of cottonwool balls are pasted all over their torsos. Fountains of leaves sprout out of the tops of their long, witch-like, cone-shaped hats.

'They are the *Wa<u>t</u>u*,' beams Ma<u>t</u>ay. 'They are your *wäwas*,' she whispers. I break out in a cold sweat, gazing at my *wäwas*. I now recognise *Wäwa* Jo. Powerful, deliberate in their movement, hands and feet paw-like, the *Wa<u>t</u>u* slink around the trees and across the road, embodying the essence of the *Wa<u>t</u>u*. It emanates through them. Rhythmical chants echo from deep within them into the air as they swish leaves and creep up to the entrance of the gateway.

Djämbutj reaches over my shoulder, she whispers in my ear, 'Now you must look down, *ŋä<u>nd</u>i*, and we will wait for the *Wa<u>t</u>u* men.'

'*Nhä?*' I say, shocked at the request. I can barely contain my excitement at the vibration of this ancestral dance, let alone pull my eyes away from it, but I drop my head down.

'Shhh. Keep your head down, don't move, don't speak,' urges Djämbutj.

Resounding beats of the clap sticks penetrate my ears. I look down, elbows resting on hard ground.

'Don't move, don't speak,' Djämbutj had said and so I don't dare budge but I can hear my heart beat loud in my chest.

Yells and cries break the suspense. We finally get to open our eyes and see the sheets thrown off, the boys revealed and greeted by the *Wa<u>t</u>u* men. The *buŋgul* is over. Everyone disperses in a flash. When something is complete here with Yolŋu, there is no hanging on.

'*Ḏatha nhe ga ḻuka,*' says Munguli. '*Ga roŋiyirr(i) yalala.*'

I return later for the fire ceremony. Once again, Bottom Camp is spilling over with an even larger crowd now. More Yolŋu have arrived from Ramingining, Maningrida, Galiwin'ku, Gapuwiyak, Yirrkala and surrounding areas of Arnhem Land. There are a few unfamiliar white faces too. I weave through the crowd to my sister Yibi's house.

'*Yä räli gu.*' Maṯay spies me, invites me to join her. '*Nhini,*' she says, '*ga nhäma.* These men are playing *biḻma* for the women's dreaming dance.'

Jessie joins us on the blanket before a sea of dancing bodies. 'In this dance, the men are looking for a camp and *ŋatha,*' explains Maṯay.

Darkness falls and the boys to be initiated are sleeping under a sheet once more near *Yapa* Yibi's yellow house but this time without their mothers.

'The men are dancing to give the boys courage. Maybe they are a bit scared or uncertain about this new path they are taking. The men are suffering with them,' says Jessie.

I squeeze my eyes shut tight, I hug my knees, the earth draws me in, and I hear *biḻma* and *yiḏaki*. I do not want to forget this moment. Yes, it is happening. Is the earth shaking?

On opening my eyes, I meet with the thud of the men's feet on the earth, naked to the waist, legs covered in eucalypt leaves that are shaking and on fire, an extreme method to relieve the suffering the boys may go through. Their masculinity, chanting, yelling and guttural sounds pierce my soul. It is through these ceremonies that Yolŋu sacred knowledge is passed on. There must be so many layers of knowledge that I will never know or understand but I do know that this moment is full of magic and meaning.

'*Wäy wäy wäy,*' they chant.

The dance continues all night, stamping, burning leaves, the men generating a powerful energy for the sleeping young boys. They will be woken up in a few hours for their initiation into manhood. I lie still, held in the belly of the earth, absorbing the aliveness of spirit and sound, my yapa Jessie combing her fingers through my hair. I'm feeling drowsy, yet not wanting to miss a moment of this potent magic.

Hours pass. Soon dawn will break.

Matay whispers, 'Come, we will sit further back now.'

The crowd has diminished through the night. There are just a few of us left and we retreat and watch from the distance in the dark.

The men form a circle just beyond Yibi's house, down near the sea. Guttural chants rise from within it; a pulse is reverberating around and around in my head, through my limbs right down to my feet. I breathe deeply to stay present. The men wake up the boys and carry them into the circle. The chanting grows louder and louder as they move the boys into a deeper stage of their initiation.

The intensity builds as the men hold the circle for the ritual. Then the circle is dispersed and the boys are taking into the bush. This part of the ritual is over and I doubt I will get to witness any more of this sacred transition. An aching wail resounds from one of my white-haired *yapas* and pierces the silence. Her tears fall and her croon echoes out through the land. Night disappears and a soft hue of daylight emerges. The softness of a new dawn touches our skin and Matay begins to cry. I reach my arm around her and tears fall down my cheeks too. These tears are haunting. Are they for the women losing their sons, the profound depth of the boys' transition into manhood, or the presence of the ancestors? All perhaps. I don't know.

'*Marrtji,*' says Matay.

We wander home, saying nothing. I am rendered speechless by this experience and the depth of Yolŋu people. Stuart and I hug goodbye near the barge ramp. The orange ball of the sun is just rising up out of the sea, birthing a new day. I drink her in and breathe deeply.

Tears continue as I walk home this Saturday morning. I do not want to sleep. I close my eyes for a moment feeling the energy of the night. I open them again and open my journal and come across part of a quote I'd written in there from Jennifer Isaacs' *Australian Dreaming*:

The sun is always a woman, and wanders across the sky spreading light and warmth, taking a long road in summer and a much shorter one in winter. The verses quoted [above] are quoted by Djankawu and his sisters as they feel the warm rays of *Walu* the sun on the coast of Arnhem Land. For the Djankawu the sun is comforting, like a mother, and its rays show them the paths to follow to the mainland.

I sit in the sunrise, sipping a cup of tea. Slivers of sun shine through the window slats onto my skin. I savour the depth of connection I experience with my Yolŋu family, grateful for them bringing me into their culture, grateful to the land and to the power of the night.

I reflect on moments throughout the night, the discipline and strength of those men dancing relentlessly with burning leaves on their legs, all for the boys and the transition they are going through, and the strength of the women in letting their sons go. Eventually, I crawl into bed as the day comes alive and I wonder how I will ever equate this world with the one I have spent my whole life in.

## 19

# Old Yapa leaves our world

> The stories you have sung to us
> Are the ones that we will tell
> This grieving from your leaving softens…knowing
> this is only one farewell
> Fires burning, soul's returning
> You have left us with the learning
> Fires burning, soul's returning
> You have left us with the learning
> – Johnnie Mac – One Farewell

Vibrant, almost iridescent blue, the sky spans for miles. I am tiny, suspended in its immensity. Old *Yapa* Muwalkmuwuy's round, beautiful face appears in the blue. Her wispy white hair lightly brushes her smiling eyes and smooth skin. There is a shimmering glow of light emanating around her. I try to speak to her but the words are stuck in my throat.

Contacting the softness of the sheets beneath me, I stir. Strips of light beam through the window onto my eyes. I wake up from this vivid dream feeling light, fresh and cool on this May morning. I have had this feeling of expansiveness before where I witnessed the sky open up, but it was not a dream. It happened the day I sat with my dying mother along with my sisters and my Aunty Margot. Dad's spirit stood at the foot of the bed.

'Dad's waiting,' I had whispered to Mum.

The room was alive with a calm vibration I cannot find words for. Mum lay still, poised, graceful as always. Only nights before, the room had filled with love and a peace that crept through every cell of my being.

'The angels have come for her,' I had said to Shaun as he sat quietly in a chair on the opposite side of Mum. 'Can you feel it?'

He nodded.

I had whispered to spirit to clear the pathway for Mum to go.

At midday, she had taken her last breath. I stayed with her for some hours afterwards, holding the heart-shaped, pink rose quartz I had put over her heart daily.

I left the nursing home and went to the home opposite the golf course in Beecroft where I had grown up. I stood in the backyard, arms wide, head back. For some moments,, I was an infinitesimal speck on the earth, gazing up at the sky in awe of the expansion. Mum was everywhere and in everything.

The closeness of spirit never seems as strong or real as it does at a birth, death or living in a Yolŋu community.

'*Dhiŋgama ŋarra?*' old *Yapa* Muwalkmuwuy says, smiling, as I share my dream with her on a visit one Saturday afternoon.

I eliminate the thought of old *Yapa* Muwalkmuwuy's death immediately.

An unsettled feeling lay in my belly for sometime after, though, and so I shared my dream with Jenny as we walked along the shore at Rapuma, one of the crocodile islands, not far from Milingimbi. Jon and Trish had sailed us there on the catamaran. It felt surreal to sail away from Milingimbi and sleep on this tiny island with billabongs, an old plane wreck from World War II and even an old school. Apparently, the Gurryindi and Gamaḻaŋga clan groups lived there. We practised yoga on the beach in the morning and then I jumped in the sea, only to witness large crocodile tracks on the sand not long after.

A month passes. It's June 2004. The nights are cooler and after the one-month holiday I'll be walking to school through the morning *wakuluŋgul*'. I have fallen in love with this word and for me the mist emanates a memorable feeling.

I am at a funeral in Army Camp. I sit behind *Yapa* on a large, pale, flowered sheet. Yolŋu women are dancing. Gracefully, old *Yapa* rises and gently, silently, walks away. Yolŋu don't always need to say goodbye.

'*Djutjutj,*' I whisper, watching her walk onto the road. Gone, just like that! The words are loud in my head.

This morning, I wake up with a weird sense of urgency. I am agitated. I have an urge in my gut to go down to *Ḍarawundhu* and to the *Djambaŋ* women, but I don't go.

I lie on my yoga mat. My bones are heavy and my breathing is laboured.

I put a bolster on the mat and lie with my chest over it and arms reached out behind me to aid my breathing. My ribs expand for a moment with new air but then it gets stuck in my lungs and I sit up gulping like a fish out of water. What can this be? Perhaps it is not even my breathing. I get up to move into a sequence of postures, thinking this may help, but then I run off and bake banana muffins between Adhdo Mukha Svanasana and Budjangasana. The heat from the oven hits my face as I put in the last batch. Gotta go, gotta go. My mind is urgent but still I continue my tasks. My breath is still short. What is this? I ask myself again. For one, this is not yoga. I am lost in the disturbances of my mind and sensations in my body. My asana practice is not bringing me to a still place. I am like a breathless bee in a bottle.

Back on my yoga mat, I look through the dusty wire screen at the beauty of green. I draw my attention to my breath and exhale all the air out then inhale slowly again until I find a calm moment. The discomfort in my lungs, however, and the tightness in my chest have already been ignored for too long. I know someone is suffering in their lungs and I don't know who or where they are but it must be at *Ḍarawundhu* because that's where I am feeling to go, and stop at the *Djambaŋ* women on the way.

The muffins are baked. I tip them out of the hot tray, wrap them in a tea towel and head for the door.

Warmbirrirr appears on the veranda, sadness in her dark brown eyes. '*Nhuŋu Waku* Munguli wants you to come around to the *Djambaŋ* tree. There's been a death. Do you know who?' She searches my face.

Boom! There's that thud in my heart. It is what it is here. There is no dancing around the truth.

'Well, I know something is wrong. I can't breathe. Yes, a death but no, I don't know who, I didn't sleep well,' I respond.

'*Bäyŋu?*' Warmbirrir seems surprised, as I often share with her when I intuit a death in the community. 'It is someone you know very well. Do you know who?' she asks, again searching my face. 'We are having a hearing (death notice) for you. Who is close to you? Mirella? Stuart? We will get them.'

Nervous sensations travel quickly from my gut, hitting my throat. My muscles are shaking as my bones carry me down the street to the *Djambaŋ* women.

Women and a few children sit quietly under the canopy of leaves reaching out from the large tree. Munguli's wrinkled brow searches my face.

My guts begin to move in all directions, churning, as it is explained to me who has died, without mention of name.

My body is cold and numb. Munguli's thick lips are moving but her words can't penetrate my ears and brain. I cannot fathom who it is. Mirella and Stuart are here now, listening to the story.

'Someone has died very suddenly down at Bottom Camp. It's Jessie's older sister,' reports Munguli, her body rocking backwards and forwards as it does when she is worried. 'Asthma, they think she died from asthma.'

My lungs lock. I am breathless again. It seems so very obvious who it is, but I am just not getting it. Nothing makes sense, yet every woman's eyes are on me, waiting for my reaction.

Munguli hands me a crab claw, a generous gift of empathy.

'*Yow, Ḏä<u>nd</u>i* Mary, you can go down there any time,' encourages Djämbutj. A gentle smile crosses her face.

'Of course I'll go.' The words scratch out of my hoarse, dry throat.

Stuart and I walk to *Ḏarawundhu*. We are walking quickly along a worn path: long grass either side of us, a palm tree or two in sight. He says her *balanda* name quietly.

'Oh, it can't be her! I just saw her yesterday at the *buŋgul*.' I look at him in horror.

'Well, just in case she's not there when we get down there, Mary, you'll understand,' Stuart says gently.

As we approach *Ḏarawundhu*, Yolŋu are sitting in groups around old *Yapa*'s house. Smoke rises from smouldering fires, large tin cans of tea brew. Black crows are hopping about and stooping around crumbs of damper.

The air is eerie: strange, silent, heavy. I can see splashes of bright red, blue, orange on the women's dresses as they huddle, presumably around a body lying on the wooden veranda.

Maṯay sits, her body like stone, yet face soft. She looks into me through wet eyes.

Jessie stands frozen, toes curled over the edge of the veranda. She stares blankly into the space ahead of her, her eyes wild with grief and desperation.

Shudders wave through my skin as she looks right through me, as if I am transparent. Now, her gaze meets mine, the flesh on her face scrunches in agony.

I extend my arms out to her and the truth hits me like a crack of thunder, shattering my frozen denial. Tears well in my eyes and stream down my face.

Time is motionless as I watch Jessie fling her arms up in the air, her hands grasp towards the sky, face angst-ridden.

Limbs flying, she hurls herself off the veranda. Her body thumps as it hits the ground hard.

Heart-breaking wails emerge from deep within her writhing body. Time starts again and I jump to stop her hurting herself. '*Yaka*, no *Yapa* Jessie, no, don't hurt yourself please.' I lean over her crumpled body.

Maṯay comes over to me and draws me up off the ground. Our arms lock and hearts meld as we embrace and weep and weep and weep. Her torso sinks into me, heart wrenched with sorrow at the loss of her mother.

This moment begins nine hours of intense grieving.

A haunting wail pierces my ears from across the way. The blue-green ocean catches my attention momentarily.

'*Yaaa-pa, Yaaa-pa.*' It is Yibi Yibi, howling for her dead sister. I move to her. There are no dry eyes on our island home today. The grey-haired old men's tears are the worst to bear.

Women's hands on my shoulders gently guide me back to old *Yapa*'s limp body, slumped on the wooden floorboards. Stuart is with me too, stroking my back lightly and, I guess, deep in his own grief.

*Yiḏaki* sounds, clap sticks and wailing create a vortex between worlds.

'Here,' a curly-white-haired woman commands.

As I crouch down, I gaze at old *Yapa*, hardly believing she is dead. Eyelids closed, she could just be asleep. Her skin is cool and she has that same soft-skinned look I know so well. My body lies pressed against old *Yapa's*, my hand across her cool chest, my face wet with sobbing. Stuart is just behind me stroking my back and staying close by.

'Thank you for your time, your ancient wisdom, your healing presence, your love and all the wonderful times we shared,' I whisper.

Physically, she is now lost to the world. Another one of our ancient ones is leaving the planet.

The ochre jeep sits, our *waku* slumped over the wheel in the driver's seat, sobbing.

I recall Christmas Day. The three of us had gone out driving around the island in that old truck, through the bush around in circles, her face bubbling with joy, as she sat between us in the front seat.

Tina Arena's voice rang out from the jeep and across the island. We played that song over and over again as we drove out to <u>N</u>ilatjirriwa and I always wondered what Tina Arena would think if she knew what a hit she is on Milingimbi Island in Arnhem Land.

The *Djambaŋ* women sit quietly on the edge of the veranda. They are here for her family and for me. I am held by their female strength and presence.

As pink and blue hues over the sea turn to darkness, more Yolŋu come and show respect. The sky is buzzing with the sound of small planes delivering her family to her side from other islands.

Haunting wail song continues to vibrate throughout the community into the night, chanting, dancing and singing her spirit.

The police arrive in a jeep to take *Yapa*'s body to Darwin. The sight of the uniformed men is alien to the whole experience. Intensity builds. A wild swirl of movement, sound and sweat vibrates across the land. Maṯay passes me Membaŋala, my baby mum. She screams and wriggles in my arms. Maṯay cries but her barefooted dance continues. A frenzy of dogs bark. Deep throaty chants spill from the men as they whirl leaves and spears around, performing ceremony at the opening of the police vehicle.

Maṯay stops and leans into me. I hold her and baby as she howls at her mother being torn from her. Removing the body is a shocking invasion at this moment. We clamber into cars and form a convoy behind the police. Perched on the back of an old red truck, sandwiched amidst Yolŋu men, women and children, I hold two long spears that are nestled in the corner. I gaze up at the billons of stars and breathe in the fresh cool night air. The dry season is almost here, the most favoured and abundant hunting season for Yolŋu.

The streets are lined with sombre faces in long procession. Wails burst the air as we drive through Bush Camp. Everyone has gathered to see this wise old lady go. Slowly we approach the airstrip. Men dance and chant, feet thumping. Grey smoke from burning leaves billows out, clearing the space for old *Yapa* to have a safe passage. Dancing wildly around the plane, resonant guttural sounds crack the air as women throw themselves on the hard tarmac with agonising cries of grief.

Finally, the white plane takes off, lifting into the night sky.

Up old *Yapa* goes, floating into her new journey.

It is a magnificent sight as she ascends into the star-studded sky. In this moment, I am moved by the unseen link between Indigenous people and the stars.

I am gutted as I realise I will never see *Yapa* again in physical form, never learn the language from her lips or weave a basket with her and hear her tales of spirit, but I know her spirit will be with me, guiding and teaching me on my path.

Late into the night, I lie in bed looking up at the luminous stars on the ceiling, I can't sleep. All those feelings I had on my yoga mat this morning – the breathlessness, the compulsion to go down to her home. Was there some way I could have helped? Something I could have done? All the signs were leading me but I was lost in the emotion of it. I was not quick enough.

Days later at Matay's house, she sits painting *Banumbirr*. Beauty exudes through her vulnerability. Using a tiny stick, she etches white, ochre and black hatching across the canvas.

'I must paint thin lines with a *nyumukuniny dharpa*. Every night I am crying, so I paint,' explains Matay. 'I would like this painting up on Mum's shelter at the *bäpurru* but it will be for you. She used to collect roots to make this paint.'

'Did she paint too?' I ask.

'No, weaving.'

'Yes, she was a beautiful weaver. How did you learn to paint, Matay?' I ask.

'I used to watch my father. He has a painting in the museum in Darwin.'

Some weeks later at old *Yapa*'s funeral, my sisters Yibi and Jessie take me over to the women in front of Yibi's yellow corrugated-iron house on the edge of the sea, and paint my legs ochre.

'Stand in the sun and dry.' They are bossy.

'The ochre represents that old woman, your sister,' says Jessie.

White clay lines are smoothly painted around my ankles and above my calf muscles. My arms and face are lathered in white clay.

The men, some distance away, are being painted up too.

An ochre strip is delicately painted from one side of my face to the other, across my nose.

'*Guku, Gupapuyŋu, litjalaŋ waŋarr,*' says Yibi.

*Yapa*'s son, our *waku*, walks over. Our eyes rim with tears on sight of each other.

Jessie witnesses this and comforts me in a firm manner. 'Remember what she taught you, *Yapa*. She taught you many things, didn't she? And she taught you well.'

'*Yow, Yapa, yuwalk'*,' I respond tearfully.

There are so many funerals.

My whole being is grasped by the energy of the place at these times. Sometimes I am heavy, laden with sorrow, so I can't imagine how Yolŋu continue to live in this state of grief. I can only think as I have thought before, that the strong ritual of funeral keeps their link to the spirit world open, the knowledge of their ancestors present, and this nourishes their souls.

Men and women are placed in groups according to their clans, some painted in white clay, some in red. Many exquisite designs relating to *waŋarr* are used on the body, holding significant meaning in relation to kinship and land. Various dances express the totems of the clans. Sometimes dances are performed with spears and leaves. With all Yolŋu ceremony and stories, there are deep philosophical and spiritual understandings shared.

Clap sticks and *yidaki* are played day and night.

At times, funerals occur right next to my window and enter my dream state.

Clap sticks as I go to sleep, dreams of hunters with their spears, piercing the bush, clap sticks when I wake.

The spiritual power is incredible. Every time.

The ground sings.

A unique frequency of sound rises through the Yolŋu into the atmosphere, thick with intensity.

Yolŋu express their deepest grief, women sometimes hitting their heads with tin cans or rocks or hurling themselves onto the concrete.

I have attended many funerals, and of people I don't know, to show respect. I am always moved to tears, my heart feels their pain, my ears receive the sorrow of their wail song and my eyes will never forget the stricken faces of the families.

And I am always left with the question, why is there so much death in our communities?

# 20

# The past

> Perhaps all the dragons in our lives are princesses
> who are only waiting to see us act
> Just once
> With beauty and courage
> Perhaps everything that frightens us is in its deepest essence
> Something helpless that wants our love.
> – Rainer Maria Rilke

Grief is not new to me. In my late teens and twenties, I spent a great deal of time sitting in hospitals with sick loved ones. Death became familiar to me.

I was twelve when my seven-year-old cousin died. My strongest memory is of my mother's grief-stricken face and tears. I think I was sixteen when Nana died and when I was seventeen my father lay in intensive care. Every cell of my body screamed that something serious was wrong. But Dad just said, Don't worry, pussy cat, it's just my appendix.'

I was in my final year of high school at the time, so I guess he didn't want to worry me but a few years later when Dad got sick again, our family doctor said to me, 'Remember back when your father had bowel cancer?'

'Well, no and yes,' I retorted. Mum put us all on a simple vegetarian diet. No more chops or white bread. None of us liked that but it contributed to why I am a vegetarian now.

Dad did get better for a few years. Then, when I was twenty-one, he died suddenly of a cerebral haemorrhage. Five weeks beforehand, he arrived home and said, 'I drove through a red light today.'

I ran to my room and threw myself on the bed with the words 'Dad's going to die' repeating in my head. The familiar scuff of his slippers padding down the hallway remained in my ears long after his death.

At nineteen, on my vibrant boyfriend Maury's body I noticed a strange mole that led to him being diagnosed with a malignant melanoma. His lymph nodes were savagely removed and a few years later a drunk driver, going up a one-way street the wrong way, knocked Maury off his motorbike. He nearly died. He learned to walk again but no longer had the use of his left arm at all, but he still wished he could ride his Ducati 900 again. With the trauma of the accident, his cancer returned. At twenty-four he died, or was it twenty-five? We were not going out at the time of his death but I had five years with him; he was my first love. I sat on the edge of the bed with him almost every day in that hospice for the last month of his life.

Not that long after Dad's death, Mum was diagnosed with Alzheimer's and suffered for years. She did not recognise me in the last few. I was with her when she passed away, as I had been with Dad moments before he took his last breath, too.

And then there was my dear friend Jacqueline, a mad Kiwi from New Zealand, librarian at the school where I was teaching. 'Celebrate life!' she'd say. 'Mad if you don't.' Her hair was wild and red, her deep blue eyes lined with black, and she smoked like a chimney, died of lung cancer. I gave her a healing treatment every week in the year up until her death. 'Quinkins, I can see the Quinkins!' she'd say as she lay there. 'They're circling around me.'

All this death made me want to live more. I realised life is not to be wasted doing things that are not true to one's heart or living via conditioned response out of mindless obligation. It showed me the importance of valuing time and how I spend it. Through witnessing the illnesses of my loved ones, I realised how important the health of my body and mind is for the best quality of life. Even though I have this knowledge, there are still times I gravitate from it, but it never completely disappears. I find it important to honour grief as it surfaces yet equally important to then let it go so that I am not going into my future holding on to it.

If I'm feeling stuck, I sit quietly or take time in nature. I want to acknowledge my feelings and transform the noise and overwhelmingness into peace. I want to experience calm yet remain alert. Nature helps me come back to me. In those years of intense loss, a seed was planted that encouraged me to know that I'm never really alone. That there is a thread that weaves through everything and connects each and every one of us if we are willing to witness it. Those deaths I experienced in my family revealed my intuitive nature to me and linked me with the spirit world. It's what I feel about Yolŋu, that they are so connected with each other, the spirit world and the spirit of the land. And what is so powerful about this is that it is perfectly natural for them, there's no shame about it. Being connected to spirit with Yolŋu is never hidden nor sought after or even discussed day and night. It just is. In fact, with my past conflict between the academic world and spirit world, here I feel transformed by the ease and acceptance Yolŋu have with spirit and healing.

*Aerial view of the blue-green waterways as you fly into Yurrwi, Milingimbi Island.*

*Yapa Elizabeth Yibi Yibi and Yapa Jessie Murarrgirarrgi.*

*Yapa Mary and Yapa Jessie Murarrgirarrgi.*

*Yapa Dorothy Muwalkmuwuy.*

*Ḏarawundhu.*

*Gunga djäma*

*Djambaŋ women weaving.*

*Waku Jennifer Munguli, Mukul Dakawa.*

*Waku Daphne Nimanydia.*

*Yapa Gwendoline Bambaniwuy, Waku Bridget Lalawan, Waku Margaret Gamuti*

*Waku Munymuy, Gaminyarr Mipururr.*

*Waku Judy Munymuy.*

*Yapa Rebecca Nunydjulu.*

*Larrtha.*

*Waku Esther Rarrinya hunting nyoka'.*

*Waku Nancy Djämbutj.*

*Waku Gwen Warmbirrirr.*

*Waku Daphne Nimanydja and waku mala*

*Nilatjirriwa gulun.*

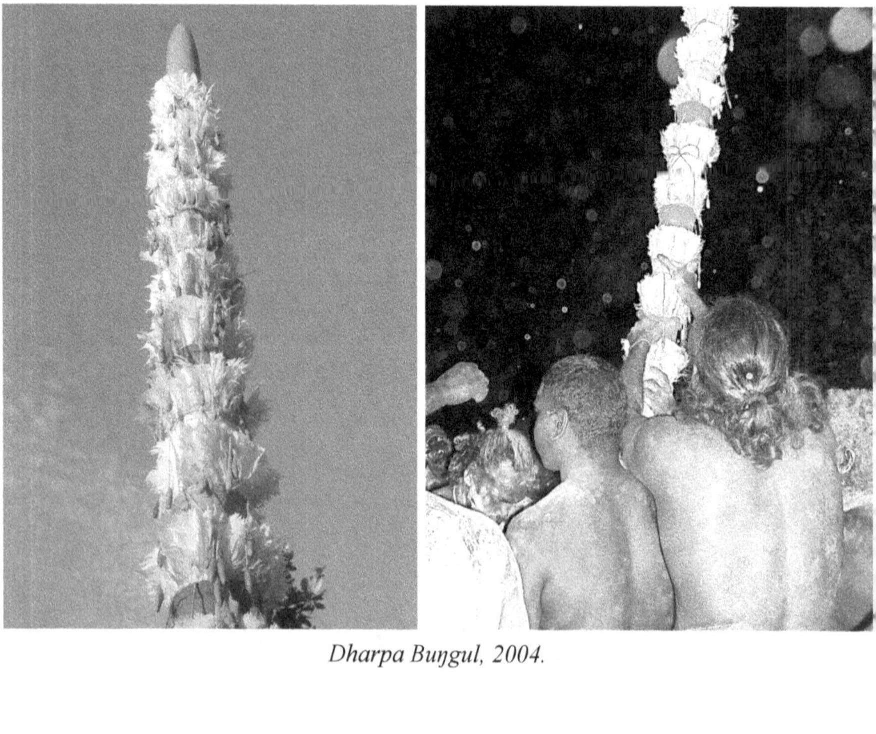

*Dharpa Buŋgul, 2004.*

*Wäwa Terry Malmaliny hunting at Yalakun.*

*Gaminyarr Wendy Mipururr.*

*Sunset at Yalakun. Waku Bridget Lalawan and Waku Joshua Buŋgalkthun.*

*Gutharra Gwen Boyukarrpi and Wutjun flying back to Milingimbi from our visit to Murruŋga Island.*

*Dhuway Laurie Baymarrwaŋa, Murruŋga Island.*

*Yoga on Yurrwi.*

*Bäpi Mundukuḻ.*

*Gutharra Kenisha Muthathani and bäpi at Ŋamuyani.*

*Ḏändi Buŋgul at Ḏarawundhu mother ceremony at Yapa's funeral.*

*Gäthu Judith Maḏupinyin Ganyawu at the Ḏärra Buŋgul law ceremony.*

*Yirritja Miyalk Mala at the Ḏärra Buŋgul.*

*Yapa Elizabeth Yibi Yibi and Yapa Mary Yibi Yibi Part 2.*

*Wäwa Jo Djembaŋu and Gaminyarr Marko.*

*Yapa and Yapa with recording of Wäwa Jo talking about Yolŋu matha.*

*Last day on Yurrwi*

Three yapas: Elizabeth Yibi Yibi, Mary Yibi Yibi and
Linda Slim Mawukuwuy at Ḏarawundhu.

Waku Vanessa Wudupilaŋu, ma<u>nd</u>a Philly Warrana
and Sandy Baladay.

Yothu Yindi.

# 21

# The spirit of Yalakun – Part 1

'Can you feel the invisible gates open, ŋä<u>ndi</u>?' asks Nimanydja, beaming a smile at me as we orbit the landing strip.

I close my eyes for a moment, feeling the powerful spirit of Yalakun calling us in.

– Stephanie Nimanydja

*'Dharrwa nyoka ŋama'*. Long white sands, *yuwalk latju wäŋa,*' says Munguli, one eyebrow cocked, striking a strong line through a word on her crossword puzzle.

There is a buzz in the air as we sit under the shade of our beloved *Djambaŋ* tree this particular Sunday morning. Children sprawl across branches of the tree; dogs nestle in the dirt, gnawing at fleas. Remnants of a fire smoulder and an array of floral skirts and dresses dries on the line strung between two wooden posts.

'It's *Bäpa* Jo's motherland,' Nimanydja explains of her husband, my adopted father. Her face shines when she speaks of him.

'It's across the north of Arnhem Land towards Nhulunbuy and near a place called Gapuwiyak. Mud crabs running everywhere, *ŋama*',' delights Djämbutj, puffing on her ciggy with one hand, the other reaching out to the ground as if she can just reach down and pluck up a crab right now.

*'Yuwalk dhäwu*, you can just pick them up and eat them.' She smiles.

Wow! Getting dinner without legs stuck in mud and ripped clothes has to be good, I think.

'We will take you there.' Judy Munymuny peers up from her latest religious book. '*Latju ŋatha, Dharrwa miny'tji mala, gunga djäma.*'

White hair swept up in a blue scrunchy, and an air of grace, Judy Munymuny picks up her stainless steel mug of hot tea and takes a sip. 'It's very relaxing, we just sit in the bush and don't have to worry about anything.' She stares wistfully into space out beyond her cup.

Glimpses of pure white sand and pristine blue water begin to appear in my dreams. I share these dreams with the women and it is confirmed that they will take me.

I recall *Yapa* Yibi and Jessie telling me about Ḏipirri, a coastal homeland, ten minutes' flight from Milingimbi. Yibi goes there by boat regularly.

'*Latju ŋatha, dharrwa nyoka.*' Yibi's face lights up whenever she talks about it.

'I want to go,' I say to her.

'We want to build our own school there, *Yapa. Nhuŋu waku maṉda* Maṯay *ga* Rarrinya can teach there.'

'Sounds like a *latju* plan, *Yapa*,' I say.

'*Yow*, at that place there is *raypiny 'ga moṉuk gapu*,' explains Jessie.

'*Nhä dhuwal, Yapa?*'

'There are two,' says Jessie.

'That's where the fresh water *ga moṉuk* water meet, *Yapa*. We can drink the water from the pool near the sea,' says Yibi.

'Wow! Sounds amazing,' I reply.

'And when they meet, those two they mix together and become stronger because they are together. They give their knowledge to each other: with respect. They are different but they can be together. That's the Yolŋu way, *Yapa*,' says Jessie.

'Thank you, *Yapa*, I have so much to learn and understand.'

And as weeks pass, talk of visiting Yalakun, this utopian piece of heaven, becomes a central conversation under our tree.

But for an unexpected cyclone, we almost get to Yalakun at Christmas.

Finally, after old *Yapa's* death, the *Djambaŋ* women take me to Yalakun in the last week of the June holidays. I was intending to leave at the end of term but with old *Yapa*'s death and funeral, I just couldn't go. I'll go *yalala*.

Munguli, Ganyawu, Djämbutj and Dorothy stay home. I'm going with my *wakumirriŋu mala*, Nimanydja, her two grandchildren Buŋgalkthun and Lalawan, who are students in my class, and Judy Munymuny. We stand on the tarmac as the pilot packs our *girri*' onto the plane. Some large blankets, tea, bread, cereal, freeze-dried milk, fishing lines, and my yoga mat are stuffed into the space under the plane, but we are not taking too much. We are going to live off the land for the next five days.

The tiny five-seater aircraft lifts off the ground, leaving our island home below us as we merge with the vast blue sky. Excitement grows in my belly as I look down at the meandering blue-green waterways. This is a dream come true, to spend the next days with the Yolŋu out in the bush.

Soon, Yalakun comes into view: sweeping long white sands, crystal-clear ocean, just as the women described and just like in my dream; thick lush green bushland on the red earth reaches for miles.

'Can you feel the invisible gates open, *ŋändi*?' asks Nimanydja, beaming a smile at me as we orbit the landing strip.

I close my eyes for a moment, feeling the spirit of Yalakun calling us in.

We clamber off the plane. I sigh at the sight of a few mangy hounds barking at us, wishing that for once there weren't any around, but I enjoy the warmth of *wäwa* Malmaliny and his wife, my *Waku* Guwalkuwalk, as they welcome us.

We walk along the grass to a light-yellow house not far from the bright blue water's edge amongst the trees.

'This is where we live with our children and grandchildren. There are about thirty Yolŋu living here, enjoying life on the land,' smiles *wäwa*.

A corrugated-iron room with a veranda stands away from *wäwa's* home near the beach.

'That's the school. Maybe you can come and teach at Yalakun sometime,' says Guwalkuwalk, her round face smiling, fuzzy hair close to her head.

We put our stuff down on the veranda of the school and wander down to the water's edge. The sand is pure white, and twisted grey mangroves grow in clumps at the end of the beach. I take a big whiff of fresh salty air into my lungs and appreciate where I am. Letting going of old *Yapa* has been a deep experience. The women bringing me here to Yalakun is not only very healing but I will learn so much.

'*Gurtha djäma*,' says Nimanydja and she bends down and picks up some dry spindly pieces of wood.

The kids and I help. We gather some dry wood and light a small fire, not far from the shore.

I crouch down to grab a chunk of dry wood. I feel Buŋgalkthun's hand on my shoulder and look around to see him showing me a tiny shell he has picked up. I look down to see hundreds of them varying in colour, shades of brown, black and cream, some pink and white, lying sprinkled on the sand.

'We can make jewellery from these, *manimani*, necklaces,' says Nimanydja, bending down and scooping some up in a corner of her blue and pink floral skirt.

I am always fascinated by Nimanydja's long spine and how she folds forward so precisely from her hips, something I have aspired to in my yoga practices for years. The Yolŋu women are naturally this way.

*Wäwa*, a tall man, lean but strong in body, a healthy glow in his face, greying hair and beard, grabs his long metal-tipped spear and ventures out into the water.

'What about the crocodiles?' I ask with a sense of trepidation growing in me.

'*Yaka Bäydhi*,' smiles Nimanydja.

Munymuny is busily arranging tea, plonking a tin of water on the fire. We sit close by adding more sticks and twigs.

I gaze out into the vast ocean, wondering what part of the earth is on the other side of it. I see the upper half of *wäwa*'s body in the vibrant blue sea. With keen focus, he raises the spear above his head and thrusts it into the water, spearing a large fish. How freeing, I think, to live here on this land this way.

Judy Munymuny throws a handful of Bushells tea bags in the tin and rounds up the cups. I pull out some banana muffins I baked at home.

Some time later, *wäwa* returns, spear across his shoulder, several fish in hand.

'*Guya.*' His white teeth flash a big smile as he throws them into the crackling flames of the fire.

We are relaxed and content to be sitting on the sand next to a fire, food cooking, blue sky above, and the fresh fish makes a tasty, luscious dinner. My whole body softens and I am in awe as the sun in its golden orange splendour sets, then slips away into the deep dark sea. This land feels old and everlasting. I watch the silhouettes of my *waku*. Lalawan and Buŋgalkthun making sandcastles on the shoreline as the sun fades.

My body is invigorated on this powerful land, still and strong. My intuition is sharp and my dreams vivid and colourful.

## 22

# Marrŋgitj

It was as if you knew me, like you stared right through me.
You met me in a dream and knew to come to me, *marrŋgitj*.
Magic happens.

Inhaling, I lengthen my arms to the lemon-painted ceiling of my lounge room. Exhaling all of the air slowly, I bring my hands into *Anjali mudra* over my heart centre and take another breath here. Inhaling, I raise my arms, exhaling I fold forward and lightly touch my fingertips to the purple yoga mat stained with the red earth.

It is Monday afternoon, after school.

'*Yow*, Mary, *yow*, Mary,' a man's voice breaks the stillness.

Taking another full breath, then exhaling slowly, I grab the long blue print dress lying over the velvet lounge and throw it over my tights and singlet. I am used to routine interruptions and am prepared.

'*Yow, nhä mirr nhe?*' I shout out loud, voice muffled

by the dress covering my face. I push through the wire door to find a tall lean Yolŋu man standing at the bottom of the concrete stairs. He is wearing a baseball cap, a long-sleeved white shirt zipped right up to his neck (why, in this heat, I do not know), long dark-blue shorts and no shoes.

'*Yow*, you Mary?'

'*Yow*, I'm Mary.'

'*Ḏarra marrŋgitj*. You want *marrŋgitj*?'

My heart jumps in its chest cavity. Oh my God, a *marrŋgitj* at my house, A rush of blood reddens my face.

'*Yow, yow, gu!*'

His long legs stride up the stairs, taking two at a time. We sit on the cane lounge, leaning into the ripped, stained, once-white cushion covers patterned with green bamboo print. The two-seater couch barely fits on the tiny wooden deck, planks missing, leaving a dangerous hole. Brown-grey birds flap their wings, playing and squawking in the trees next to us. Within minutes of us sitting down, I am filled with serenity.

'*Nhe bones.*' Straight to the point, this *marrŋgitj* gestures to his back right where I have pain in mine.

'*Yow,*' I confirm his insight.

'I can feel it, I got *marrŋgitj* and I help everyone, then they are *manymak* so I can help you.'

This *marrŋgitj* has an ageless face. His presence exudes strength and calm at the same time. Rarely here on Yurrwi is there a reference to one's age in a conversation. To know someone's chronological number is not a point of understanding about how that person is in life. I love this, that there is no generation gap, or traditionally there wasn't, and everyone is together. Perhaps with the age of mobile phones and technology, things are changing. But I notice wherever I go on Yurrwi that all ages are comfortable with each other. I find this very freeing, relationships not being limited by a number.

'I drank the water, now I am a *marrŋgitj*. I was in the bush and two-spirit *miyalk* came to me. They have always been spirits, never human and they moved inside me and I drank the water. Now I am a *marrŋgitj*. They told me to help people so I do,' the *marrŋgitj* continues. A soft smile curls upwards as he cups his hands together, palms lighter in colour than the rest of his rich black skin.

His English is clear. I am listening and attempting to speak some Yolŋu *matha* too. Though the cells of my body are racing around I am also calm, fully engaged and captivated by this outpouring of information. This is incredible for a Monday after school and so unexpected. Magic is in the air and I welcome it.

'It comes from spirit,' he continues with a glint in his eyes.

'While I am healing, I hear things. People are *manymak* straight away after the healing.'

'But,' he raises his long finger and eyebrows, 'there are bad witch-doctors too. They want to drain people's blood and kill them.'

I shiver at the thought of bad witchdoctors, scribbling down '*gulaŋ*', the Yolŋu word for blood, on the back of an old envelope.

'Sometimes they take someone's hair and the sting from the stingray and hang it around a body part.'

Yeww, are my thoughts again, and my body freezes for a moment, resisting this notion of evil.

'They take people's clothing and inflict harm upon them. But I bring light.'

Immediately, I feel lighter.

'I help people feel safe. People give me *ŋarali, rrupiya, ŋatha*.'

My body relaxes again.

'Do you want healing *djäma*?'

'*Yow*, healing *djäma* please,' the words fly out of my mouth.

We stand up to go inside. I linger at the door as I pull it open, awkward, wondering if it is a culturally acceptable choice to invite this witchdoctor into my house.

My body urges me in the door, that split second of doubt gone.

In the kitchen, I pull a tall blue glass out of the cupboard, fill it with cold water from the fridge and offer it to the *marrŋgitj*.

As the *marrŋgitj* takes it, he says, 'I can use this.'

I lay my yoga mat out on the middle of the lounge room floor. 'Lie on my front or back?' I ask, concerned with the logistics of the healing.

He silently casts his eyes on what I am wearing.

I look down at my dress. 'Oh, I'll get changed. Hang on.' I run to my bedroom, wondering if he understands 'hang on'.

I throw on a skirt and top so he can work on my back. Butterflies dance in my gut, goosebumps spring up on my skin, and I know this is right.

'*Guḻun*,' he directs me.

I lie on my mat, reaching my arms over a cushion so I can turn and watch the *marrŋgitj* at work. My heart is pounding louder than the clock tick and I wonder if he can hear it.

His long fingers press around my spine, feeling cool and then warm.
'I'm checking, I feel your pain in my body.'

Tell me about it, I am thinking, reflecting on all the years I have felt the pain of others in my own body.

Then he smears his whole hand across the sharp pain in my sacrum and gathers it into his hand, forms a fist and then blows on it. A pulling, tightening, tingling sensation occurs in my back as if something has been taken out.

For a split second, my mind and vision take me back to the big round Aboriginal shaman at the café in Sydney. The one that told me I was 'Saltwater'. His large hand had snatched pain from my bones and muscles. Scooping it up, he had opened his hand and whisked it to the wind. Gone!

'This is *yindi' djäma*.' The *marrŋgitj*'s soft voice brings me back. 'Now exercise and see if it's gone.'

I rise up off the floor and walk around.

'Still there,' I inform him, wondering why I am such *yindi' djäma*.

Long, bony fingers reach into my flesh again. His hands are so black on my stark white skin. 'Sheww,' a swishing sound comes from his thick lips as he hastily blows the pain away. He repeats the whole action.

'*Wäy*! I have been doing this technique in my healings with the Yolŋu these last months.' The words spill out of my mouth.

'I know. Because you are a *marrŋgitj* too.' His chocolate eyes widen, revealing large whites and a mischievous glimpse. 'How did you become a *marrŋgitj*, Mary?'

We have so much to share and I want to understand and speak his language. 'Where do I begin?' I sigh.

His hands gently press on my back. 'Do you have *yothu*? The blood here is dry, it is not moving.'

'*Bäyŋu djamarrkuḻi*'.' I stare out the window at the green leaves and vast blue sky. The light of day is fading.

'*Bäyŋu djamarrkuḻi' ŋarraku*, but I tried to have them. Maybe you can help me with healing *djäma*,' I say.

He smiles.

The *marrŋgitj*'s gentle even tone of voice continues. He is lean but his arms are strong and muscular. I can see a long vein running down the centre of his smooth hairless biceps. The veins are very prominent on the backs of his hands too.

I naturally soften in the presence of his masculinity.

He continues, 'Your body is healthy. When I look into your eyes, I know you are a *marrŋgitj*. Sometimes your spirit goes away. It flies. Two-spirit *miyalk* are coming to help you, help more sick people. I save people's lives from bad spirits and sometimes I take bad things into my own body. I am healthy. I go hunting and eat *guya*, *nyoka*, *we*t*i*, but I smoke *ŋarali* and then feel *yaka manymak*,' he confides.

His coarse black hair is short aside from a few funky spiral dreadlocks that fall over his high cheekbones. Wide nose, thick eyebrows resting on a strong ridge across his forehead, and thick lips.

The *marrŋgitj* dips his fingertips into the glass of water and rubs it into his willowy hands. Forming fists, he rubs them under his armpits and goes to work on my back again.

'You use sweat and water?' I ask.

'*Yow*, it helps spirit through. I will take you to where I got *marrŋgitj* power and do business if you want and go hunting.'

'That's all I want to do' are the words in my head. 'That would be really *manymak*. When?' I ask excitedly.

'*Babalarmirri*. You are the first *balanda* I have ever given healing to,' he says over and over again with a smile on his face.

'I am honoured. Thank you.'

Wide-eyed, the *marrŋgitj*'s hands propel, dancing in the air,

'*Winyiwinyi, winyiwinyi*,' he says. 'They help me with healing. We are bats,' he says pointing at himself then me. 'We fly.'

Momentarily, I am gripped by a pang of exasperation at not fully understanding what he is saying.

'I can only drink cold tea or my *marrŋgitj* power will go away,' he says.

God, I love hot tea. I'd be in trouble it was the same for me.

Tck tck tck. He clicks his fingernails together next to my ear. 'When you hear this sound, you know the *marrŋgitj* has come to visit you. Listen and you will hear it.'

'I will listen, thank you, and my back is feeling *manymak* now.'

The sky is black outside.

I get up off the floor and stick my head in the fridge. I find some oranges and apples and give them to the *marrŋgitj*.

'I'll bring some *rrupiya* later, okay?' I ask.

'*Ma.*' His wide smile flashes white teeth.

I sit in the dark. My body is light. My cells tingle. Finally, I have met a *marrŋgitj*. I light a candle and watch the glow from the flame fill the room, shadows flickering on the wall. I think back to my dancing days. In addition to dancing, I was doing Aboriginal studies at Tranby College in Glebe in Sydney.

'*Sorcerers and Healing Spirits*, that's the book you want, love,' the Aboriginal woman had recommended when I asked her what I could read on Aboriginal spirituality. I remember lying under a tree in Birchgrove Park after a day of dancing, sun bright, ferries crossing the waters of Sydney Harbour. My eyes were glued to the pages of the spirit book I had found in my favourite, musty-smelling bookstore in Glebe.

'*Marrŋgitj* Yolŋu healer.' The cells in my body stirred with vital energy as I read on.

He possesses special powers which enable him to heal the sick and to divine the cause of illness or death.

Stages of Gaining Power
• A frightening supernatural experience by which he becomes 'clever'. Encounter spirits who confer power onto him. Confrontation by spirits dead. Experiences of dying and coming to life again. Living for some time in a death-like state.
• must show that he can cure sick – demonstration of powers.
• must attract clientele & establish a practice. Once validated the sick begin to seek him out for treatment & his or her practice expands.

- healing stones
Gilapa…magic things

— Janice Reid, *Sorcerers and Healing Spirits*

I gave my copy to Paul, a clairvoyant mentor of mine on his way back to England and did not lay eyes on the book again until I came to Milingimbi. There it was on the shelves of the Milingimbi School library. I picked it up and read it again, astonished to find that all its stories related to Yirrkala and Milingimbi. I wonder if the *marrŋgitj* uses *gilapa*, healing stones. They probably have a different name. A pang hits me, though. All these amazing experiences are culminating and yet I have made a huge decision to leave my home here and go back to New South Wales.

I am sad now. I have finally met a *marrŋgitj* but I am going to leave my island home in just a couple of months.

## 23

## The marrŋgitj's mother

And here this is a dream within a dream
We the Winywiny, little bats
Casting shadows in the moonlight
Flutter do our wings
Deep into the night
As we fly together

Nightly I sit perched on my doorstep at the top of the concrete stairs, writing everything down, every conversation, every word, every dream, every visit I share with Yolŋu. My heart is wide with happiness, I am learning so much, and it feels great to record it all and lay the thoughts and experiences down on the page as they occur. I have been doing this for my entire time here on Yurrwi now, often late at night when I have finished school planning. I have always liked to document life experiences, but life on Yolŋu land seems especially important to take note of. Everything is flowing effortlessly and naturally. Being held in the energy of the land, the Yolŋu spirit is guiding me.

Each night, electricity charges through my limbs. The cells of my body are invigorated and pulsing. Sleep is not always possible. I am in the underbelly of the psychic world. Whoosh, disembodied I fly up, hovering at the ceiling sprinkled with tiny luminous stars. Whoosh, up I go and look down on my body lying on the bed. This goes on for weeks. I am quite comfortable with my aerial nature. This began in my very first days on this tiny island and then dissipated somewhat over time. But now it has been happening every night since the day the *marrŋgitj* came to visit. I understand that I am going through a huge transition of a subtle realm nature, one that I do not fully understand. My experiences with the spirit world as I grew up have prepared me for this.

It is not the first time I have left my body. In earlier years, I spent a lot of time practising Tratak: candle gazing. It is a powerful way to increase Dharana: focused concentration. This practice encourages nourishing sleep and helps to create clear vision and relieve anxiety from the mind. For me, it has been a spiritual practice, awakening intuition and more importantly, according to the ancient yogis, one must move beyond one's psychic powers and take the opportunity to raise consciousness.

From a young age, I read the works of Edgar Cayce, Harry Edwards and other original healers. I read Robert Munroe's books about near-death experiences and astral travel. Both reading and studying with experienced teachers in these fields helped me make sense of my own experiences and develop these skills further. I spent plenty of hours lying on my bed visualising myself lifting up above my body and expanding out to the world. Initially, though, all the experiences occurred naturally without knowledge or study. The study came after my experiences. I was hungry to understand my spiritual nature even though it was nothing like the religion I grew up in.

Since childhood, I have often met people I know and love in my dream state but I had a desire to experience this in my waking state also.

At times, in silent meditation, I experienced glimpses of being a bundle of vibrant molecules larger than my body, larger than my minuscule life. The mystical is alluring and yet these experiences help me become more present in my body and in my daily life. They aid me in being aware of how I am in the world, bring clarity to my mind and offer a chance to grow as a human. This is what offers me the most inspiration from these explorations.

Here on Milingimbi, I am committed to the kids at school and my days are filled with other more academic thoughts now. In addition, though, here in the Yolŋu world, spirit is palpable and I experience it in ways I never have before. Still today, these spiritual experiences unfold organically in my waking and dream states.

I step outside and gasp at the moon, a huge stunning ball, dressed in a glowing field of light. A large bat wings its way across her milky white face and I think of the *marrŋgitj*.

*Winyiwinyi* flit around the light shed by lamp posts and the *marrŋgitj* dances at ceremony. His blue-black skin shines with sweat and his bare feet thud the earth. Dancing *ŋerrk*, his being expressing white cockatoo, chanting, singing, calling me with his eyes, I am held in his gaze as he expresses his blood, bones, land and spirit.

'*Nhe manymak*,' he asks.

I am mesmerised yet confounded and sometimes I cringe back, looking around to see who is watching, wondering what people are thinking, scared I am breaking some law. But I can't help but fall into his gaze. I mean, he's a *marrŋgitj* after all, and anyway everyone seems perfectly happy and encouraging of our connection.

'Mary, there he is.' A big beaming smile shines on my *Waku* Maṯay's face as she dances her clan songs and calls my attention.

I smile back and look over, aware of her eyes peering into me, perhaps scanning me for my reaction. But who knows what she is thinking. In this life, I am learning to stop assuming another's thoughts.

A wad of fuzzy black hair circles her round face. She wears a loose, black-and-white, floral dress. The *marrŋgitj's* mother lathers her limbs with white clay as she prepares to dance at the funeral in the house a few metres away.

I have come to visit the *marrŋgitj* at his home.

I look out at the *ṉinydjiya*, grey cracked salty earth stretching out for miles, fringed with *ḻarrtha*. Green leaves hang on gnarled roots deeply entrenched in mud, hunting ground for juicy mud crabs and shellfish.

The *marrŋgitj* leans against a tree, inhaling deeply on his cigarette.

I sit in the shade. Kids clamber all over me lightly touching my hair, one twirling my nose ring, another snuggled against me, circling her finger around my elbow. There seems to be a fascination with my elbows here.

'*Nhä dhuwal?* Earring?' the girl twirling my nose ring asks.

'*Yaka, ŋurru nhawi.*' I prise it back into the tiny hole before it slips down into the earth with the many others that have gone before it.

'The spirits took my son,' the *marrŋgitj's* mother announces, casually looking me right in the eyes.

Wow, she doesn't waste any time, I think.

'For two weeks when he was young,' she says, looking over at him.

'Were you scared?' I look over at him now too.

'The first time but not the second,' he says smiling and sitting down next to me.

'They took him into the bush to teach him *marrŋgitj.*'

I'm getting the story from mother and son at the same time now.

'I came to you. I saw you in a dream and knew to come to you, *marrŋgitj.*' He looks directly in my eyes.

My bones jump.

'Yes, he found you and flew to you,' reveals his mother. 'He went to find the other *marrŋgitj*. You are bats, and at night you fly together.'

'*Winyiwinyi,*' the children repeat, their faces alive with joy.

I can feel tears well in my eyes, happy ones.

'The *marrŋgitj* tree is not so far away,' says his mother. 'Show her the healing *marrŋgitj gunda.*'

The *marrŋgitj* pulls a black stone out of his pocket. 'Hold it.' He hands it to me.

'Oh, it's smooth,' I say, 'it feels cool.' I roll it around in my hand.

'Yes, hold it,' he encourages.

I have two kids sitting on my lap now and another two huddled over my shoulders, pressing in closer, giggling and looking at the stone, but they don't try to touch it.

'*Nhe marrŋgitj*, Mary?' a little girl asks, fingers heading for my nose ring again.

'*Yow, marrŋgitj ŋayi.* Take it: hold it and you will feel your pain. Let it take your pain,' says the *marrŋgitj.*

I take the stone and place it on my lower back, cupping my hand over it. The kids giggle even more. The pain in my back becomes apparent and the stone grows warmer. I can't believe I am now holding a *marrŋgitj*'s healing stone.

'I was dreaming. The spirit came to me under the tree and gave it to me. I woke up with it in my hand,' says the *marrŋgitj*. 'There are three stones: this one is to see through a person, see their sickness and heal it, fix it. The other one is to help me fly.'

'Fly. Look,' I point in the sky. 'Eagle.'

The *marrŋgitj*'s eyes grow big. 'Yes, the stone helps me change into eagle, cat, bat, snake and does what I ask.

'Like what?' I ask.

'Maybe someone is in trouble or lost. I can change to cat and find them.'

In the corner of my eye, I notice the *marrŋgitj*'s mother heading over to the funeral now.

'You love hunting, don't you?' I ask.

'Yes, I'm a good hunter, *guya, weṯi*.'

'And you are a *manymak* dancer?' I ask.

'Yes, sit here and hold this stone. Take it home and bring it back *yalala*. Sit now and I will dance for you.'

Beaming faces, the little ones cuddle into me even more.

Teenage boys sit on red flour tins and beat sticks together. The *marrŋgitj* joins them. Donning his white baseball cap, he is handed a *yiḏaki* that has been wrapped in thick red tape. He blows into it and the *buŋgul* begins. The kids squeal with delight; I can see he is a hit with the children. A young boy takes the *marrŋgitj*'s *yiḏaki* and he rises up, bare feet thudding the earth and flicking the sand in ancient dance.

'*Marrŋgitj buŋgul,*' the children whisper in my ear, squeezing my arms.

I walk down the road back home from the *marrŋgitj*'s house. The black healing stone rolls around in my hand. It feels to have a strong power of its own. Memories flash in my mind of all the meetings I have had with Aboriginal people up until this day. It is as if there has always been this link alive in me but certain experiences in life have provided a nexus for its gradual rich unfolding.

I can still hear the beat of the clap sticks as I pass the Maccassan well, a place once said to have been 'living water', a place where according to history the Rainbow Snake visited, came flashing like lightning and created the waterhole.

My dreams since the *marrŋgitj*'s first visit have been filled with the two of us out bush together, swimming freely in water holes, catching fish and cooking them in a fire.

Lying under billions of stars, learning Yolŋu *matha* and sharing *marrŋgitj* talk together, the mysteries of spirit being revealed to us. Visits from elders; their faces appearing in the flames of the fire and in the sky and stars, giving us their knowledge, their long-held wisdom.

Despite my lack of deep sleep, I am energised, inspired and filled with creative thoughts. I am light and joyful.

Perhaps these visions will always remain dreams in semi-sleep states or perhaps they are very real experiences we were having in some other parallel dimension together.

# 24

# Baymarrwaŋa

This place is a Yan-nhaŋu place. It is the place the ancestors gave us. These are the seas given to us by the ancestors, of the Yan-nhaŋu speaking people, The Gamalaŋga, Gurryindi and the Malarra. Together we share the stories of the ancestors. We know the songs of the seas and of the islands.

Listen to me, listen to me closely for the children. I have made a school for the children to learn their language A homeland on their country.

My name, the name of these places, the languages of the islands, and the seas were given to us. These were given to us by the ancestors when they made the world. These are the places and the things that I have taught generations of young people here.

But is it a good thing or bad thing?

Now that the government can see my place and hear my words, will they help? What will they do?

I want the children to live on their homelands, to learn about their country, their language and stories, so when they grow up, they can continue to look after the spirits and the sea. And learn to live in the right way.

This award makes me think, I have done the work on the homelands and now the government is interested in me.

Will they help me keep my homelands before I die?

– Laurie Baymarrwaŋa, from the film *Laurie Baymarrwaŋa –*
*Senior Australian of the Year 2012*

Her bare feet make tracks in the sand as she strides across the island of Murruŋga. I crouch down and lightly touch her footprint. A shiver goes through my spine. Baymarrwaŋa's thin hair blows in the hot wind. She wears a red skirt with white flowers and a large grey T-shirt that hangs on her slight frame. A long greenish-brown net she wove years before hangs from her head down her back.

I walk behind her. The edges of my feet hang off my thongs. It's almost October, *Dhuludur*' season, and my skin cooks on this scorching land. It's so hot and humid. Soon the heat will build up, big black clouds will appear and threaten to burst open with rain. I've been told it's referred to as troppo season, as the intense heat creates high pressure and short tempers before the arrival of rain finally brings relief. I've a T-shirt wrapped around my head to stop the direct hit of the sun on my skull.

We are tiny on this island, like the minuscule shells that dot the far-reaching shoreline here. There are only six of us on this island right now. The old lady, her son, two grandchildren and Sally, who flew over from Milingimbi with me on the five-seater. Baymarrwaŋa and I are going hunting for oysters on the rocks.

I wipe the sweat off my face and gaze at the sea, desperate to get in and find solace in water on my parched limbs, but this isn't going to happen, for crocodiles abound.

Baymarrwaŋa finds a spot on the sharp rocks and squats down. She is in her eighties yet full of energy and her limbs are fluid. She goes to work with her long steel rod, prising oysters from their shells and putting them in the empty freeze-dried milk tin beside her.

I crouch on a black rock at the edge of the infinite sea. I lick my salty, dry, cracked lips, attempting to moisturise them. There are piles of brown and black rocks covered with white shells containing precious fleshy food. I think back to my very first trip to Yirrkala in 2001, where I collected oysters with the women. Back then, I dreamed of returning to Arnhem Land and now here I am this 2004 with Baymarrwaŋa. I take a breath, exhale deeply and stab my stick at the oysters, happy to be here again hunting for my own food in the company of a strong Yolŋu elder, a custodian of this great land, no less.

I finally crack a tough shell open and pop the white oyster into my mouth. It slips easily down my throat, the salt stinging my ragged lips. I am content to just sit here eating my catch but Baymarrwaŋa isn't doing that. She is collecting them and filling up her tin. So I stop eating and do the same. Every now and again, she looks over to me and then goes back to work. I take my camera off my shoulder and snap a few shots of her. The lines etched in her face tell a million stories of ancient times gone, but she is still present here, making history.

I am not close enough to speak with her, so the next time she looks across at me, I catch her eye and make motions with my arms to physically show myself lying in the water. She nods. Fully clothed, I slide into a shallow rock pool and lie there. The water is hot, acrid, and it trickles through my knee-length red shorts onto my skin. I lie motionless, eyes fixed up into the huge sky. Then I let my eyelids close, breathe deeply and sink down, relaxing my body until a sudden shock of fear jolts me up into a sitting position and my eyes open to check for crocodiles.

I drag myself out of the soup-hot sea, clothes sticky, but feeling refreshed. I perch on a rock and begin to dig my stick into the white jagged shells once again and continue the oyster collection. I stay focused on the hunt for a while, my plastic container filling up. A flock of black birds lift off the rocks; their large wings synchronise as they soar across the blue cloudless sky, thin legs dangling down.

My eyes fix on Baymarrwaŋa again and I think about what a wise courageous woman she is, living here for decades. Tiny, yet a powerhouse of a woman, her strength is evident. She must have so much knowledge about the rocks, plants, land, animals and fish that live in the immense blue ocean surrounding this island. In her years, she would have seen the arrival of the missionaries on Milingimbi, fishermen from Japan and Europe, and even witnessed war.

Murruŋga is a small island off the coast of East Arnhem Land, one of the Crocodile Islands, about twenty-five kilometres from Milingimbi. There are about three houses on the island. One is the schoolhouse. Baymarrwaŋa has worked hard to maintain culture and develop a school and a home for the few families that reside here. The corrugated-iron houses face the sand dunes and beyond them is the ocean.

Pandanus trees grow behind the houses. That is where Baymarrwaŋa collects pandanus for all the traditional *bathis* and mats that she weaves. Here she is living day by day, not gnashing her teeth at life and being tossed away by its challenges. I can learn a lot from her. Not far from her house is a public telephone box. I still can't get used to hearing the shrill of that phone ring out here, far from anywhere.

A massive *guḻun* lies behind a ridge. You can see this mottled green swamp from above as you fly in. It is a huge dark pool adorned with waterlilies, paperbarks growing around the edge and most likely, no definitely, is full of crocodiles.

Baymarrwaŋa sits on the wooden veranda of her house, weaving a basket. It is a small long cylindrical one woven with rich brown and yellow pandanus string. Next to her there is a white plastic fan blowing air on her as her nimble fingers thread and weave the pandanus. Her son, a tall, bony, lean man with a wide nose, big lips and white flaky skin on his arms holds a large fish. He and the two boys are not long back from hunting on the other side of the island.

I am here because, after eighteen months, I could not leave Milingimbi Island without spending at least a few days with this woman, and Sally is here with us to record Baymarrwaŋa's language for the dictionary being developed. Baymarrwaŋa is one of the last speakers of the Yan-nhaŋu language. It is wonderful that Sally is contributing in this way, so the old women's language can be recorded and documented for the future generations. Sally's parents lived on Milingimbi many years ago. She grew up in Melbourne hearing the Yolŋu *matha* language.

Sally and I decide to go for a walk along the sandy ridge. Baymarrwaŋa's long fingers are working their way through the string as she weaves. She stops and hands us a box of matches and says something to Sally.

'To light a fire, we need one,' says Sally.

To keep crocodiles away, I imagine. I can use some words and sentences in Yolŋu now but not in Yan-nhaŋu, although Baymarrwaŋa can speak other Yolŋu languages.

Tall paperbarks grow around the billabong. Golden light shimmers on the weeping willow and the white Stringybark. A green vine twists its way through the willow. Hues of green and yellow light flicker in the sunset. The whole scene looks like a watercolour painting. Tufts of thick grass grow out of the sand dunes.

We reach the beach and find tiny tracks etched in the sand.

'Turtle tracks,' says Sally. Her skin is very clear and she has light brown hair and big blue eyes.

We collect a few sticks and twigs and make a fire high up on the beach. The hot red flames add to the sweat that is already dripping down our skin.

Staring at the sea, I find an eye peering at us.

'Turtle?' asks Sally, spying it too.

'Nah, think that's a croc,' I say, feeling immediately freaked out.

We stub out the fire and hurry back to tell Baymarrwaŋa's son and the two boys about the tracks. They grab their spears and head off in the direction we just came from.

Baymarrwaŋa, nimble in body, squats next to the fire, placing a large tin of water on it for tea. She tosses some Bushells tea bags into the pot.

The big scaly yellow fish the guys had thrown on the fire is baking in the embers.

'_La̱lu_,' says Baymarrwaŋa.

'That's the type of fish it is, a parrot fish,' says Sally.

The guys return and Sally chats with them in Yolŋu *matha*.

'They saw crocodile tracks right where we were sitting on the beach, Mary,' she explains.

Baymarrwaŋa's son stands leaning against his spear. He points back to where we had just come from.

I shudder.

The water tanks in the distance form black silhouettes as the burnt-orange sky turns to night. Oysters bobble in a tin in the flames and Sally buries some yams in the hot coals. The smell of the yams makes me realise how hungry I am after this magical day. Baymarrwaŋa inspects the _La̱lu_ boiling in another tin. What a feast.

After dinner, we sit under a canopy of billions of stars. Baymarrwaŋa picks up her corncob pipe and stuffs a few strands of tobacco in it. She shoves a small skinny stick into the fire and then lights the pipe, toking on it until a stream of smoke wafts up into the dark. I sit in the starlight, listening to her, watching the lines of her face. She talks and talks and every now and then she points her bony finger up into the black night sky with its shining jewels and I know she is sharing great knowledge. Somehow it doesn't matter that I can't understand all the words, though I wish I could. The melody and tone of her language, the stillness of her presence and the land are profound.

Sally and I squash into a mozzie dome on the veranda and Baymarrwaŋa sleeps inside the house.

That night, a spirit woman comes to visit me in my dreams. Swirls of light hold her ethereal presence. Big eyes, her cheeks are round, thick silver hair falls around her shoulders as she smiles at me. I wake up wondering if it was one of the women the *marrŋgitj* had told me about at our healing.

The next day, we connect the run-down old trailer to the tractor and ride across to the other side of the island. After several attempts, we tie the broken bits of trailer together with old rope. Baymarrwaŋa's son drives the rusty tractor and the two boys sit on the top of the fenders over the wheels, flashing white-teeth smiles. Beyond the guys, huge white puffy clouds hang in a clear blue sky.

Sally and I sit with Baymarrwaŋa on the trailer. I sniff the air, enjoying the salt and smell of the bush.

We dig for yams and go for a walk along the sand and collect tiny shells.

I wander off and carve a big circle in the sand and place smooth stones around it. This is my vision quest. I sit in the middle, staring out to the sea. I stretch my hands up in the air and say, 'I am living beyond my wildest dreams!'

I run down and roll fully clothed into the sea, very quickly, though, as crocodiles are sure to be near.

I dry off quickly in the sun and join Sally and Baymarrwaŋa. 'When you were taking a dip, the old lady said, "She sure likes to be in the sea,"' Sally tells me as she pokes the fat yams in the crackling fire with a stick. I wish I could stay with Baymarrwaŋa and learn from her for the rest of the year, I think, forgetting completely that soon I will be leaving my island home.

As the sun begins to set, we sit around the fire, and Baymarrwaŋa brings out a large book written by the anthropologist Donald Thompson in the 1930s. Baymarrwaŋa names the people in the black and white photographs and speaks about some of the rituals and hunting practices. Silver, wispy-haired with some strands of grey growing out of her chin, her whole body frame shakes when she giggles. She is childlike yet exudes an unshakeable strength and determination.

'*Buḻaŋgitj,*' she says.

'*Buḻaŋgitj,*' I repeat. '*Nhä mayali' bulaŋgitj?*' I ask.

'*Manymak,*' she says.

'*Yä, buḻaŋgitj* means *manymak* in Yan-nhaŋu. *Latju.*'

Baymarrwaŋa turns a page and chuckles again as she comes to a photograph of three women and points to herself.

'Wow, *bulaŋgitj,*' I say. 'How amazing!'

Baymarrwaŋa loves photos so I take lots of pictures of her and promise to send them to her. As I am snapping away she holds one hand to stop me for a moment. Resting her other hand on my arm she points inside. I nod. She walks briskly inside and comes out with an old *maḏayin bathi* that she has worn at ceremonies. She walks away from the veranda onto the sand, puts the string around her neck and stands proudly while I take a picture of her.

I remember vividly the day I met Baymarrwaŋa. It was a pivotal moment in my Arnhem life because meeting her was to me like meeting a monk in Bhutan, Nelson Mandela, or the Dalai Lama. It was one of those moments when you know you have met a great living spirit. We met at the school on Milingimbi Island.

I walked past the staffroom at lunchtime one day and caught sight of two women inside, sitting on the old cane lounge.

Baymarrwaŋa sat there, her thin arms circling a long, traditionally shaped *bathi*. Her younger sister sat next to her, greying hair swept up in a bun, blue and white floral dress.

'She wants to sell that *bathi*, *yapa*,' the tall woman said.

'I'll buy it!' I said without consideration. A pulse ran through my veins as I gazed at the old lady. I wanted to learn more about her. She emanated ancient wisdom and knowledge.

Her gnarly fingers collected the string handle on the *bathi* and she placed it on her head. The *bathi* hung down her back. She chuckled and the lines in her face deepened.

I smiled back in appreciation of her sense of humour.

'I'll go home and get some *rrupiya*,' I said and ran out the door.

A young man with strong shoulders, blue eyes and short brown hair met me in my stride. From what I am learning, this guy is very dedicated in supporting Baymarrwaŋa in living her vision.

'You have no idea about what you just bought. No idea of the value of this basket and what it will be in the future. I'm not talking about money.' His accent sounded British but he was Australian.

Yes, I do, I thought, but didn't say. I know she is an ancient spirit and I intend to know her well if I am so lucky.

## 25

# Living between worlds

> Between two worlds life hovers like a star,
> 'Twixt night and morn, upon the horizon's verge.
> How little do we know that which we are!
> – Lord Byron

On arrival at Milingimbi, I surrendered to the timeless wild force that took hold of my being and allowed it to pluck me deep into its stratosphere and envelop me in its snake-like magnetism. Still to this day I know I am in a totally unique dimension, a rich vortex of energy like no other, a meld of land, ether, spirit and kin.

Most holidays, I leave Milingimbi to go to Darwin or New South Wales. If I have been on Milingimbi many months, ensconced in a demanding school life, *buŋgul* and weekends of hunting and weaving, it takes a while for me to find my feet again at the other end. I purchase lipsticks that I will never wear, wander down large supermarket aisles, marvelling at shelves of chocolate and fresh greens – well, fresher than anything I usually taste, anyway. On occasion, I fall into the arms of my sporadic Latino/Italian lover in Darwin. Our random closeness provides a radical shift from the rest of my life.

Riding on a bus, I feel like I'm eavesdropping on conversations held in English. I am shocked by slang terms and Northern Territory humour. I just don't get people's use of sarcasm any more. I stare at the colour of people's eyes, skin, the shape of their bodies and fashion sense. I literally prepare myself to walk across a highway. My senses are heightened. Colours are brighter. I squint in shops lit up with fluorescent lights. Café and coffee smells are stronger and traffic is loud. Deep in me, a sense of serenity dwells but at the same time sometimes I am not grounded. The world outside my bubble is a shock to my nervous system.

When I travel overseas, I love the feeling of anonymity, when no one knows me. I could be on a plane to Paris or Istanbul or walking the streets of Chennai in India. Anything could happen in those moments. As a child, in addition to family life and religion, I dwelled in the worlds of nature, healing and intuition. In my teens, I entered the yoga world.

Although there are connections between all these worlds, traditionally, yoga is not about healing and intuition. Though one may experience these aspects as their practice develops, one is encouraged to grow beyond the psychic realms. I have tried to move beyond the psychic and healing world, but I've come to the conclusion now that these qualities are an innate part of my being and are useful for me and to share at times with others.

These are different kinds of between-world experiences. Right now, I am talking about the transition from the Yolŋu world – where spirit is alive in everything and everyone, and traditional life is independent of time – back into the world in which I've experienced the rest of my life. The Indigenous thread woven in me through my adoption by the Yolŋu extends way beyond this tiny island. Strolling through the Smith Street Mall in Darwin, I discover how I am related to a seemingly complete Yolŋu stranger I happen upon from Galiwin'ku (Elcho Island). I cannot ignore the face of a Yolŋu woman I see by chance, sitting in a four-wheel drive in a car park in Byron Bay. She is from Yirrkala. I must speak with her, hear her language, learn her skin name, and she will know how we are connected in the lattice of Yolŋu kinship.

I am going to leave my island home. Yes, I have tossed and turned over and meditated on whether this is the right thing to do. I love my life here but I miss people, romance, swimming in the ocean, and yoga and healing work in New South Wales. Still my skin hasn't adjusted to intense heat, healthy food is hard to come by. Im sure, though, that eating fresh food and bush *ŋatha* would alter that. My soul is captivated here, though, and I feel a great sense of purpose. The depth of intimacy through kinship here is sometimes beyond my comprehension, but what to do? Really, it seems mad to leave. I'm 'between two worlds', as Lord Byron would say. I see this struggle in other non-Indigenous people too and we understand each other for it.

Today is my last day. Last night, my Yolŋu family had a *buŋgul* for me. We danced down at Yibi's place at Darawundhu. Sally was dancing too. *Wäwa* Jo and *Wäwa* Clancy played the *bilma*, and some of my *waku* played *yidaki*.

Jessie sang the Leaving song for me in the staffroom at school and I couldn't stop crying.

> Do not hurry to tell us goodbye.
> From this island, they say you are leaving.
> We will miss your bright eyes and sweet smile,
> just because you are weary and tired
> You are changing your home for a while.
> Come and sit by our fire before you leave us.
> But remember your Milingimbi Island,
> And the people who love you so well.

I run my fingers along the worn, tattered, eagle feather Jo Buchanan, a dear mentor, healer and friend brought back for me from sacred Sedona some years ago. I poke it into the wire screen of the back door where I have spent so many evenings perched on the top step, looking at the stars, scrawling down my thoughts and absorbing the community. This old feather has smudged, smoked and cleared many a body and energy field, including my own, and countless spaces, inside and out, but now its work with me is complete.

'I'll have to get another feather,' I say out loud, perusing the house fondly once more. I love this big old house so much. How different I feel in it now in comparison to those first few fearful days.

At the Milingimbi airstrip, my *Waku* Warmbirrirr stands, also waiting for the Air North plane to Darwin. I am glad we are travelling together. A feather is sticking out the top of her hair.

'*Nhä dhuwal, Waku?*' I ask.

'It's for you,' she smiles, pulling it out of her hair and poking its long spine into mine. 'Eagle feather, *Dändi*,' she says.

Wow, that was quick, Spirit, I think, laughing out loud: but of course. 'This is so right, *Waku*. I was just thinking about this. Thank you so much,' I say, hugging her.

*Yapa* Gapan and Warmbirrirr sit with me until the plane for Brisbane comes after midnight. We laugh and share stories until I cry.

'*Yaka nhe ga ŋäthi, yak*a.' *Yapa* hugs me tightly into her heart.

I am held in the women's loving gaze until I walk through gate number two and disappear back into my other world.

I move into my apartment near the beach and the tea tree lake in Lennox Head, New South Wales. I wake up, swim across the lake, make a juice, teach yoga and take long barefoot walks on the sand. Hour upon hour, I sit on a purple bolster in front of my computer, looking at photos of the Yolŋu, listening to the Djambaŋ Band, Saltwater Band and reading my journals. I send Baymarrwaŋa photos of her holding her sacred basket. The *marrŋgitj* calls me from a phone box on Murruŋga Island and runs out of coins. Bats smash against my window at night and I wonder if I have made the right choice.

My dreams are filled with kids clambering all over me in the classroom, days out bush with the women, dancing at *buŋguls* and the beating of *biḻma*. The memory of dancing at my *buŋgul* with *Yapa* Yibi and my *wäwas* under the stars is vivid in my mind. That last night on Yurrwi, I lay awake, energised by the *buŋgul*, grains of earth still stuck on my feet as I stared up at the luminous stars for the last time. My arms had been laden with several beautiful baskets the women had woven for me as gifts on my departure. They now adorn my Lennox Head lounge room.

Here at Lennox Head, I am enjoying the yoga and healing worlds I am immersed in once more. I drive to Sydney and see clients on the Northern Beaches again. I'm feeling healthier, fitter and enjoy being closer to people I have missed and I even start a relationship of sorts. I read through the journals I wrote late at night on Yurrwi Island and begin writing a book about my Milingimbi days and how I landed there. Writing is not new for me. It has been a practice since childhood. Like the practice of yoga, writing down my thoughts has been a long-term companion that I cherish.

I love to get the words out of my head onto the paper. Writing does something profound. It gives a new perspective. It connects me with who I am, beyond the incessant stream of critical thoughts flowing through my mind. When I arrived on Milingimbi, it became essential to write everything down, as important as yoga practice. Now, here at Lennox Head, my life on Milingimbi remains alive as I write the story.

In my in-between-world confusion, I sit in the lounge room with the hot pink wall I painted and meditate with the intent to ground myself in my body where I am right now. I aspire to align my mind, heart and soul, and experience stability. I breathe, relax and bring my mind once more into the world I now dwell in, but somehow I am in limbo, I belong nowhere. I sit on my yoga mat, knowing that the strength I desire lies inside me, but a great sense of disconnection envelops me. I am not even Yolŋu but I am made to reflect on how challenging it must be for Yolŋu when they are not on their land with their kin.

Life beyond my island home unfolds naturally now, filled with encounters with Indigenous Australians and Maori people from New Zealand. We are in the rural north coast of New South Wales. The surrounding landscape is green, spacious, with undulating hills. My eyes squint in the sun on this warm day. The sky above is vast and a perfect blue.

The large rock beneath me is one of a circle of cool, smooth boulders around a fireplace. I sit listening to the Aboriginal healer and talk about the stones he uses in his healing treatments. For years, I had heard his name in healing circles in Sydney, yet our paths never crossed in the flesh until I had a healing treatment with him recently. I thought perhaps he could help me with my great sense of disorientation.

I imagine flames roaring and crackling in the centre of the circle of stones and sense the presence of eyes on me.

I look up to see an Aboriginal woman with long straight black hair.

'Hey, sister,' I hear.

I jump on hearing these familiar words once more in my life. Memories of the *yidaki* player and the shaman in Sydney speed through my mind.

'*Yow!*' I respond. 'I mean, yes.'

'Hey, sister, you bin sung. That mob up there are calling you back,' she says. 'You've been sung!' she says again.

The words etch my heart. I look up, screening the sun from my eyes with my hand so I can see into her face. 'Really?' is all I can muster.

'You won't hang around here,' she says.

Goosebumps ripple through my skin. In my soul I know she is right.

I am moved and honoured by these words but also confused by the between-world state in which I dwell.

I am not ignorant of this incredible alchemical spirit that I am connected to in Arnhem Land. I'm also fully aware of the grief, politics, suffering and deaths that challenge me, not to mention the heat; but there is a pulse that calls me to experience this interconnectedness yet again.

I dream every night of being back in Arnhem Land.

One night, I dream I am back at Yalakun with Wendy Mipururr, Judy's granddaughter, my *gaminyarr.* Her face is beaming with joy as we stroll hand in hand together along the endless stretch of white sand.

I sit at my computer writing in my lounge room at Lennox Head. I stare out the large glass sliding door at the frangipani tree I planted in the courtyard. I wonder what else I can grow in such a small space.

I jump when the phone rings and almost spill my tea.

'*Yow, Dändi, marrkapmirr.*' I hear Nimanydja on the other end of the phone.

'*Yä Waku, marrkapmirr,*' I reply.

'Judy Munymuny *ga rirrikthun*,' Nimanydja's worried voice comes through the phone.

'*Yuwalk Waku? Gurrupuruŋu*,' I respond.

'*Yuwalk! Nhätha Yapa dhu roŋiyirri Yalakunlil? Bitjarr Wäwa waŋan.*'

I hang up the phone, knowing in my heart I am not ready to never see *Waku* Judy Munymuny again. I begin to receive more calls from Yolŋu saying they had heard I'd be up there for the next festival.

'*Yaka bäyŋu*,' I respond, but now it is clear that my time on Yurrwi Island is not complete, and so I choose to return.

# 26

# Return to Yurrwi

> From a long distance away
> I heard my Yolŋu *gurruṯu* calling me back to my island home
> Tears in my eyes, I could already see the vivid blue sky, the storm clouds, the rich earth
> I could smell the rain and the saltwater.
> I could hear thunder and Yolŋu language
> I could hear my *ŋerrk mala*, my dreaming
> And I could hear the laughter of children,
> the *biḻma*, the *yiḏaki* and the thud of barefeet on the earth in ceremony.
> My Yolŋu *gurruṯumirriŋu mala* called me back and so I followed my heart and I went.

I peer out the window and see the woman's wispy hair, her brightly coloured floral skirt layers trailing as she runs barefoot along the tarmac of the airstrip. One arm reaches towards the light aircraft ahead of her that has taken off and is flying away, the other hand clenches her heart. I'm in the Air North plane, on the way back from a trip to Darwin; it hovers in a puff of white clouds.

This was my first flight back to a city since I returned to Milingimbi in July. We have circled the green gums and cycad trees below three times now, but cannot land. The plane this woman runs after has ascended higher in the sky now. She is lost in despair. Yolŋu women are good at revealing what's in their hearts. Right now she cannot let go of her loved one; she is torn by this unbearable separation. Her feet cannot move her fast enough. Her trembling body and guttural wails cannot raise her up off the earth to grab hold of the plane that has taken her loved one's body away. Finally, she flings her self on the ground and lies there, writhing in sorrow. Other women, also in tears, come to her aid and usher her off the tarmac.

My gut wrenches as we finally land. 'I'm home' are the words in my head.

I step off the plane, onto the tarmac. The force of sadness thuds my stomach as I witness the grieving faces of those suffering their loss.

There is no way to ease back into this world, no way to soften the depth of spirit that exists in every rock, stone, animal, tree and person, creating a thick impenetrable web that I am once more ensconced in.

And I never want to change this but so much sorrow hangs heavy on my heart.

After all this time away, someone yells out to me and I jump on the back of a white ute full of Yolŋu family and get a ride back to the red pole house where I lived the last time I was on Milingimbi Island.

I lie on my mat in the lounge room. It is surreal that I am living in the same house I left before I returned to Lennox Head and I have come back to the same teaching position. It feels so natural and right to be back with Yolŋu again and the work I'm assigned to, but the heat and biting dogs challenge me.

Geckos scurry up and down the wall, after their next meal, a spider or perhaps a juicy fly. Red-brown dust, residue of the wind, sticks on the window glass, contrasting with the green leaves of the trees. I watch the golden sunlight on the pale-grey tree trunks fade as day dissolves into night. Birds squawk as they cluster in the treetops before flurrying across the sky to retire for the evening.

'*Wäy, räli marrtji,*' calls a mother to her wandering child.

Children's laughter rings out. The fan above my head whirrs. The door rattles in the wind.

A soothing breeze touches my face momentarily. A child cries.

'*Sha,*' yells a voice at a barking dog.

As the moon grows full, the mangy hounds' barks become one voice crooning in the night.

A random clap stick sound resonates with possibility of the beginning of a new ceremony.

Orange-footed scrub fowls synchronise and overlap their calls.

Through the slat windows, my eyes can reach a slice of night sky covered in stars.

Cane toads rummage in the compost heap. Yes, a few made their way onto this island on the barge one day and now they are everywhere.

'*Yaka, yaka,*' a child screams over at *Bäpa* Jo's house.

Christian songs in Yolŋu language burst out through a loudspeaker.

I lather my face and hands with moisturiser.

I am not alone at all. In this moment, I feel a part of the potency of the web that weaves us all together here.

Yes, I am home. I relax again but my dreams reflect the dichotomy of the worlds in which I dwell.

After a day out bush staring into the smooth waters of <u>N</u>ilatjirriwa I dream I am in the bush on the edge of the <u>n</u>inydjiya. Smoke billows from a fire under the paperbark trees. A group of Yolŋu faces and limbs painted with white clay and yellow ochre appear dancing: their feet flicking up the earth. A resounding, deep 'wha wha' emerges from their insides, silhouettes incandescent in the subdued light of the sunset. *Wäwa* Jo sits in the sand and sings, another *wäwa* plays clap sticks, and a *waku* plays the *yi<u>d</u>aki*.

I am compelled to join my two sisters dancing close by, yet I hesitate. The cracked grey earth of the saltpans crunches yet is soft and powdery between my toes. My clothes hang heavy on my sweaty body, but my feet move me to dance as if in a trance.

Then in the corner of my eye I catch the sight of my brothers from the world I was born in, their wives, my nieces and nephews. They are looking at me and then they walk away. My heart thumps and my legs carry me after them.

'Come back, come back,' I scream in my dream and then hurl myself to the ground, mournful cries burst forth from within. Then bodiless, I float above the earth and look down. I see a Yolŋu woman's body in a heap on the ground, thick black hair, round cheeks wet with tears. Yellow ochre is streaked across my nose and cheekbones.

I wake up still sobbing and with the question in my head, is this what I must do? Choose between worlds?

## 27

## The spirit of Yalakun – Part 2

Feeling so tiny on the long white sands.
Sit by the fire
Tea on the boil, stories, and women's wisdom shared.
Luminescent stars in the night sky.
Led by children who know how to play.
Never let the beautiful light in your eyes
fade away.

I walk along the far-reaching white sands with Wendy Mipururr at Yalakun. Her face is beaming just as I was shown in the dream I had back in my apartment at Lennox head.

It is 2006. I returned to Yurrwi Island in July and now it is the September school holidays. Munymuny has brought me back here to Yalakun. We are all here together enjoying some timeless space. My heart is at home immediately with Dorothy Guwalkuwalk and *wäwa* Terry Malmaliny.

*Waku* Guwalkuwalk walks us over to a lush garden of fat orange pumpkins, tomatoes and other vegetables. 'We are growing *dharrwa ŋatha* and the *ḏirramu mala* go hunting everyday. We want to build a strong community, *ŋama'*,' she says.

An old black stove and large silver bench create an outdoor kitchen not far from the house. The men chop up the *buliki'* they hunted today and the girls and I cut up vegetables from the garden and cook up a huge stew for our first night here.

The Yolŋu would love a bigger school with more teachers and a clinic.

At sunset, *Waku* Judy Munymuny and I stand among the trees as the burning orange ball of the sun melts down into the sea, leaving purple and pink streaks across the sky. I am relieved to be by her side once more and that she is okay after her near death experience at the hospital. Apparently, her heart had stopped for some minutes. That is when Nimanydja called me at Lennox Head. Munymuny's face glows and wisps of white hair gently touch her eyes and high cheekbones. Calm exudes from her. Tiny *winyiwinyi* swoop and dart close to us and I think of the *marrŋgitj*.

'*Winyiwinyi marrŋgitj,* is that you?' I whisper.

'I'm here to help some teenagers who want to stop taking drugs or sniffing petrol. It can harm them and make them angry, violent,' says Judy Munymuny. 'I can talk to them and help them stay strong.'

A crowd of Yolŋu have gathered around Munymuny under the night sky. They listen intently and receive inspiration and courage from her words.

We sit in a circle on a patch of land the Yolŋu have marked out.

'This space has enormous healing power, *ŋama*', so we gather here to align with its energies and receive healing,' says Guwalkuwalk. I sit quietly next to *Waku* Munymuny. I do feel a very clear and potent vibration here and I breathe deeply and absorb it into my cells.

Late in the night, I leave the women chatting by the fire and head up to the classroom with my *gaminyarrs*, Mipururr and Gulikuli. Our blankets and pillows are piled together in the centre of the classroom. Desks and chairs are stacked at the window ledge. Bookshelves spill over with old readers and magazines.

I pick up *Where the Wild Things Are* by Maurice Sendak to read to the kids and settle into my sleeping bag.

Giggling, the children grab books too and we snuggle together, laughing and sharing stories and pictures.

'And the wild things roared their terrible roars and gnashed their terrible teeth and rolled their terrible eyes.' I growl as I read, then look down to find the children fast asleep. I smile and rest the book on my chest, fall into a deep, deep sleep and wake up to find the children gone. A feeling of concern washes through my blood stream, as I am normally such a light sleeper. How come I didn't hear them leave? Usually, I wake at the slightest sound but not this night.

*Waku* Munymuny returns with them; they had gone looking for her. Back to sleep I go and dream of spirits and fleeting faces. I wake up unable to move. Someone is grabbing my foot and trying to drag me away. I am immobilised in my body, unable to stop what is happening. 'No, no. Munymuny, Munymuny.' It takes a moment before I realise it is my own voice saying these words. My eyes open to find Mipururr's large, wide eyes peering through dangling strands of her hair into mine, a puzzled look on her face, and Gulikuli's eyes round too and his brow wrinkled.

'*Bäydhi manymak, manymak ŋarra*,' I reassure the children and pull them close, but I lie awake for a while, fear alive in my bones, heart thumping loud in my chest and until I finally drift off again.

'Mary, that was spirit. What you were experiencing was someone being taken away and you could feel what that person was feeling,' says Judy as we sit weaving the next morning.

That's normal for me, I thought, taking a sip of tea, to experience someone else's feelings and experiences.

'Actually I was wondering if the spirit had come to take me to the bush for *marrŋgitj* and I had resisted with fear,' I say.

'Oh, so you want to be a magic *miyalk*?' the woman next to *Yapa* Guwalkuwalk says, smacking her hand on her knee and laughing out loud.

'That was our uncle, *ŋama*',' says Guwalkuwalk. 'His spirit lives here.'

There were a few theories about it. I sat staring into the flames of the fire that night, deep in thought and intrigued with this spirit talk.

'*Napurr ga marrtji huntinglil Momu.*' Mipururr takes my hand and leads me down to the rocks on the edge of the sea.

I squat on a rock in the shade of the tangled mangrove roots. Lost in my activity, I stab with my stick at oysters glued to the round boulders. I look up to see Mipurr smiling at me through strands of hair hanging over her eyes. She is smashing the shellfish off the rocks with a sharp rock she has found. Gulikuli and several other children are collecting too, bits of oyster shell stuck on their lips. I smile back, pick up my camera and click away, catching the beauty of spirit in their faces at that moment.

As I stab at the rocks, I reflect on everything Munymuny has told me. This discussion about spirit I hear often from the women.

Mipurr has already filled a container with oysters. She picks it up and runs back to our camp and gives it to the women. Today they are stripping back pandanus ready to weave baskets.

One of the boys has a long wooden spear with a steel tip. We amble along the beach. The long white sand goes for miles and I have to pinch myself at where I am.

'Look, *momu* Mary, *miyapunu dhurrpa*',' says the boy with the spear and he pokes it deep into the sand to look for turtle eggs.

Immediately, two of the other the boys lie down and become turtles. They drag themselves across the sand, their arms flapping alongside them. I wish I knew how all the children are related to me. People are always telling me who is who but the kinship system still confounds me. Slowly, though, I am beginning to understand more about my relationships with people and also that it is very important for me to know my relationship name, like *waku* or *yapa*, or *wäwa* or *gutharra*.

When I first came to Yurrwi Island, I spent a lot of time focusing on learning Yolŋu names because I did not want to just refer to people with their *balanda* name. I wanted to be able to pronounce names correctly. I did not comprehend the depth of kinship at all. I know Gulukuli and Mipurr are my *gaminyarr* and I have only recently learned that the *marrŋgitj* is my 'poison cousin'. I should have realised he was Yirritja all those times I watched him dance *ŋerrk*. I am Yirritja too and traditionally I do not speak directly with my poison cousin, although there are correct ways to communicate. It worries me that I am not even aware that I am not aligning with the culture. How patient the Yolŋu are.

The boy with wild curly hair sits amongst the shrubs, holding branches of leaves around his face, flashing his white teeth. 'This bush [is] my home, Mary,' he says.

I enjoyed a lot of time down by the creek in the bush after school where I grew up; it gave me a strong connection with nature, but this experience here seems so far from the activity of my own school days, I think, as I laugh, join in and snap photographs. We run with barefooted wildness along the edge of the cobalt-blue salt water. How free these children are to express themselves, to explore nature. How happy they are and creative as they play on the land they are so entwined with. Their culture and language is alive for them, embedded in their cells. The elders carry it for them and continue to pass it on through time. I look out to the vastness of the sea. I look up at the brightness of the blue sky. The children and I are but dots on the sand of this compelling land.

Another of my *gaminyarr,* a little girl with huge eyes, a round face and long thin hair, picks up two sticks and begins to clap them and sing traditional song. Mipururr begins to dance, her footprints marking the sand with ancient tradition. Knees bent, she claps her hands in time with the girl's clap sticks. They create perfect rhythm together. Mipururr lifts her long thin arms and a strange look of pain grows on her face, then she hurls herself onto the sand, landing with a thud and remaining motionless just as her mother and grandmother would if grieving at a funeral.

I am speechless initially, just watching and marvelling at the life force of these children.

'Wow, *buŋgul latju!*' Some words finally come out of my mouth.

At the end of the beach lies a pool of clear water. The strong roots of the mangroves create a barrier to the rest of the sea and the children laugh, splash and swim about. Apparently, we are safe from the box jellyfish and *bäru* here. The women have moved close to us now, sitting in the shade around the fire, boiling tea and cooking damper.

I stand knee-deep in lukewarm water.

'*Luplupthun, momu?*' says Gulikuli, inviting me to join the fun. His wild curls are slicked back now by the water, revealing two big ears.

'*Yow,*' I laugh and stretch my arms out wide and fall into the pool fully clothed.

Two boys sit with hands cupped on the water's edge. They scoop sand up and rub it through their hair and down their limbs. I dig my hands into the wet sand and do the same. I glide sandy hands down my arms, legs, whole body, until I am caked from head to toe. Right now, I couldn't care less about how I look or how perhaps I think I am meant to act. I rest on my back, my whole body slumping into the warm moist sand. I lie grinning up at the sky. Nothing can faze me in this moment. I slip into the water again, wash off the sand and am soothed by liquid rippling on my skin.

Two of the little girls wriggle out of the water and pull themselves up onto the sand. One's face wrinkles up into a very stern look.

'*Bäru,*' squeal the kids and drag themselves along the sand like crocodiles, roaring, laughing and slithering along the shoreline.

By night, I am joyfully exhausted. We have walked for miles up the beach and collected turtle eggs for dinner.

I lie on my back, trying to stay awake, looking at the stars. I'm so happy for this experience right now.

The children fall asleep snuggled together and I am not long after them. Tonight, under the strict orders of the women, we are sleeping around the fire close to the children. I lie on my purple yoga mat under the brilliant stars, a few stones poking through it jabbing me in the back, but I'm too tired to be disturbed by them. My clothes smell of wood smoke and eyelids become heavy. Tiny *winyiwinyi* flutter and dart around the lamppost above.

'Hello, *marrŋgitj*,' I murmur sleepily.

I feel safe from the possibility of being dragged away in the night again with the presence of the *winyiwinyi* and the women sitting next to me around the crackling fire. They sip bottomless cups of tea, and share stories all night long. I'm lulled to sleep by the sounds of their beautiful language, my heart once more nourished by the spirit of the land and the Yolŋu.

# 28

# Djutjutjnha, Waku

> Waves of grief wash through me like a wild sea
> My whole being sucked deeper and deeper into sorrow.
> I'm lost in loss.
> There is no other way but to feel these unfathomable feelings of grief.

Two years have passed since my second trip to Yalakun. It's now 2008. After I returned from our beautiful time on the land, I moved into a smaller blue house on Balanda Boulevard, so-named because several of the non-Indigenous teachers live in this strip of relatively new houses. This house is different to my red pole house; I'm closer to the ground and have a big deck looking at an entanglement of trees and plants I call my jungle. My days on Yurrwi Island have continued to be ensconced largely in school life, community, relationships with young and old, ceremony, trips out bush, yoga, spirit and healing, but a tinge of sorrow that was not there before now hangs in the air.

I lie on my yoga mat with my legs up the wall in *Viparita Karani*. Hands placed on my chest, I exhale all of the air out and intend to relax. The skin on my face softens a little and I feel the earth holding my body. It's about six a.m. I take another breath. A loud crashing din splits the silence of the morning as the workmen build new houses next door for teachers. Thoughts of yesterday are still vivid in my mind.

I came home from school and sat on my mat. Focusing on my breath, however, wasn't having its usual immediate affect after a challenging day, so I headed outside into the garden, armed with a shovel. I dug and dug, turning the soil upside down: creating a new garden bed for the green capsicums, eggplants and broccoli I plan to grow. The soil, a mixture of brown and red, looked a richer, deeper colour after I added some potting mix. I wiped the dirty sweat off my brow with my long sleeve and gazed at the remainder of sunlight through the leaves of the jungle. Despite the heat, long sleeves are necessary at this time of day with the sand flies injecting their sting into my flesh. I was covered up from head to toe and my feet were safe in my old favourite Blundstones that my friend Jacque gave me when I left Northern New South Wales back in 2003.

I sniffed the smoky air and looked around at my banana trees, five of them, sprouting long, round, fresh green leaves nicely. Stu had given me a couple of them as a birthday present. I am having more success with them than with pawpaw trees. The politics of school weigh heavy on my mind, thoughts vivid as I pull weeds out of the earth. At times at school, a lack of sensitivity towards Yolŋu is expressed in regard to ceremonies and when they are held. But this is a huge ceremony about the law, and we're invited to learn and understand.

Words whirl in my head. In these situations, I watch the Yolŋu people's response. They are patient. Year after year, people arrive on Milingimbi with big ideas, announcing how things are going to be now that they have arrived. Then one day, they just wake up and leave. And let's face it: I'm one of them. I'll probably get up and leave one day too but at least I intend to collaborate while I am here. In situations like this, I desire to be less reactive. I want to be patient with what I see, too. I wish to become present where I am, in what I am doing, what I am learning, what I can offer, and remain in community spirit without being consumed by someone else's opinions.

My mind reeled back to that day in June in 2007. It was the last day of term before the month-long school break. The women and kids were dancing. I was taking photographs and we were all laughing. I remember Maṯay's brilliant smile and the joy of her being as she danced. But an uneasy churning stirred in my gut. 'It won't be the same when I get back from holidays' were the words in my head. By the time I reached Darwin that evening, the government of the time had announced the Intervention. An emergency response was organised to make changes in Aboriginal communities. From my perception, there was little collaboration or acknowledgement that Aboriginal people have any strength within them at all. This was an attempt to rescue and fix the issues at hand. How can strength emerge from this attitude?

'*Napurr marrtji bala Dipirrilili,*' said Yibi Yibi a few weeks later. 'We're taking the kids to *Dipirri, Yapa*. We don't want them to take our kids again.'

Back on Yurrwi, there was a sense of foreboding darkness.

After the initial Intervention, our school was no longer a bilingual education centre. Important teachers and the Yolŋu support network are no longer employed. It is expected that four hours of English a day must be taught to all students, beginning from the moment they step out of their home into the school.

I wipe the sweat off my brow once more, take a last look at the garden for the evening and head back inside. I shower the dirt, sweat and anger off me, sit down on my mat with a bowl of dhal, a pen and a scrapbook, and begin to pour everything that's been whirling around in my head down on the page. I put the pen down and sit on the edge of a cushion on my mat, close my eyes and begin practising my mantra. Finally, I experience a moment of calm and of understanding.

It is not only school that is disturbing. I am staring death in the face yet again. I'm sitting beside someone I have grown to love and cherish and in a moment they will be gone; well, physically anyway. Fleeting painful memories of the deaths from my past wash through me. But although they are gone physically, they are still ever-present with me. Sometimes I just hear their words of strength in my ear. 'Just sit down, love, have a cup of tea, just sit calmly' are the words of my mother. Sometimes at the end of my practice while still lying in *Shavasana* (corpse pose), Maury is present, smiling at me and quietly holding my feet.

It seems here on Yurrwi Island I have developed a level of comfort around someone who is dying. With my meditation and grief counselling skills, I worked voluntarily in palliative care some years back at a hospice in Sydney. I feel I have something to offer someone who is experiencing his or her last days on earth. I choose to sit with them. Perhaps the death of my parents gave me this strength. Yolŋu often ask me to come and sit with someone who is dying, even if I don't know them that well.

Each involvement with death offers opportunities for growth, understanding and connection. Experiencing a death or loss invites us to appreciate life, live more fully and increase capacity for depth in our relationships. We realise that time, and how we spend it, is precious. These challenges instigate change whether we want it or not. Lifestyles we are comfortable in and that we perceive will last forever are cracked apart and it is demanded of us that we move on to some new way of being. In general, though, our society does not encourage this. It commands that we stay wherever we are and hold onto a job, relationship, or habit forever, whether it is true for us or not. In our culture, we fear change. I know I do sometimes, yet radical change has been forced upon me frequently from a young age. And perhaps if I had followed the intuitive messages deep in me in certain situations rather than holding on for dear life to what was familiar and comfortable, then some of my transitions might not have been so shocking.

The Yolŋu face death far more frequently than I have. They invite everyone to be with a dying person, to witness them in their last days, to provide comfort. What is also notable is that, whatever the age, all are included. In fact, it is important that no one be left out: the young and old are there for each other. There is no fear or need to hide the dying member or the death from anyone. It is vital that everyone in the community and extended family are notified and granted the opportunity to respect the loss. There is pain but somewhere there is an acceptance of it, a willingness to go genuinely into sorrow and come out the other end. To grieve and cry is a skill to be cultivated, an important part of life. It seems that celebrating death is not only healing but a way to intimately connect with earth and spirit, and experience union with everyone and everything.

*Wak*u Munymuny has been sick for over a year now but in the last weeks her health has deteriorated so much that she can no longer walk down to Munguli's and is at home a few houses up from our usual spot under the *djambaŋ* tree. Gäthu Ganyawu shares with me everything the doctor has told her; Munymuny is in the last stages of cancer now. She is dying.

We have been an integral part of each other's universes and now *Waku* Munymuny will be gone. It will throw me off balance for a while, bring up old grief, turn everything upside down, make me think about my choices and what I am doing, as every other death or loss has, but something new will grow from this experience and my connection with her will always remain alive. It cannot die.

Today, my Saturday morning plan is to clean the house and go straight to Judy Munymuny, my *waku*.

The phone rings and it is my dear friend in Mullumbimby. We are chatting away when there is a loud bang on the corrugated-iron wall of my house outside.

'*Yapa, wanha nhe?*' Jessie has arrived.

I hang up the phone and now go with the flow of the day as it unfolds.

We eat bananas and Scotch Finger biscuits, and drink cups of milky tea.

I am confused about poison cousins again.

I tell Jessie about the time at the airport, that *Ɖapipi* Matchawuy stood between me and Maṯay's husband, my *gurruŋ*, passing messages. I still don't really understand these avoidance relationships.

Jessie sits looking intently at me, sprigs of black curls falling around her cheeks, and says, 'When you see Maṯay's husband.you should say, *Nhä mirri nhuma*, not *Nhä mirr nhe*, because that way you are addressing both of them and not using his name. Say, *Nhä mirri nhuma* for poison cousin.'

'*Nhä mirri nhuma*,' I repeat.

'*Yow*. That's the Yolŋu way, *Yapa*.' She looks me in the eyes. 'That's our law.'

I hear a clap stick beat and freeze for a moment.

'I have to go to Munymuny's,' I announce urgently to Jessie. 'Why are those clap sticks playing?'

She ignores my question and anyway, I know why.

'*Yapa*, can I have that lap lap?' She points at the rainbow-coloured fabric draped around my waist.

I pull it off and hand it to her. She wraps it around her head.

'*Wäy, latju* African *miyalk*,' I say.

Her white teeth flash a big smile.

We often share clothes, always have. What I witness in Yolŋu culture is sharing. It seems expected that you just give and share what you have. It is not like this in the culture I grew up in. I am not saying there is not generosity nor am I judging. Just saying that it's much more about what's 'mine' and 'yours' in the world I grew up in and if someone just takes, uses or expects something, it can be considered rude.

We amble outside the front of the house, hand in hand.

'I'm going over there for *ŋarali*,' she says, pointing to a group sitting under a tree across the road.

We squeeze hands. I let go and follow the sound of the clap sticks.

The street is full of men, women and children walking this Saturday morning.

Gäthu Ganyawu is walking in my direction. 'I am just coming to get you, *mukul*.' Her brow crinkles like her mother Munguli's. '*Munymuny yätjkurr dhäwu*,' she says, holding my shoulders. 'She is calling for you.'

*Waku* lies in the corner of the bare room of her house on a mattress covered by a pastel pink sheet. Her eyes wide open, she looks almost dead. I sit quietly, touching her cool gaunt face. The whites of her sunken eyes are yellow. Cheekbones protrude from her face and the breath left in her body moves noisily in her chest cavity. Sounds move through her nostrils.

Elaine, my *gutharra*, lies alongside her, resting against her arm. Silver-white hair and big eyes, she has flown from Gapuwiyak near Yalakun and is by her side day and night. Her face looks tired.

Angela (also Munguli's daughter, also my *gäthu*) is standing on the freezer and is cleaning the blades of the fan.

'*Yow, mukul.*' She wipes her brow and looks over to me for a second, then keeps scrubbing.

'*Yow,* Gäthu,' I say.

I take a deep breath and look at Munymuny's frail body. I pull my watery eyes off her and look outside for a moment. I gaze at *bilitjbilitj,* a beautiful green and red parrot flitting about in a tree Munymuny planted herself. *Guṉinyi*, its cone-shaped fruit, is used as medicine for coughs and colds.

Women and children are beginning to gather out there on the grass, under the shade of a tree, but for now while the cleaning is going on, there are just the three of us in the room. Nimanydja's blue house is next door. There was a fence between houses but it has been pulled down to open the space between families and make room for as many people as possible to be around. When it is time for the funeral, the men will put sand on the ground to make it smooth and even for all the dances that will take place in her honour. The big red corrugated-iron house I used to live in is just across the road. I loved that house and being so close to Nimanydja, Munymuny, my *mori'Bäpa* Jo, and Nunydjulu, Banbaniwuy, Melissa Natuyŋa and all the family members.

'I was sitting outside under the stars last night, and I saw a witch-doctor under your house, *ŋama*',' Munymuny would often say. 'I'm watching over you.'

I knew she was. Once I went away on a holiday and left a blue towel on the line.

'*Yow, Ḏä̱ndi*, we were looking after that blue towel, making sure no one would take it,' said Djämbutj when I returned from a holiday.

We push the mattress with Munymuny on it into the centre of the space under the fan so that she can receive a skerrick of cool relief from the heat. There is a morphine patch on her left shoulder. She is wearing an orange flowered skirt up around her breast line. Use of a skirt this way is common and much cooler. Maximum comfort is needed now. Her blue scrunchie holds her wispy white hair in a bun.

I stroke her frail arms and her forehead. Gutharra is lying on the other side. *Waku* Munymuny is very quiet these days: hardly murmurs a word, but her presence is powerful. Anyway, we have talked so much these last years.

'Is this really you, *Waku*?' I murmur, moving closer to her.

This woman who has been so prominent in my life, who has taken me into her culture, given me her stories and language, sat with me under the stars on the long white sands of Yalakun, interpreted my dreams and shown me grace. A religious woman, people gather to hear her wisdom and yet steeped in her roots, there at every funeral with the Djambaŋ *miyalk mala*, Munguli, Djämbutj, Dorothy, Ganyawu, Gamuti, Warmbirrirr, explaining every dance, never seeming to tire of my questions as I sit by scrawling language on post-it notes.

I must know that woman, I thought, the day I met *waku*. Well, this is not the strong healthy woman I have known but, yes, it is your spirit present here. Pure. Vibrant: a great spirit in a dying body about to depart her sacred land and expand beyond the deep red earth. This day has come so quickly. I shall miss your voice, soft like water.

Pressed against her for one of the last times, we slowly stroke her arms and her legs. The room fills up and empties throughout the day as people come to say goodbye.

Munguli is outside, grandkids clambering on her as she sits for her sister.

Boys run around, in and outside, batting dead cane toads to each other with long sticks. One lands on my skirt and one on the pillow above Munymuny's head.

'*Yaka*,' shout the women. '*Outsidelil djamarrkuḻi'.*'

Nimanydja comes in and out and then settles for a while on the large blue sheet spread on the concrete outside with Munguli. Large tin of tea at hand, she reads the Bible, her voice shaking with sadness. Her face is washed out, her body moving slowly, seems crumpled, yet an air of grace exudes from her. Nimanydja and Munymuny have always been the two women to stand up at funerals and share the Bible and words of comfort. Now she must do it without her sister, but her husband *Bäpa* Jo, the minister, will be next to her.

Tea is constantly on the boil on the fire and cigarette smoke wafts through the air.

Maṯay arrives with her daughter Lisa Membaŋala, my little mum, and her sister Rarrinya. They are here to attend to Munymuny's every need. She is their *märi*. They are her *gutharra* and it is their role to assist her now. There are many responsibilities that need to be fulfilled by Yolŋu in every part of life.

Men sit in a circle under a tree, chanting, playing clap sticks and *yiḏaki*.

'A *märi buŋgul*,' says Elaine.

A few days before, the men had entered the space and asked Munymuny if it was okay to start *buŋgul*.

'*Yow*,' she had murmured.

'Sometimes they are singing the spirit to help the person get better, but then when it is the right time they begin to play and help the spirit move on,' whispers Elaine.

Once, as we sat beneath the soap tree on Murruŋga Island, my *gudi* had told me, 'Sometimes the singing and clapping of *biḻma* is to wake up the brain of the dying person. It goes into the ear to stop sleep, to wake up and not die. Keep noise in ear to stay awake and not die.'

Ganygulpa's mother, black bun and glasses resting on her nose, sits holding Munymuny's hand. Her own grandchildren join in the dead cane toad game.

I am holding Munymuny's feet. She is disappearing under the big blanket over her, sweating and shivering at the same time.

Ganima, a little girl with sweet chocolate eyes who is in my class, runs around like a bee in a bottle, then in an instant stops and gently touches Munymuny's face with her fingertips. Knees bent, she crouches under me and peers up into my eyes with her own huge ones. I wink at her through tears. She is my little *yapa*. I hug her. She is still for a moment and then races off once more. At times, no one and nothing will contain her.

A woman sits in the corner, breastfeeding her baby.

*Waku* Buŋgalkthun, lean, with a huge smile like *Bäpa* Jo's, peels a dead cane toad from under the layers of my skirt. He was almost still a toddler on our first trip to Yalakun.

Lapuluŋ and his wife, my *yapa*, arrive, and Jenny and a couple of the teachers from school come and sit with Munymuny for a while.

I go outside and sit with Nimanydja and Munguli. The air is thick with continuous sounds of *yiḏaki, biḻma* and the intense lyrics of *manikay*. The women's soft, serene island voices sing hymns. I look around; more people are gathering for Munymuny. There must be fifty or so people now.

Ganyawu sits with us too. There isn't much to say.

After a while, Nimanydja touches my face and says, 'Be with your *waku.*'

'*Yow,*' says Ganyawu. 'Sit with her and help her spirit move on, *mukul.*'

I go back inside and sit with Munymuny and Elaine and more Djambaŋ women, our ex-school principal, Djuwandaŋur, and Djämbutj.

*Waku* is uncomfortable, writhing. A pang hits our hearts at her discomfort as we move to calm her.

'*Latju dhukarr nhuŋu,*' Gutharra Elaine whispers in her ear, calming her, stroking her face.

I look about, counting ten women and two children circled around her at this moment.

The sound of the ironwood sticks pounds in my ears. Men's voices and *yiḏaki* sounds reverberate through the earth. A familiar atmosphere of death settles in my cells and there is so much of it here on Milingimbi, so much death.

Again, the words of my *gudi* are in my ear, helping me understand what is happening: 'Then they sing the song for her when it is time to die and the person can feel their grandchildren, husband, mothers and family with them and they know it's time to go but it's *yaka manymak.*'

'Now we will call her Guminḏa,' says Gutharra Elaine, sprinkling lavender talc under Waku's arms. 'This is the last time we call her by that name, the name you have always known for her.'

After five hours, I come home, eat a banana sandwich, drink a cup of tea and go back.

Guminda is still with us. It's afternoon and I am lying on my bed, beyond tired, exhausted and restless. The builders and their tractors are making a din. The air is like it was in that movie *Blade Runner*: filled with the buzz of tiny planes arriving from all corners of Arnhem to see her move on. My hand rests on a cup of tea and I look out at my parched jungle through the window slats. I'm not stopping long. I just need a quick rest. This morning, I scrubbed the lounge room and kitchen. Whenever someone is dying, I start scrubbing and cleaning. I think most people do. Perhaps we are clearing the way for ourselves after our loved one is physically gone from our lives. Perhaps on some level we are clearing the way for their spirit to move on. Perhaps we are just freaked out and busily doing, doing and doing.

I stand on the veranda and shake out the dust from my new woven mat from my *dhuway* on Murruṉga Island. I place it on the floor in front of the altar where I practise yoga asana. I decide in that moment I will meditate on my mat in front of Tara, Lakshmi, Saraswati and Ganesh deities. I will have a candle burning and in its flicker, the statues will cast shadows on the ochre painting backdrop. Usually, I meditate on my bed, facing the jungle at dawn. I observe night become day. I may change my mind about this, though.

I amble back round to *Waku*'s yellow house about four p.m.

Guminda's daughter, my *gäthu*, sits holding her mother's hands. She begins to speak of a prophecy that means her mother will live on. I thought yesterday she had realised her mother was going but she keeps talking as if at any moment she will rise up and be fine.

Gutharra touches *gäthu* lightly on her shoulder. 'She is waiting for her husband and then she is going,' she says gently.

As if the words broke her numb denial, a deep wail rises up from within Gäthu and tears spill down her face.

'*Brayer, brayer.*' Her face shakes as she begs her mother to pray.

Gäthu's tears unleash the pain in Mipururr and Gulukuli. Her children and *waku*'s grandchildren huddle together on the freezer. Large drops fall out of their eyes, faces scrunch in pain as they clutch each other and realise their grandmother will soon be gone.

*Waku*'s breath is more laboured now. Her lips round as she gulps for air, and then she becomes still for a moment. I take hold of her thin wrist in my hand. It is cool and her pulse is fading in and out. Gutharra smears pawpaw balm on *Waku*'s dry cracked lips.

Hymns fill the air from the silver CD player in the corner of the room. 'Jesus, my soul is in your hands,' are the words of Guminda's favourite hymn. Everyone in the room is crying, some silently, others letting out strong wails of pain and sorrow.

The brown-haired nurse enters the space and kneels down next to Guminda. She gently pats her face with medical wipes.

Nimanydja and Ganyawu are in the room again now.

'Munymuny can have whatever Munymuny wants now,' the nurse says, eyeing us all.

I flinch a little at the sound of *Waku*'s name once more.

The nurse leaves the room and again we huddle close around *Waku*.

She wriggles, and murmurs that she can see spirits and she wants us to tell them to go away.

It is late afternoon when she sees spirits again.

'*Ḏarra marrtji*,' the words come through her lips.

And I know she means it.

Already a wave of peace is filling the room as it had done years ago when I sat at my own mother's side as she passed away. It won't be long now at all, I think.

*Waku*'s thin legs curl up to her waist.

'Guḏurrku *Märi*, that's her dance, it's *Dhuwa*, she's dancing the brolga dance,' whispers Gutharra Elaine.

*Waku*'s thin gangly arms reach up to the baby blue painted ceiling, her fingers delicately curling this way and that softly spiralling the air.

'*Boṉba*, '*Ḏändi*, she is dancing the butterfly,' says Nimanydja.

The sun is setting outside, golden light filters through the trees, forming soft patterns on the sand, birds twitter as they fly to their nests for sleep, and bats begin their dusk squawk in the trees.

There are about twelve of us women and a couple of kids. We lie around *Waku* in a big circle on mattresses we pushed together. We fall asleep, waking to check her pulse and see if we can feel her breath, and then fall back to sleep.

The men continue *buŋgul* outside.

At one-thirty in the morning, I pull myself up off the ground.

'*Wäŋalilnha?*' asks Gäthu Ganyawu.

The women seem surprised.

'*Yow.*' I hesitate.

*Waku* lies very still on her back resting on two pink pillows, the beanie on her head almost hiding her sweet face. Her grandson Gulikuli lies on a wide mattress next to her in our circle. He came in around nine-thirty last night, still in his red school uniform and black shorts. He pulls the shirt off over his head and lies on his side next to *Waku*. He is growing into a tall lean boy.

'Gerome Gerome (Gulikuli),' utters *Waku*.

He looks over to her and then in an instant falls asleep, their arms linked.

I lean down and kiss *Waku*'s cool forehead, knowing it is the last time I will see her breathe. I take a photo of her in my mind, her face and our hands joined, as I had with my first love so many years ago, two days before his death.

I step out into the night, the sky crystal clear, moon bright. Shining stars look down on me. My bones are heavy but they carry me home. Not even the hounds can worry me tonight.

I can't sleep. I don't know why I didn't stay there. Finally, I sleep a little while. I wake at three thirty-three, dazed, and get up.

At one point in the night, I think I heard wailing.

'Mary, *Baŋaḏitjan, gu!*' I think I hear *Bäpa* Jo yell out so loud.

I get up, gulp a glass of water, light a candle, put a bolster on my knees and lie over it in Pascimottanasana on my pandanus mat. After some time, feeling calmer, I sit up and meditate in front of the goddess Green Tara. I watch my breath and connect with her qualities of calm, compassion and her ability to assist when one is passing over from this world. I have heard her described as 'She who ferries across', a female Bodhisattva of compassion. I peer into her. I chant,

> *Om Tare Tuttare Ture Svaha*
> *Om Tare Tuttare Ture Svaha*
> *Om Tare Tuttare Ture Svaha*

The candle flickers. I gaze into the flame. *Waku*'s face comes into view. She looks soft and peaceful. Light is shining, emanating from her. My heart softens.

A piercing wail breaks the dawn, that women's cry that will help *Waku*'s spirit go back to her ancestral homeland. A sharp pang slices my heart but it is mixed with relief in my cells for *Waku*.

I look up at the clock on the wall. It is five-ten and *Waku* has passed from our world. Without thought, I get up and run barefooted out of the house. As the slow, still dawn tints the darkness, I scurry back to join the circle of women around *Waku*. Her skin is still warm.

## 29

# Yirritja Ḏärra' Buŋgul – the spirit of Yolŋu Rom

The past. Really in a profound way the past has got the bitterness in the history of Australia but we would like to appeal…common ground…common understanding…non-indigenous Australians and Yolŋu of this great fertile land.
A common understanding where we walk together clear up our past way and together we achieve our destiny. Yolngu and balanda. Treat us in the scale of reality. Through justice law and order.

– Lapuluŋ Dhamarrandji, from the film *Riyawarray: Common Ground*

It's Sunday morning and so lovely. I'm snuggled under my blue sheets in bed, a grey yoga blanket over me. Yes, it's cold here in Milingimbi town and delicious to feel the crispness in the air touching my skin. What relief from the usual sticky ceaseless heat. Half the year has flown by and it's June 2008, *Dharratharramirri* season again, the dry season. Fresh breezes blow, it's warm and sunny, cooler and without rain.

*Ḏerrk*, my *waŋarr*, fly through the clear blue sky. Loud resounding screeches echo out, white wings span wide and yellow feathers fan out from their heads. I lie here peering at my green jungle through the slat windows. I look fondly at my tall, spindly pawpaw tree that has grown higher than the roof, but I just found out it's a male so it won't give me any pawpaws. How boring is that?

What is thrilling about this particular Sunday morning is that I have a whole month off school. I love working with the kids at school but it is a huge job all the time, so it is nice to have some time to replenish myself and healthy to have some balance. I don't want to leave my island home these holidays. I want to stay here and do whatever I please.

I take a sip from a large cup of tea and gobble a piece of raisin toast. As well as rest, I have lots of projects planned for this winter break. Singing as much as possible around the house is one of them. I love singing. It lifts up my soul. It really is the nicest time to be here weather-wise too, and yet I always go away.

'Will you have any art work soon, *Wäwa*?' I ask my brother Milay.

'C'mon, *Yapa*, you know me, I'll be out hunting all day,' Milay says.

There is an atmosphere of excitement and lightness as this season is abundant for *guku*, *yuṯa guya*, *miyapunu*, *djanda* and *nyoka'* among other favourable Yolŋu dishes caught fresh from the land.

It is superbly sunny and cool at the same time. Long narrow brown pods dangle in one of the trees outside my window. I look forward to going hunting with everyone and doing lots of yoga asana and meditation.

Yesterday I rode my new bike – well, a second-hand one. I bought it here from one of the teachers. I rode to the airport and back. I am getting better at riding now. I never had a bike when I was a kid. Stuart encouraged me and he taught me: bless him. Milingimbi is completely flat so it's a good place for a beginner.

Out at the airport I stopped at the tap for a drink, cupped my hands, slurped water down my parched throat and splashed my face. *Gurrutjutju*, my *waŋarr*, soared above me, two of them. Their clear descending whistle drew my attention up to the sky. Dark sandy-brown wings swooped down low, hovering and leaning against the air. They rose again, slicing the blue with their wings. I could have watched them all day. I spotted more, silent in the distance. About eight of them veered closer and circled low, their long feathers well splayed; they shrieked their call as they swung across the skyline.

I am going to rest, read and write, write, write. Today I must write at least until midday or one o'clock. I want to be focused and present with my writing and at last I have some time to give to it.

'*Dhäkay-ŋäma*,' I said to the women under the djambaŋ tree the other day. 'Did someone die?' I asked. I always go straight to the women with the feelings I have. They understand.

'*Yaka bäyŋu.*'

But as the day progressed I felt worse, engulfed in a sense of pending doom. Then I found out someone had passed away. The woman are used to me sharing in this way, we share together in this way. They taught me the word *dhäkay-ŋäma* meaning to feel and experience. Like many important words though, its meaning is much deeper and more complex than I can explain. *Dhäkay-ŋäma* means to feel deeply, to experience the presence of the land and the ancestors who are still with us, to know the *rom* experience it inside, and experience oneness. This is what the old women want the children of the future to know, to experience in their lives and to keep this alive within the generations to come.

Now we will have another funeral. The *Därra' buŋgul* is on now too, down at *Ḏarawundhu*. The *Ḏärra'* is a *Rom* ritual performed by Yirritja clans and will go on for three months in total. I'm looking forward to going to it in the afternoons.

I lie asleep, my head resting on the hot-pink sari-covered pillows. I stir with the smell of smoke in my nostrils. I wake up suddenly and sit upright, a crackly sound in my ears. I look through the window slats: my beloved jungle is on fire. It is perfectly normal, the Yolŋu burn off every dry season and right now they are burning off in the backyard behind mine. The bright orange flames, however, are hungrily spreading through the wire fence into my jungle.

Flames leap across the lawn and eat their way towards the house. I run outside and turn on the hose and set water on the jungle.

'*Gapu marrtji*,' yell the young men next door, completely relaxed about the whole scene.

I can see their sleek lean bodies shimmering in the flame light as they throw buckets of water on the fire over the fence from my *mukul*'s backyard.

Smoke billows into the blue sky. I pull the thin green hose as far as it will reach and spray water into the flames.

'Don't let that bamboo catch on fire. It will blow up and burn the houses down,' I hear one of the tradesmen yell from a few houses up, but he is not coming to my aid.

All the teachers are away. I am the only one here in this line of houses. A giant thicket of bamboo grows in Anne's backyard and a blaze of fire is almost up to it. I run next door but the hose won't reach the bamboo. I run back into the house, leave a wet trail of footprints across the lino floor, fling open all the cupboard doors and grab the biggest pot I can find and run back to Anne's tap. I struggle for a few minutes to wrench it on, and then fill up the pot and race to the bamboo. The fire is moments away from its thick roots. Back and forth I run. Black soot streaks my arms, clothes and up my nose. Sweat drenches my skin, but I can't stop now.

'*Gäŋu dhipala! Gapu bulu,*' I yell to the boys at *mukul*'s house. '*Guŋga'yurru!*' I scream.

'It's to clear the snakes, *mukul*,' Gäthu Ganyawu says as I sit under the *djambaŋ* tree later that day, relieved to have saved my own house and a few others.

A few days ago, as I lay on my bed, I saw a long green snake whip across my garden. It almost flew. I swear it was airborne for seconds at a time.

'They are smoking for other reasons, *mukul*. Land *ga* spiritual,' *Gäthu* Ganyawu tells me.

The next morning, I wake up to a charred mess. Ash lies there in place of my jungle, tree trunks still smoulder and the smell of smoke permeates the house, curtains and everything in it, including me. A layer of black soot remains on the window slats.

'Oh well, *bäydhi*, the jungle will grow back in the wet season,' I sigh.

These have been a mixture of two powerful ceremonies. *Waku*'s funeral is over now and the *Ḏärra'* ceremony is in full swing.

The last *Ḏärra'* was held in 2004, not long after I left Milingimbi and headed back down to Northern New South Wales.

'When will you do *Ḏärra'* again?' I ask *Wäwa* Djembaŋu every now and then.

He just looks and smiles, and now it's here, perfectly timed.

'When there is no *buŋgul*, *wäwa* gets sick,' says *Yapa* Yibi Yibi.

These words make sense to me as, in the midst of *buŋgul*, many Yolŋu are fully engaged. The body painting, song and dance invoke the presence of the ancestors and an even deeper spiritual connection is experienced once more. So when a ceremony draws to a close, there is a feeling of disconnection – at least that is how I feel at school on a Monday morning after a whole weekend cocooned in ancient ceremony.

*Wäwa* Jo is conducting this ceremony. This is Yolŋu *rom*, expressing the nature of the Yolŋu and their law through ceremony and *miny'tji* .

'We want to share our law *dhiyaŋu bala*,' says Yibi. '*Wäwa* has asked those lawyers to come from Darwin, so they can see our law.'

'*Nhaku?*' I ask.

'We want them to see our law, understand our law, not just tell us their law. We need to share law.'

'*Manymak, Yapa,*' I nod.

'We want them here to see. *Ga* all our Yirritja clans from Ramingining, Galiwinku, *Yapa*.' She points her head in every direction.

'*Ma*. This feels very important, *Yapa*.'

'*Dharraḏayirr*,' scolds *Yapa* Yibi Yibi as she slaps *miku* onto my face with her hands.

We sit in front of her yellow house down at *Ḏaruwandhu*. *Yapa* Mawukuwuy is here too, her face and arms covered in red clay. She is a tough large woman with long grey curly hair and is always cracking jokes. She is Dorothy number 2 but we call her Linda Slim. She comes and goes between Milingimbi and Darwin and has the twins, my *waku*,

Ada and Bobby, and four other children too. She heads over to some other women in a circle near a tree branch that has been planted in the earth.

Yibi is already painted with red ochre too, her arms, her feet, and her greying hair slicked back into a pigtail now has a red tinge, ciggy hanging from the corner of her mouth.

I sit on the ground and roll up the sleeves of my light blue Indian top. My hair is tied in plaits. Yibi digs her hand into the miku on the rock next to her and rubs it through my hair. I love the feeling of thick earth being lathered on my head and I enjoy having red hair for a few days too.

I pull up my green and blue circle skirt so Yapa can lather my legs but I keep my Blundstones on.

'We will wait *ŋunha bala.*' Yibi points with her mouth pushed to the side.

I look over to the thin, bare *dharpa* in the middle of a clear space in front of my old *yapa*'s house.

'We will hold that *dharpa* and call to the *ḏirramu mala.*' And that's all she says.

Yibi doesn't speak unless there is good reason. It took me some time to understand but I have grown to love her for it and to enjoy being with her in the silent spaces. At first, I thought she was mad at me all the time because she often looks quite serious, even stern. But over the years, I have grown to feel her softness and her love and sense the pride she holds for her culture and especially her *Wäwa* Djembaŋu, our brother. I'm glad she adopted me as her sister and into such a big family. It is during a *buŋgul* and while dancing that I learn so much from her and all the *Ḏarawundhu* crew. With Yibi, it is not so much through 'telling' but through our being present in the incredible ceremonies that take place at *Ḏarawundhu.*

The women, children, babies and I gather around the tree in a circle. Some rest one hand on the tree. A mixture of bright floral dresses, bare feet on the earth, and women lathered in red ochre holds a powerful space.

Eventually, we hear the reverberation of men's feet coming through the bush. Dogs howl. Sounds of chanting, clap sticks and *yiḏaki* resonate and my skin ripples as the two long lines of men holding spears emerge from the bush.

This is the core of life happening here, the witnessing of spirit, alive, potent and connecting us with each other, the land and the ancestors.

They reach us at the tree and we disperse and sit on the ground. *Wäwa* Djembaŋu climbs the tree today. The men circle him. Dancing, their feet thud the earth. Every afternoon, the men get painted up in the bush and the women get painted up near Yibi's yellow house by the sea. Then ceremony begins. *Wäwa* Djembaŋu climbs down the tree. The dances begin.

I've not seen these particular ancient ceremonial dances before. Fresh sand has been laid out on the ground for the dancing. A group of men stand at one end, some in red lap laps, some in yellow, white clay through their hair and on their limbs. *Maḏayin miny'tji* of yellow, red and white ochre have been painted on one side of their upper bodies and one leg, and ochre markings cross their noses. Two lines of men dance, leaping up and down on one leg, waving *galpu*.

It's the end of my holidays now, but the *buŋgul* will continue.

'Are you going to get *nhuŋu rumbal* painted?' the Djambaŋ women ask, chuckling among themselves under the *djambaŋ* tree after my first day back at school.

'Of course,' I respond every time. 'I'm ready.'

'*Nhuŋu dhuway* will be painting you, *mukul*, *manymak*?' Ganyawu asks, waving her hands across her breasts to indicate where exactly on my body I am going to be painted.

'*Yow, manymak*,' I reply, thrilled at being part of the law ceremony. I wouldn't miss this for the world.

According to Yolŋu kinship, I have lots of *dhuways* and *galays* but in this case it is not a husband like it would be in my world outside of Milingimbi. *Galay* and *dhuway* are reciprocal kinship terms. They can be defined as wife, or sister-in-law, husband, brother-in-law, or mate.

With their giggles and questions, the Djambaŋ women certainly prepared me for this last day of *Ḏärra'*. Unaccustomed to being half naked on Milingimbi, I feel surprisingly at ease and content to be here amongst family. This is the most crowded I've ever seen the island. Earlier this Friday morning, though, I felt I would break out of my skin at the slight possibility that the powers that be were not going to allow us to leave the empty school.

The school term has begun and this rare ceremony is now coming to a close. In essence, it is about non-Indigenous Australians and Yolŋu meeting and sharing power as equals. It is not a performance but culture expressed through the Yolŋu in a sacred way. Everyone is getting painted up. Everyone. People are here from all over the world, coming together to share law. The law of both worlds respecting each other.

Yibi had painted me up every afternoon and the Djambaŋ women had shared so much with me these last weeks. I found it almost impossible to accept the way this sacred ceremony was being dismissed here at the school.

Please, no! I had stood in the empty classroom thinking. This ceremony is about healing between cultures, about us being able to open our eyes to Yolŋu law and sharing law, not just one or the other but the union of our cultures. Finally, a reluctant 'yes' and I walked at a fast pace, an unnecessarily fast pace, down to *Ḏarawundhu*.

I move through the throng of Yolŋu, yellow ochre, white clay, and find Yibi Yibi.

'*Räli*, lie down.' She gets straight into it.

'*Ma'*,' I respond.

The orange and brown swirls on my skirt match the blanket beneath me as I lie down ready to be painted up. The vibe is busy yet relaxed as Yolŋu prepare for this auspicious last day of the law ceremony. It's chilly this morning. My skin shivers as my *dhuway* Ronnie Barrmala paints a yellow ochre square on my stomach and two ochre stripes up to my neckline. Tall, lean, with a greying moustache and wearing a grey jacket and baseball cap, my *dhuway* delicately paints along the edge of the yellow ochre with white clay. Yibi and my *yapa*s are not far away, and my *gaminyarr* lies next to me, getting painted up too. Tash from school decides she wants to as well and lies down on the ground. I stare up at the clear blue sky. I am so happy to be alive in this moment. Crows squawk in the trees; Yolŋu language fills the air.

'*Guku, nhuŋu waŋarr*,' Yibi says proudly.

I close my eyes to receive and absorb the sacred honey dreaming design being painted on my upper body.

*Dhuway* carefully paints white clay across my belly, making diamond shapes on the yellow ochre.

'*Räli*,' says Yibi.

*Dhuway* moves over to paint Tash.

Usually, I can't wait to move out of the sun, but this morning I welcome its warmth on my skin. I look out to the blue-green ocean and sniff the salty air.

Yibi starts lathering my sides with miku and then my *galay*, *Wäwa* Djembaŋu's wife, steps in and slaps *miku* on my back and down my arms. I love the sensation of cool clay on my body before the sun hardens it.

'*Dharradayirr*,' *galay* says.

It's a very well used word. Yibi always says it too. She must like saying it because I think I am standing or lying perfectly still and then she says '*dharradayirr*' again. All the women do. In fact, I am always saying it to the kids at school as well. One day, one of the non-Indigenous tutors who was assisting me teach a yoga class said, 'Mary, who is *dharradayirr*?' I said it so often.

I look around at the women and girls lying on the earth, being painted in the honey dreaming. Laughter is plentiful and just about everyone has a camera or a mobile and snaps away, taking pictures. There are just a few men, only the *dhuways*. The others are in the bush preparing for this powerful last day of the *Ḏärra*. Thuds and wild sounds emerge from the bush now and again.

*Galay* passes me onto another *yapa*, a large woman with streaks of red ochre through her hair and white clay smeared around her lips.

'*Ḏarra marŋgi, dharraḏayirr,*' I say with a giggle.

'*Yow, marŋgi nhe,*' says *Yapa*, smearing both hands, caked with red ochre, over my head and through my hair.

A white guy I don't know circles us, snapping photographs.

'*Mel-bambaydhi,*' *Yapa* snaps. Her hair is pulled back tightly in a bun. Hands caked with white clay, she digs her hand into a pot and scoops clay into her mouth. '*Mel-bambaydhi,*' she says again with her mouth full.

The white guy kneels up close to us with his camera. I'd like some copies of these shots, I'm thinking.

I close my eyes and feel spots of white clay hit my skin as *Yapa* spits it all over my face. Finally, a yellow ochre strip is painted across my nose from ear to ear.

'*Yow, yäa Baŋaḏitjan, Gupapuyŋu,* tribe, *marrkapmirr,*' she smiles.

The *miny'tji* have been painted on everyone now. Women sit clustered around the *dharpa*. I try not to get ochre on my camera as I flit around taking photographs. I peer through my lens at women and girls painted up in their clan group colours. *Gutharra* Ganygulpa's group have white clay faces and a triangle of white on their upper bodies.

'Lie down, *mukul,*' calls Gäthu Ganyawu.

I scurry back to my honey dreaming group. The ground beneath us is hard. Tash and I try to muffle our giggles as we lie with maybe a hundred or more other women and girls under a canopy of sheets held up by the Dhuwa women. This sacred knowledge is passed on from a long lineage of ancestors, both Dhuwa and Yirritja. Today, the Dhuwa women and girls are doing 'labour' work to support this Yirritja ceremony. Yirritja clan nations from all over Arnhem Land are here to express ancient law.

Tash teaches in *Yarrawarri* class next to my little room at school. I first met her on the phone in the school office. She is from New South Wales, but she and her partner were working at a community called Ngulu on Bathurst Island at the time. She had rung Milingimbi to see if there were any teaching positions available. 'Oh, you must come and teach here,' I remember saying to her. I liked Tash immediately. We are the same clan and *mälk*. She feels like my sister but is my *marratja*. We often walk through the bush together and try to remain calm when approached by scary dogs. Both of us love dogs but we are afraid sometimes.

I know the Yolŋu love their dogs. They are kin. We are kin.

One morning when I was walking to school, in my fear I got upset at a dog wanting to bite me.

'Märi, Märi, Märi,' called my *gutharra*. Please do not worry. I will always look after you. *Dhuwal waṯu nhuŋu galaymirriŋu*'.

On hearing how I am related to this dog, I softened, relaxed, and my fear dissipated. I really do want to trust my *galay*.

I had less fear of the dogs in my earlier years on this island. I often walked on my own in the bush, or sometimes with Banana and Potato. Those two dogs followed me everywhere. They belonged to everyone and we all loved their light, calm presence. A few times, I walked with Banana, Potato, Witney and a flurry of dogs with pointy dingo ears and long snouts. I thought I'd become the dog woman but that changed over time.

Once, as I walked along a dirt track out to the *ṉinydja*, goosebumps errupted on my skin as I felt that I was being watched. I turned to see three dingoes quietly lounging in among the trees, tongues panting and the breath expanding their bellies in and out. We made eye contact and they stood up. My heart pounded and without thought, I looked ahead and began to sing and sing. I looked back: they were drawing closer, the pads of their paws silent on the earth, their presence ethereal. Ears tweaked, they seemed rather inquisitive at the sound of my voice. Perhaps these dingoes were harmless, but fear gripped me. I picked up my pace and sang until I finally had the courage to turn around again and found them gone.

Tash and I have very in-depth conversations about school and the environment, healthy food, massage, and life on this island. I treasure talking with her, as I do with Stuart and as I did in the early days with Maria, Ingrid and Mirella. Mirella and Stephan came all the way from

Austria to live here on Yurrwi Island. Mirella was the special needs teacher. Stephan was a silversmith. Mirella loved coming to yoga and we shared an interest in the healing arts.

Tash lives here with her lovely husband who is doing a PhD in Environmental Sciences. They both love coming to yoga and are super at growing fresh vegetables. They even have chickens. They live in respect of our earth and I learn a lot from them.

In the stifling heat, the sheets held above us provide some shade. Right now, we are hidden from the men and it is taking some willpower for us not to peek out beyond the sheets.

Silence falls. The men emerge from bush. I imagine their bodies marked with the golden ochre of honey dreaming, spears in hand. A deep humming, whirring sound penetrates the area as they draw nearer. I lie perfectly still, fully present and in awe of the deep, throaty chants and pounding of their feet on the earth as they circle us. The ground is shaking, vibrating through my bones, and my heart thuds. Round and round they circle us, the power of the masculine presence infusing the space and pulsing through my veins.

Finally, the sheets are lifted and the biggest *buŋgul* I've seen on Yurrwi Island begins. The air is electric as earth and spirit meld through Yolŋu dance song and *miny'tji* painting.

We are a throng of mingling bodies. Yolŋu and some *balanda*, we dance down to the blue-green water's edge. I'm seized in that trance-like state I've experienced before at a *buŋgul*, the hypnotic beat of clap sticks, guttural chants, the sweat, the heat and collective thud of our feet on the sand is mesmerising.

'Wooo,' I yell, dancing on one leg along with everyone else.

The elders wave spears and lead the way into the sea, flicking up the salty water. We all enter the ocean for the ritual cleansing, immersing ourselves in the salt water. A momentary pang stabs my heart in my resistance to let go of the carefully painted design on my body. But I release a breath and join everyone again as we rise up out of the ocean, renewed and refreshed.

Every cell in my body is invigorated with life force. The salt water is warm and there is no thought of crocodiles.

Emerging from the sea, we walk back to the place where the *dharpa* is planted, our bodies wet, skin mottled with streaks of ochre mixed with salt water. I look up and see the *marrŋgitj*. He spots me at the same time. For a moment, everything stops as our eyes lock. Then he moves into a group of men and begins another ancient ceremonial dance.

Silence falls. Streaks of ochre and white clay pour down my skin. We stand still to honour the presence of the ancestors, the lives of those who have gone before. Wails split the cocoon we are ensconced in. I look around through watery eyes at sombre faces weeping for their loved ones lost, crying for the ancestors.

*Ḏärra'* acknowledges death but it is also about regeneration, cleansing, renewal and creation. This particular *Ḏärra'* has been performed to help change the thinking of the Australian government, to show the strength of Yolŋu *Rom* and Yolŋu people, and to join together as one people.

Land is the essence of Yolŋu people.
Very strong ties with the land.
*Ḏärra'* ceremony is asking you to share the power.
Intervention disempowered the Yolŋu people, put a negative image of Yolŋu people.
What we are asking is for both of us to see from another perspective that is full of grace
A perspective that is full of richness and come together and unite as one.
*Nhäŋal ŋarra bala.*
*Nhäŋal ŋarra räli.*
*Nhäŋal ŋarra ḻiw'maraŋal.*
(I look over there, I look here, I look all around me.)
And I wonder what it took yesterday to create today. Yesterday it took the knowledge, courage, strength, faith, integrity of these very people who are now asking you to please have another think of the Intervention.

    – Gutharra Ganygulpa Dhurrakay, from Milingimbi CEC administration, from the film *Riyawarray: Common Ground*

## 30

# Ḏarraku matha – my language

> When you lose your land, at least you can fight to get it back. But when you lose your language, a whole way of being, a whole cultural universe is lost.
>
> 'Avoiding a Silent Future', *Land Rights News*, June 2002

It's 2008 and I'm in my final semester of a Graduate Certificate in Yolŋu Languages and Culture at Charles Darwin University. Initially my education took place out bush with Yolŋu family, writing down words and sentences, integrating culture, language and kin. It was important for me to start this way and it is to continue this way. I find language challenging and I don't know if I will ever be any good at it, but I feel it is a significant way to grow relationships and, quite clearly, relevant as a teacher in an Indigenous community.

I will also be updating my teaching skills with a few units of English as an Additional Language (EAL), a more appropriate term than English as a Second Language (ESL) for kids who can already speak several languages. These studies contribute well to my work in the classroom with both Yolŋu children and teachers.

My final assignment for the Graduate Certificate is to do an independent study that the Yolŋu would like me to do. I am desperate to do bush medicine but I put that aside and go out and ask everyone what they want.

'*Wäwa ŋarra dhu wäŋa*,' said Yibi Yibi when I asked her about it.

'We don't want to lose our language, *ŋama*'. We want you to talk about our language,' explained Nimanydja, Munguli and Djämbutj as we sat under the *djambaŋ* tree one day.

'You mean like in that video *Not to Lose your Language*?' I ask.

'*Yow*, that's the one. We need to update this one, *ŋama*'. We need to preserve Yolŋu languages for the future of the *djamarrkuḻi*.'

Elizabeth Milmalany is my *mukul rumaru*. We do not call each other directly by name and use some appropriate sign language. She is an important teacher of language and has agreed to speak with me and help me plan my assignment for Yolŋu studies. Mukul sits on the old cane chair on my wooden veranda. She is a plump woman, hard of hearing. Deep brown, her eyes are large and gentle with a hint of sadness. Smooth-skinned, sometimes *mukul* looks so serious and then her face breaks into a broad, heart-warming smile. She is strong in culture and religion. I've often seen her, Djämbutj and Nimanydja down at Jessie Smith Park near the barge ramp dancing to hymns playing over the loudspeaker, their hips swaying, arms reached out, eyes closed, with a serene look of reverence on their faces.

She is always correcting my Yolŋu *matha* efforts and once when she was teaching me a traditional dance, she said, '*Yow*, use *warrpam'rumbal nhuŋu*, move your whole body when you are dancing.' Perspiration slips down her round cheeks. She wipes it off with a corner of her dark blue dress.

We move slowly in this blistering heat. The air is still but the backdrop of my bright green backyard jungle is alive with birds squawking. Woodsmoke from a nearby campfire drifts across my yard to where we sit.

'*Gapu nhe ga ḻuka, mukul?*'

'*Nhä?*' Her eyes squint when she can't hear me properly and she sounds grumpy.

'*Gapu. Nhe djäl?*'

'*Yow, gurruŋ guyiŋarr gapu gurruŋ.*'

My eyes linger on her face for a moment. I feel great affection for her. I have a flash of her lathering her face with red ochre, and I remember her dancing around the body of my dear *waku*, also her loved one, in a room packed with Yolŋu. I am moved by her strength but I feel a sharp pang in my heart when I witness her grief over and over at funerals. She is always there fully present as she watches her loved ones leave the earth plane. *Mukul* works on creating the Yolŋu *matha* teaching resources at the school so that the children will continue to speak Yolŋu language.

I bring out two tall blue glasses of cold water clinking with ice cubes and sit before her.

'*Latju,*' she says as she takes a long drink.

'*Manymak?*' I ask, and hold up the camera ready to film her.

The sounds of kids laughing and birdsong fade into the background as she speaks.

'*Yow*. Traditionally, Yolŋu learned their father's language. The Yolŋu people speak different languages, different dialects, but we understand each other…it's very important for us to understand what dialect we are using…it is very important for us to understand what other people are saying to us in their own language.'

I film her speaking Djambarrpuyŋu first and then English. I put the camera down.

'You must go and talk to all the elders and ask them about their languages,' explains *mukul*. 'Let's see, there's Jacky Maŋala, your *gutharra*. He speaks Waŋgurri.'

I scrawl down the list of about ten elders and the names of their languages on an A4 notepad.

I visit each of the elders and interview them about their original language and ask how they feel about what is happening with it today in the community. I really want to take on this worthwhile project but I am bamboozled. It's impossible to undertake in one semester while I am teaching full time at school. So, under the advice of my supportive university teacher, I decide to focus on one elder, my *wäwa* Jo Djembaŋu.

'*Nhini, nhini,*' orders Jo Djembaŋu's wife. Hair swept loosely in a bun, thin strands brush her round cheeks. There is a nervous energy about her and her young face is tired. Lines of worry crease her brow and her large brown eyes widen as she spreads a cloth out on the brown earth, sweeping bits of sticks and leaves off it with her hand.

'*Yow, galay,*' I respond, looking around for Yapa Yibi.

She was here a minute ago, she brought me here, but now I see she has wandered over to the circle of women sitting under the shade of the *Djambaŋ* tree. They are chatting away together and playing cards. Only on the odd occasion would I visit *wäwa* without her. She brings me to him when he is ready to speak with me. He is my brother and in this culture I do not ask of my brother directly, nor do I call him by his name directly. She has already organised this interview with him, though.

Yibi lifts her hand and gives me a short sharp wave and a smile, then slips her attention back into the circle.

*Wäwa* Jo Djembaŋu sits down next to galay and my heart pounds as I sit before him. I always feel a little nervous around him, though I have no idea why, as he is ever present, warm, his eyes smile and he shares his message openly and generously. His hair is snow white and chin covered by a wispy white beard. Today he wears a red headband across his forehead. Within minutes, I am in stillness in his presence.

'*Ḏarra ga rirrikthun, Yapa, rirrikthun mirithirri,*' he informs me.

'*Yuwalk, Wäwa?*' I ask. But I look at him and I sense there is life force alive in him.

I'm aware of the illness in his body but I know that the minute he begins a new ceremony, his being will be activated by the rhythm of deep tradition and it will pulse through his veins. He will inhabit the energy of ancient *manikay*. It will echo from his lips and the clap of his ironwood *biḻma* will reverberate throughout the community.

Remnants of yellow ochre still mark *wäwa*'s skin from the recent ceremony. His grandson, my *gaminyarr*, leans across Jo's leg. Marco is one of my students at school. Smoke wafts up from the fire close by and I gaze out for a moment at the blue-green ocean and take in its breeze. I can taste the salt on my tongue and feel it sticking to my skin. My thoughts about the sea have changed over these years in Arnhem Land. I have always seen the ocean as a place to swim and luxuriate in cool water, a place to wash off any unwanted heaviness in my body and mind. But here, my eyes look to see who is out waist-deep with a spear, looking for food, or if there are women and children collecting *maypal* around the rocks and in the mangroves.

I brush flies off my face and fiddle with the small, archaic, battery-operated tape recorder in my hand. I wish in this moment that I had a video camera.

'Oh well, this will have to do. *Bäydhi*,' I mutter to myself.

I put the tape recorder down, prop the camera, zoom the lens and shoot a few photos of *wäwa* and *gaminyarr*. His tall yellow house, blue mozzie dome tent, and smoke wafting from a small fire provide the backdrop. I zoom in closer and capture a portrait of *Wawa*'s engaging face. He is perfectly at ease being photographed.

Here are a few of the words *Wäwa* gave me when I asked him about his language.

Mary: *Yow, Wäwa, nha nhuŋu dhäruk? Nhe dhu dhäwu ḻakaram ŋarraku? Manymak?*'

Jo (with warmth and interest): *Yow*. My language. I speak Djiliwirri, Dhuwala'mirri language like this. Here old people like me speak Dhuwala'mirri. But where I live here, the whole clan is gone that speak Dhuwala'mirri language. I am the last person speaking Dhuwala'mirri language.

*Wäwa* lifts his hand and points a finger towards the graves set in between his blue house and Yibi's yellow one. I look over at the brightly coloured plastic flowers adorning the mounds of earth. A white wooden cross sits at the head of *Yapa*'s grave. Black crows flap their wings and peck around for a morsel to eat. Several *Djambaŋ* trees dot the shoreline out to the vast sea. I smile as I remember the day Yapa told me that crow was her ŋä<u>n</u>di, her mother.

Jo: This sister was speaking Dhuwala'mirri language but now she passed away, there's just me, that's it! [*Wäwa* looks directly into my eyes.] I believe that no more children will speak Dhuwala'mirri language. Yes, they speak Djambarrpuyŋu language. They are already speaking lots of Djambarrpuyŋu language now. But anyway, sister, I have a big problem because the children can't speak Dhuwala language. It's bad.

Mary: What do you think we can do about it?

Jo: We can't, no. Big worries, big. You know the children at school. All the kids are only speaking Djambarrpuyŋu language. No Dhuwala language, no Wangurrri, no Warrami, no Birrikili, no Yan-nhaŋu, no Gurryindi, no Gamalaŋga. There are many tribes but they are only speaking one language – Djambarrpuyŋu. *Ga balanya.* I am the last man.

Mary: The last man, *Wäwa*.

Jo: Yes, I am the last man. When I pass away, my language Dhuwala will be finished. There are no more children here who can speak Dhuwala language, only on the other side at Ramingining. Yes, sister, like this. Only one. Myself. Yes. No more speaking Dhuwala language here at Milingimbi. I am the last man. Last man.

The tape recorder clicks off just as we finish. What can I possibly say? I gaze at *wäwa* through watery eyes. I just sit and let these words sink in. The shroud of grief hanging about us is palpable.

*Wäwa*'s response to my asking what can be done – 'We can't, no' – spins around in my head and weighs on my heart. Imagine what this is for him every day. I can see the sorrow in his eyes and the responsibility pressing upon him.

There is nothing more to say.

And here we are dwelling once more in this silent lingering stillness at the end of a conversation. These moments command not only reflection but call us to listen more deeply to what has been shared here. In the silence, a deeper understanding is possible.

'*Ma'!*' says *Wäwa* Jo.

'*Ma', ŋarra!*' I slowly get up.

That's it. In Yolŋu culture when what has been said is said, it's over, so I split.

I learned that traditionally, Yolŋu languages were oral, not written. As the Yolŋu moved around following their Dreaming tracks, new languages evolved from dance and song. Every part of the land holds rich stories that are an expression of the animals, plants and land itself. Yolŋu know how they are related with the land and the animals on it. They can tell me if this is their fatherland or if the moon is their *yapa* or if a *djetj* is their *waku*. Different parts of the body represent an aspect of relationship; for example, heart is mother, womb is child.

Paintings are inscribed on bark or on a boy's torso when being initiated into manhood or on a girl as she moves into womanhood. Sand carvings are created on the earth at a ceremony. These sacred designs have been passed down over the generations.

The essence of culture is embedded in language, oral language, and I wonder if in being written something of this sacredness is lost.

As I walk back through Ḏarawundhu along the seaweed-covered beach, I sneak quietly past the few hounds lying asleep in the sand. I don't want to disturb them and have their barking rattle my nervous system. A dozen children are splashing and swimming in the ocean. They smile at me and wave. They are playing so lightly and freely, but as I walk on, along the hot sand, I am still holding such a feeling of loss in my heart. I feel helpless.

'We can't, no,' Wäwa had said. I am learning that these oral languages are not just words at all, but an expression of being, a manifestation of living culture, the spirit of the Yolŋu, potent, rich, whole. And though I can feel *Wäwa*'s enormous responsibility, I have an inkling of acceptance in him too, like the sense of acceptance I witness in Yolŋu about the frequency of the deaths that occur in our community. Perhaps it is this continuous thread the Yolŋu possess that links them with the spirit of the land, animals, law, each other, the ancestors and the cosmos itself that sustains them. The eternal spark that resounds itself through ancient tongue. I am not speaking of a linear world here and it's hard to find the words to describe it but the vibration of this thread lingers in the silent space between words and in the gentle lull of Yolŋu matha.

## 31

## Mimi, Warrabunbun and the Marrngitj dharpa

Stars and white owls in the dark of night
Traditional ways of the bush wisdom shared.
Listening.
Held in a cocoon of inquisitive ethereal beings
Allowing, I learn and I receive.
Inspiration awakened.
Answers come in synchronistic moments.
Gratitude.

I fly into the tiny remote school in Arnhem Land on a five-seater light aircraft. I have my mozzie dome, sleeping bag, boxes of flashcards, various teaching resources and food supplies like rice, tea, Indian food in packets, nuts, fruit and muesli. It is a ten-minute flight from Milingimbi. It's August 2009 and after the long June holiday. I've started teaching in the surrounding, smaller, homeland communities. I love flying to school in a light aircraft, floating in the clouds, peering down on the bushland, saltpans, mangroves and the maze of vein-like, blue-green waterways of the Crocodile Islands. I think if I could, I'd fly the plane myself.

When I arrive, the kids are already having class with my *galay* in the classroom, a blue corrugated-iron building in the bush. There are just a few other houses here, nestled in amongst the tall eucalypts here in remote Arnhem Land.

I step off the plane and draw in the scent of the gums. A tall Yolŋu man waits for me. He leans on an old red lawnmower.

'*Yow*,' we greet each other and stack as much of my gear as we can on the lawnmower.

He pushes it and I carry the rest down the worn path to the classroom. Tables and chairs fill the space and there is a blackboard with English words chalked on it. Slat windows reveal a view of gum trees, red earth, birds squawking and vivid blue sky.

A mixture of boys and girls of various ages smile and welcome me. I join in with *galay* as she finishes her Yolŋu lesson, then I take out a small tape recorder and walk around the class, speaking to each child in English.

'Hi, what's your name? How are you today? Where do you live?' I ask. I encourage them to share so I can assess their levels and work with *galay* to plan appropriate programmes for them.

A thin man with wild grey hair enters the room, his wife with him. She is tall and lean with long wavy hair and big eyes. They have come to sit with the children and help out in the classroom. He is not the usual teacher – his brother is, but he's away today.

At morning recess, we sit on the wooden veranda that looks out to eucalypts and xanthorrhoea (grass trees). I discover these two brothers are my poison cousins. The one here visiting me now does a lot of painting. We call each other *gudi*.

Munching tuna sandwiches, *gudi* begins to speak about his paintings. 'It is done in yellow ochre and white clay,' he explains.

'You mean the Gupapuyŋu *Guku miny'tji*?' I ask.

'*Yow*,' he nods, his brow deeply furrowed.

'Last year at the *Därra'* ceremony, my *dhuway* painted that design on the front of my body,' I say.

He sits quietly listening and looking deep into me. 'That was the law,' he said. 'When they painted that on your body, they gave you our law and now you must share it.'

That familiar jump in my belly occurs again. It astounds me how casually information is given to me at times.

'Thank you!' is all I can muster.


I grab my torch, leave the classroom, and head over to find *galay*. It's night now and so quiet our here in the bush, but for the bush creatures.

'*Ḏali nhina ga.*' *Galay* pats the ground next to her.

I crouch down and sit close by her. Though it isn't cold, I enjoy the warmth of the crackling fire on my face. Two boys lean, one against each of my legs, and we stare into the bright orange flames that sparkle and dance, casting shadows on the earth. Our flickering silhouettes are long in the darkness. Much as I enjoy talking with galay, I love these moments where we are together in nature and stillness, saying nothing.

And then a new language – new to my ears – breaks the silence. The Yolŋu seem to understand each other no matter the difference in tongue, but every single word I am hearing right now is completely foreign to me. They are speaking the Burarra language.

The energy here in the middle of this thick bushland is different to anywhere I have been in Arnhem Land. It's a whole new world without the smell and sight of the sea in direct proximity. There is a gentle yet light ambience in the air and I have a sense that playful, fairy-like spirits abound.

'We saw those white owls last night and we knew you would come today.' *Galay* smiles at me as she points into the trees.

I peel my eyes from the bright orange flames and turn to see three white owls perched on the tree branches behind us. Their white feathers are bright in the darkness. I gasp in delight, recognising the auspiciousness of their presence. Owls are often around me in my life. To me, they represent truth, omens, and are a symbol of spiritual energy made tangible.

My eyes reach further up to the sky and marvel at the billions of stars shimmering over us.

'*Ganyu latju*, I love the stars,' I say, sighing.

'*Ḏayipi djäl niŋyipa*,' translates one of the twins as he pokes the fire with a long stick, the whites of his eyes vivid in the night sky. The twins are about seven years old. Thin boys with huge, liquid brown eyes, round cheeks and curly hair.

'*Ḏayipi djäl niŋyipa*,' I repeat the words.

And so I'm introduced to Burarra language without my even having to ask. My skin tingles. I lean my A4 notepad close to the fire to catch the light and scribble the words down as they come flying out of the mouths of the kids.

'*Godjula.*'

'*Arrawa.*'

'*Ininjaya?*'

I'm still not sure why I am so fascinated by these ancient languages but it seems the Yolŋu know I am before I even say anything and just start teaching me wherever I go.

'It's too hot for the kids to come with us now,' says *galay* as we walk away from the corrugated blue school building.

We have finished teaching for the day and *galay* is taking me out into the bush.

'We'll get some of that *nhawi* to make a fish trap.'

'*Ma, manymak,*' I reply. Beads of sweat form on my brow and slip down my face.

'I'm going to hang it in the classroom,' she adds.

'*Latju guyaŋa,*' I respond.

*Galay* has a round moon face, fleshy body and big fuzzy hair. I love being with her. She generously shares her knowledge. I feel like we are making good friends and we are a good team in the classroom together and enjoy planning for the children.

I draw in a big breath of the scrub air as we head further away from the school and houses. Tall thin gums surround us on our walk. Stout palms and red anthills dot the area. There must be so much food and medicine right here, I am thinking. The heat is sticky and the air has a different quality than anywhere else I have been. Leaves crackle under our feet. *Galay* is looking around intently.

I spy a white cockatoo feather lying on the ground, pick it up and stick the long spine into one of my plaits.

'*Ɖerrk*: Yirritja *waŋarr ŋarraku,*' are the words in my head. I don't speak much Yolŋu but I'm no longer surprised at the fact that I think in Yolŋu sometimes and I dream in it too.

'The Warrabunbun trees are up here, *Dhuway*,' says *galay*, pointing ahead.

The kids have been telling me about the spirits that dwell here. 'Many many people, they come here for healings from them, these spirits. They been here a long time.'

'*Galki, galki,*' *Galay* almost whispers.

I am surprised when she points to two long, slender, palm trees ahead of us. I wasn't expecting such palms in this thick bushland.

'There they are, those two old men, *Warrabunbun*, healing spirits,' she says.

But as I approach, I sense that soft ethereal presence again. 'The Mimi spirits!' My heart pounds with pleasure. Tears form in my eyes.

'*Yow*, the Mimi spirits,' repeats *Galay*, smiling, her cheeks wet with sweat. 'Some Yolŋu paint those spirits. You can see them in the art centre,' she adds.

A strange headachy sensation fills my skull. I put my hand on my stomach and notice a sense of nausea as we approach the spirit trees.

'This is the place.' *Galay* bends down and begins to tug at some dry green shrubs at the bottom of the trees. 'Where is my *gunga* stick?' She bends her knees and reaches her hand right under a thick, bushy green shrub. 'Ahhh here it is,' she laughs, and drags out from the bushes her long stick with a hook at the top for pulling pandanus.

The Djambaŋ women and Baymarrwaŋa come to mind immediately, as we have spent so many weekends out bush together collecting gunga.

'*Warrabunbun* look after it,' says *galay*.

I smile.

Last night I lay in my dome tent talking to the spirits. Creatures rustled in the leaves; their whistling, buzzing and clicking created a bush symphony. *Galay* and I had planned our lessons for the next day at school and I had cooked up and eaten my palak paneer Indian meal in a packet. The air was warm but I still snuggled in my sleeping bag, with my green headlamp perched on my forehead, shedding light as I scribbled thoughts from the day. I paused from writing to tune into the strong sensation of being wrapped in something light, ethereal, expansive, calm. I squeezed my eyes shut for a moment and then dared to look up beyond the dome. Encircling my tent were thin, long, lanky beings with unusual-shaped heads. They were not invasive at all; if anything, a little reticent themselves. Large eyes peered curiously into me. I breathed deeply and smoothly to relax the hesitation in my cells but I knew I was safe. They were pure innocence. 'Well, Mary, you invoked them and here they are,' were the words in my head. I lay very still and I remembered *gudi*'s words from our conversation earlier today after we finished teaching the class.

*Gudi*, the teacher, had come into the classroom to make a phone call. 'If you feel strange at night, *gudi*, don't worry,' he chuckled. 'Just let him know who you are. Say, "Jo Djembaŋu *ŋarraku wäwamirriŋu. Ga märimirriŋu wäŋa*. Jessie Murrragi *ŋarrakun yapapmirriŋu. Burrkun ga Baraŋitji ga ŋarrkun* blood aunties from the Gupapuyŋu tribe." They might give you *marrŋgitj* healing powers,' he giggled again, raising his eyebrows, and picked up the phone to make the call. 'That *marrŋgitj* can change like a chameleon. They are good spirits and they will come to you. Sometimes they come and tell you things. They will look after you.'

'Thanks, *gudi*,' I respond. 'I'm not scared but happy to meet them.'

'Tck, tck, tck.' The sound the *marrŋgitj* had spoken of so often now whirred in my ears as I lay in my dome. My spirit touched and nourished by their presence, I fell asleep dreaming of the Mimi and *winyiwinyi*.

Now *galay* stands, stroking the tree and speaking in the Burarra and Djambarrpuyŋu languages.

I understand bits and hear the words '*Bäpa* Jo', my dear adopted father. She is asking them to give him healing as he is gravely ill. I hear her mention my name and my Gupapuyŋu family. I open to receive the healing and gently touch the thin, cool tree. I become still and soothed by the sound of *Galay*'s voice and the unearthly impression of the *Warabunbun* trees. A small brown pod is growing out from the bottom, containing red seeds. I touch them lightly.

'You can take those, *manymak*,' *galay* says.

I bend down and scoop up the red seeds and stuff them in my camera case as we walk further into a dense spot tangled with long vines, green leaves attached to them.

'I like a straight one. Come on, spirit, please help,' *galay* calls, 'help us find the right tree for string for the grass skirts. *Brrrr, Brrrr*,' she shrills to call on the spirits for help.

Further into entangled vines we tread and *galay* finds what she is looking for. '*Manymak*, it is the right size for a fish trap!' she says, her face softening. She raises the axe and slices the sharp blade swiftly through the vine. She wipes her brow and creates a circle with the vine to see if it is the right size for a fish trap. '*Manymak*,' she repeats.

I snap lots of photographs and then wipe the sweat off my camera. We pull some pandanus and find two *raki'* trees to make string for the grass skirts.

*Galay* sighs in satisfaction. 'The *marrŋgitj dharpa* is just around that corner,' she drops casually.

'*Yuwalk*?' I yell much louder than I mean to. Oh my God, the *marrŋgitj* tree. Is she serious? My thoughts are loud again.

'I'll take you,' she offers.

My heart beats fast. This must be the tree that the *marrŋgitj* has promised to take me to so many times since 2004. I'd given up on ever coming here.

Ahh, the *marrŋgitj*! He is still with me. Snippets of memories flash through my mind as *galay* leads me through thick bush to the *marrŋgitj* tree. I remember all our talks and how painful it was for him to see and experience so many people's pain and suffering, I remember him describing my first love's spirit transfixed over my face. He said, 'Your d̠irramu is helping me,' yet he knew nothing of him. I remember him telling me he was going to drink hot tea to make the X-ray vision and *marrŋgitj* power go away. One Saturday night at my place, he had picked up the book *Healers of Arnhem Land* and pointed to a picture of his father lying down with smoke swirling over his chest. I had gasped, not quite believing yet again how these books I'd read so long ago had returned to me in the very places they were written about.

The sky is no longer visible and leaves crackle under our feet as the bush thins out and reveals a massive banyan fig tree.

'Look, there it is,' points *Galay*.

Its wide trunk is a collection of entangled roots that descend deep into the earth floor that is covered in leaves and brown dirt. Patches of sunlight stream through the trees. It's quite dark here, though, and smells damp. My body melts in its presence.

'This is where Yolŋu come to get *marrŋgitj* power,' whispers *Galay*.

So this is where the *marrŋgitj* lay down and received his powers and his *marrŋgitj* stone. He had shared this experience with me as we sat at a buŋgul some time ago. It is at these moments that I feel timeless: yesterday feels like today, as if no time has passed.

'Lie down there and I'll talk to that tree for you,' instructs *galay*. She reaches out and takes my camera to take a picture of me.

I lie on a bed of brown leaves not far from the giant roots of the tree. I decide not to be overwhelmed by the swarms of mosquitoes. My muscles and bones relax. *Galay* stands close by, and her voice like a soft breeze speaks to the tree on my behalf. I cannot understand any of her words. Maybe she is speaking a spirit language. I open myself to the power of her intention, her words, and to the spirit of the *marrŋgitj* tree.

I lie still. Piercing fierce mosquitoes drone in my ears. I'm drowsy and my eyes want to sleep but I keep breathing consciously to remain alert. I can feel things crawling on me but I am not going to resist. I open myself to receive the power of the healing tree. I breathe deeply, drinking the oxygen it produces into my lungs. I open to receive *marrŋgitj* for my highest good. I ask for healing for the planet and everyone I know.

I freeze in a moment of reservation: fear. Resistance in the form of high tension tries to seize control, giving me an impulse to get up and run away. But quickly I realise what a profound moment this is. I open once more to the spirit of the Yolŋu, the *marrŋgitj* tree, and the spirits of the land addressed through my *galay*. Waves of warm currents of energy stream through my body and I fade in and out of awareness. My eyelids are like lead and my bones are sinking. I relax. Vitality circulates through my veins and blood. The weight of the earth holds me.

'I asked for healing for you, *Dhuway*. I asked that you may receive the knowledge and wisdom and healing and whatever that *marrŋgitj dharpa* wants to give you, *Dhuway*,' *galay* tells me later as we walk home with our fish trap and *gunga* materials.

'Thank you, *Galay*. I'm honoured.'

I am also silenced by the experience. Wow! I made it to the *marrŋgitj* tree and I'm exhilarated. Synchronicity: yet again.

I fly back to Milingimbi the next afternoon after school.

The sound of bilma resonates throughout the community. Three of my *waku* I have watched grow up are being initiated around at *Bäpa* Jo's house. It is his last wish to see their transition into manhood.

Though exhausted, my legs carry me round there.

Women dance in a circle. *Waku* Lapuluŋ is in the middle, beating rosewood sticks. The boys' torsos are painted with their *waŋarr*: the *bul̲ 'manydji miny'tji*.

Nimanydja greets me. We embrace. Sadness dwells in her eyes but she is serene too. '*Bäpa. Nhe dhu nhäma*,' she says.

My *bäpa* lies on a simple wooden bed, looking peaceful. He opens his eyes, looks into mine and squeezes my hand, but not so tightly today. I lightly stroke his arm, forehead and his hand. His skin is cool.

'I know it's my time to go. I am ready,' he had told me on one of our previous visits when I came to give him healing.

This is the last time I'll see *Bäpa* alive are the words in my head.

'*Yä Baŋad̲itjan, Baŋad̲itjan*.' He always called me by my skin name and I shall miss that.

I lie in my bed, focusing on the rise and fall of the breath in my chest down into my belly. The night is still and hot and the fan clunks above my head. I'm still aware of the presence of the Mimi spirits, *Warrabunbun*, the *marrŋgitj* tree, *Galay*'s words and the generosity of her teachings. Yet I am alert and waiting expectantly for the first wail to let us know *Bäpa* has passed over. And then it comes: not long after the boys' initiation that fulfilled *Bäpa*'s last wish. A deep penetrating wail spans the island with its unique resonance as only a grieving wail can. The timing is always perfect. How tuned in the Yolŋu are to spirit.

*Bäpa* has left the world.

I sit up and think of *Bäpa*. I think of Nimanydja losing her husband and all his children. I let out a long exhalation, close my eyes and see him in a strong light, smiling.

'*Yä Bäpa marrkapmirr*,' I murmur. '*Yä Bäpa marrkapmirr, Yä Bäpa marrkapmirr, Baŋaḏitjan, Baŋaḏitjan, Baŋaḏitjan*, you would call to me. *Yä Bäpa marrkapmirr.*'

I let my tears flow. I lie back down under the sheet. Something has shifted in my awareness yet again. I have allowed and surrendered to these experiences. My moments with the Mimi spirits, the *marrŋgitj* tree and the last days with *Bäpa* Jo as he lay dying have brought spirit to life and reminded me again how powerfully connected we all are. I've long held the thought that whatever we are experiencing in life, there is something larger than ourselves in existence that we are a part of. And when we connect to this knowing and surrender to it, we become in tune with a flow that can lead us to live life beyond our wildest dreams.

## 32

# Yoga and Yolŋu
# – the collaboration of two ancient worlds

I'd like to introduce to you Mary McCarthy, who came as a teacher to Milingimbi to work at the school here at Milingimbi. I'm sitting at a place called Ṉilatjirriwa. This place belongs to the Gamaḻaŋga, Gurryindi *ga* Marraŋu tribes. Yoga: Mary *ŋuli ga gäma*. Yolŋu *rom* is about body (*rumbal*), mind (*ḻiya*), *ga* spirit (*birrimbirr*).

Yoga is about spiritual connection and Yolŋu people here at Milingimbi are connected to the spirit, the land, and Mary found that similarity here: the parts of the land where the billabong is, *Ṉilatjirriwa*, *Ḏamuyani*, the Rocky Point and *Ṉinydjiya* the mud flats, Yolŋu ways and Mary's yoga is about body, mind and spirit.

Gutharra Ganygulpa Dhurrukay, 2010

Mrs Barlow was my history teacher in high school. Her hair was silver-grey yet she had a glow to her skin and a calm radiating from her like no other teacher in the school, actually like no other person I knew.

After teaching us some yoga postures, she instructed us to lie on the floor of the classroom among the wooden chairs and tables.

'Let your body relax into the floor.' Her voice was soothing.

I tried to relax, feeling constricted, though, by the red bow tie around my neck, heavy grey uniform, and pantyhose we wore every day in the heat. Wild worries and burdensome thoughts about home and school whirled around in my head.

'Breathe deeply in and out. Picture a mountain. Imagine yourself walking up the mountain. Stop on the way and feel your anxieties dropping away.'

My body relaxed more and more as she spoke in a quiet reassuring voice. The student snoring next to me did not bother me.

'Now you are at the top of the mountain. Breathe. Relax. Be free of all worries. Look out across the space below the mountain. Feel the relief.'

I could no longer feel my body. It dissolved. I was light, floaty. It was the first time I could remember experiencing silence inside a room full of people. I remember a calm silence the times I sat in the shade of a tree in the backyard, or perched on a rock in the creek on the golf course across the road from where I grew up, but this was different. I was cocooned in a quiet stillness I had never experienced before.

'Breathe life back into your body,' Mrs Barlow said, bringing us back to the room.

In the next days, I was tranquil. Nothing bothered me. A weight had been lifted.

I couldn't wait to do this again. There was something strangely familiar about it all. I knew something had been changed in me, a potential awakened. My history teacher gave me one of the greatest tools I have ever received: yoga. Since then, though initially to varying degrees, yoga has been a way for me to come back to my true nature, a way to connect with the still, strong part within me during the chaos of my own mind, emotions and the world. Yoga for me is an ongoing journey to cultivate and stay connected with my centre and then connect with all other beings and the planet. It is a way for me to cultivate inner strength.

It's now 2010 and I think back to the first night I ever spent in Darwin city, in February 2003.

It was more of a snippet of a night really. The taxi pulled up in a driveway where a line of tall, sleek, palm trees stood. I think it was about one a.m. My skin was clammy and the air thick with moist humidity. I had flown from Sydney. I sat up drinking a cup of tea, pressed close to the locked window; trying to feel into this hot tropical place I had never been to before. It was still wet season, but I was in an air-conditioned room and couldn't see anything but concrete.

I fell into a deep sleep and dreamed I was practising yoga asana. Perspiration was flowing down my skin, my body liquid, at ease moving in and out of postures with a strength and lightness that in a waking state was a rare experience. I certainly hadn't mastered the postures I was doing so effortlessly in the dream.

Practising yoga with Yolŋu *buŋgul* going on outside has become the norm for me here on Milingimbi Island. As I stand in Virabhadrasana, *bilma* are clapped together outside. The sound meets my ears through my backyard jungle. Yolŋu breath swirls through *yidaki*, its hum rises out of the earth, mixing with the sound of my breath. I am aware of my weight sinking through my feet. I am aware of the earth holding me. I breathe deeply and enjoy the strength and courage warrior pose has to offer. I wonder how I will be without this blend of yoga practice and ceremony when I leave here. Ceremony does not always occur so close to my house every day and, more often than not, I am attending the ceremony, but somewhere on this island a pulse of it is usually present.

Contrary to my original thoughts that yoga would make me into an illuminated being free from all negativity, I find if anything it helps me be more accepting of the toing and froing of the mind, my human condition, my lapses into feeling separate from the world, and all my foibles. It also helps me become clear about where I'm at and those around me.

It is hard to say what I am like now, as in recent years life has been an amalgamation of a somewhat hermit-like state and an immersion in a culture where people would rarely, if ever, even consider being alone.

In my practice here in this unique world, my body is fluid in the heat, my heart opened by the experience of this spiritual entwinement in which I dwell. I have always loved ritual.

As I practise, I'm aware of the Yolŋu outside. Their earthy guttural chants imbue the environment with the presence of the ancestors. I connect with this too. Om sounds rise from my belly up into my throat and the vibrations of these two ancient cultures entwine deep in my core, bringing balance, harmony, and collaboration between earth, heart and spirit.

I don't have to do this practice; there is no semblance of the religious obligation I grew up with. I want to do this. I love it. My emotions are more in balance and my mind steady. My body feels awake, alive and nourished by these postures, and this experience affects the moments in my day. I loved certain rituals at church, too, when I was a child, but strict religion gave me an image of God as a man sitting in a chair in a cloud, watching me. I have always found solace in the essence of Christ but I can no longer live by the view that God is a punishing man. It took me some years to untangle from this philosophy. Perhaps I am still untangling from it. I was constantly terrified of doing something wrong as a child, and when I did I would have to confess it and be punished.

In yoga, Isvara Pranidhana is one of Patanjali's five Niyamas or codes of conduct. It means to surrender to a higher power. I do not see this form of surrender in the same light as giving my power over to God in a religious or conditional sense.

While I hold the view that there is a larger force at hand to tap into, that I am a part of, yoga assists me in accepting where I am, wherever I am and whatever I am feeling at any given moment, covering a broad spectrum of feelings: impatience, happiness, grief, frustration, lightness, ease, or perhaps fury. And sometimes I can accept where I am better than other times. Yoga has supported me through many of life's challenges. Meditation has many benefits and allows me to have moments beyond the duality of the mind and brings clarity. Mantra, though, can change our thought process through the use of sound. The spark of connection, however, exists in me whether I take on this practice in this particular setting or not. But for now, here is where I have chosen to reside and so I align with it. Living here has been the deepest spiritual experience of my life.

So I sit on this piece of earth, absorbing extraordinary ceremony as if it were a common occurrence, and guess what? Here, it is just that.

Practising and teaching yoga in this community has been like no other yoga experience I've had. Here in the raw belly and bones of the earth I am challenged to apply all I learn through my practice and studies to life as a schoolteacher and life within an ancient culture. I feel a strong bond with the teachers and nurses and sometimes the doctors that come to my classes, because we are exploring yoga in such a unique environment together. It's a raw space and yet life goes on around us, kids play outside and jump on the roof, maybe the rain pelts down, maybe the shop has been cursed and closed so there is a disgruntled feeling, maybe a death occurs, or a ceremony. Sometimes we are all exhausted after school, and then yoga helps us. The mixture of heat and rasping noisy air conditioning we surrender to at times become part of our practice. I love teaching the Yolŋu women yoga. Our classes organically unfold. Sometimes there are teenage girls, babies even. I've still got a picture of a girl holding a baby in Trikonasana. Sometimes no one turns up and I stroll home, my yoga mat on guard for some dog that may want to bite me. I reach my doorstep and then someone comes to find me.

'Mary, *räli gu, miyalk dharrwa ga nhina ŋunha bala, wanha nhe?*'

But generally Boyukarrpi and Maṯay, my two co-teachers, always come. They love it and express themselves freely and I learn so much from this. I am not writing all the names of the dear people who have attended my classes through these years but if you are reading, then thank you for joining in and creating such a wonderful space, a community within a community, and yoga and Yolŋu are both about community.

I love to practise yoga asana with the children. Their bodies are fluid, light and agile and they move easily into postures.

'*Dharpa*, Mary.' A child steps into tree pose when we are out in the bush.

They relate so well to turtle, eagle and snake yoga postures. These animals are their dreamings and, some of them, their meals. The kids love all these poses. Not only can they relate to them, in ceremony they become an embodiment of the essence of their *waŋarr*.

Here on Milingimbi, I have found parallels between ancient worlds. I am not saying they are the same. They are not the same.

But somewhere deep in me I have been truly nurtured by this meld of the essence of two old worlds.

## 33

# Bäpi Mundukul'

*Mundukul* – Yirritja snake. Python connected to water. The Maccassan well belongs to the Yirritja moiety. It was made by a snake called *Mundukul*, He came flashing lightning from Worral. When he was at Worral, he was the Balamwuy tribe. [But] when he got here, he was of he Walamangu tribe.

Tom Djawa in The Native Born

I race to the door and pull it open. The March rain beats down hard on the tin roof. Yolŋu kids run through the streets laughing, their sleek bodies wet and shiny, legs dancing in the caramel-coloured puddles growing on the black tar road. Steam swirls up from the earth. The tall green grass grows longer every day, though it's still hot and sticky and mosquitoes, blood-sucking creatures desperate for their fill, buzz wildly around my head at night as I sleep. The billabong is overflowing. Water seeps through salt-crusted cracks, gushing into the broken earth, forming large mud pools on the *ninydjiya*.

Over the years, Stu and I've headed out there some afternoons after school. We'd walk on the saltpans, revelling in the open space, and clear our minds from the pressures of school life. I love to lie fully immersed in the thick, black, warm, salty mud, the sky vast above and land quiet and spacious. Relief comes when the billowing black clouds finally break and spill rain down on our parched, heat-stung faces.

I stand at the staffroom door, shaking the rain off. I snatch a corner of my skirt and wring out the water. Milay, my *wäwa*, is just behind me. We laugh at how soaked to the skin we are. Thunder cracks the sky. Lightning hits the ground and we hurry ourselves. *Wäwa* holds a large parcel covered in a blue garbage bag under his arm. I push the staffroom door open and we enter the darkened space.

'*Nhä dhuwal?*' I ask as he peels off the plastic, revealing a long carving he has just finished.

'*Bäpi.*' *Wäwa* places the long, thick serpent on its side on the bench.

'*Yolku dhuwali?*' I ask, entranced by the ochres of this piece. Milay is a born artist.

'*Dhuŋa ŋarra.* I just finished it,' he replies.

'*Ḏarraku,*' I smile without thinking, marvelling at the intricate design of smaller snakes engraved into its long, thick body. '*Wanha Gamuti?*' I ask, but before he can open his mouth to tell me where his wife is, I am out the door in search of her as she will be the one to tell me the price. Not that I care; there is no price on this work.

By night, the snake is mine. Milay and Gamuti come around for a cup of tea and to tell me its story.

I've always been intrigued by owls, bats and snakes. I often see them, and snakes of all shapes and colours appear in my dreams frequently. I'm fascinated at the sight of shed skins lying on the earth or hanging off a tree branch. Whenever I see either a snake or its skin, it seems to synchronise with the occurrence of significant change in my own life. Apparently, snakes have small bones in their heads that can conduct low-frequency vibrations as they travel across the earth. They can tune in to the magnetic resonance of Mother Earth, demonstrating their deep interconnectedness with nature.

For me, they represent change, potent creative energy, sexuality, fertility, the development of the ability to transform oneself and grow spiritually. Of course, in yoga there is the rich symbol of the Kundalini. This Sanskrit word means 'coiled'. Kundalini is perceived as a powerful energy that lies at the base of the spine like a coiled serpent. Nestled in the sacrum, it is often referred to as sleeping power. And there is Sesha, the coiled serpent lying at the feet of Vishnu, the preserver of life. Lakshmi, his wife and Hindu goddess of beauty, light, grace, love and prosperity, massages her husband's feet in devotion.

I have two small wooden snakes from my trip to Uluru in the desert. I have another carving of *Wititj*, a snake I received when I helped out with some work at the Yirrkala Art Centre on my first Arnhem journey, and of course there was the powerful serpent dream/vision I had on the sands of Cape Arnhem.

'That was the serpent guiding you to Yurrwi,' one of my Yolŋu family had responded on hearing of my experience.

'Your hands inside me feel like *bäpi marrŋgitj*,' I have been told several times after giving healings.

Aboriginal art holds the very essence of the Yolŋu spirit itself.

I climb up on a chair and suspend Milay's snake between the curtain rod and the wall near my front doorway. A protective quality radiates from its serpent body. I look around at the pandanus baskets hanging in various parts of the room, the two Gupapuyŋu *mokuy* carvings also created by Milay, the grass mats and bark paintings, and I welcome the presence they exude.

At night, thunder splits the silence, lightning flashes through my jungle, and sparks of it bursting into my eyes and keeping me awake.

I give up on sleep and wander out to the kitchen, eyes half-closed, and flick the kettle on. Again, lightning flares, illuminating the lounge room to reveal Milay's fine snake sitting majestically on the pandanus grass mat in the centre of the lounge room floor.

The sight of it jolts me fully awake. The snake had been carved into such a shape that it is impossible for it to sit on the floor the way it is. But here it is sitting perfectly balanced, lightning ablaze around it.

'Thank you, spirit. Welcome to my world.' I smile, no longer surprised by art works coming to life in my home.

I know in that moment the spirit of the snake has landed and is with me. I sit before my altar, and light a candle. The flame flickers wildly on this stormy night, creating shapes on the wall of Natarajasana, dancing Shiva statue and the Lakshmi statue. I trace my finger around the shape of the Rainbow Serpent on the card leaning against the Ganesh statue and stare at its ochre colours.

Time has rolled on and it's April 2010.

'We'll take you to that *bäpi dhiyaŋ bala, ŋali*.' Djämbutj points to herself and Djuwandaŋu, my *gäthu*. '*Räli gu*,' says Djämbutj.

'*Ma'*,' I respond and get up from under the *Djambaŋ* tree.

Munguli looks up from her crossword puzzle, raises an eyebrow and waves her hand in approval for me to go.

I climb into the troopie with *Waku* Djämbutj and *Gäthu* Djuwandayŋu.

'Everyone wants to see *Mundukul̲*, that Rainbow Serpent, *ŋama*',' says Djämbutj, her smile beaming into me.

We stop again and *Gäthu* Paula jumps into the car too.

We arrive at Lapuluŋ's house by the sea. The frame of the shelter from the last funeral still stands on the earth. A few weeks before, this framework of sticks now standing bare had been covered in leaves and provided shelter for the body of Lapuluŋ's mother, my *yapa*.

'*Yow*, Mary,' my *waku* greets me with a big smile. A wild tangle of hair on his head, Lapuluŋ has a strong body, piercing eyes and a mesmerizing ability to speak about the spiritual world.

I hang on every word he says and he appears completely oblivious to the effects of his charisma.

*Yapa*, Lapuluŋ's gentle wife, sits on the edge of the veranda, barefoot, navy blue skirt with white flowers and striped top, a grandchild clambering on her.

Djämbutj and Djuwandaŋu sit down on the sand near her.

Djämbutj picks up Yapa's green enamel mug of tea and begins to sip on it. '*Yow, Yapa*,' she smiles at me.

'*Yow, Yapa*,' I reply.

Lapuluŋ's aunty stands singing. Her thin arms hang by her side. She has white wispy hair and she wears a red top with bright yellow flowers printed on it, and a red skirt with an orange, green and yellow flower-print.

She is singing a *manikay*. '*Bäpi, bäpi*.' Her voice is low and almost a chant, with a tone of sorrow in it.

'*Bäpi manikay*?' I ask.

'*Yow*, for *Mundukul̲*.'

The long python with the yellow underbelly spirals around the pole of the large wooden frame outside the house. She moves closer to the snake.

The children step down off the veranda and gather close around the snake. One boy carries another child barely smaller than him.

Lapuluŋ and his granddaughter stand closest to the snake. 'Put your hands under your arms like this, ŋändi, and then touch the snake. Then it can recognise you,' says Lapuluŋ. '*Nhe ga barrarirri?*' he asks.

'*Gaŋga,*' I say.

My heart is pounding fast. I watch as my *gutharra* calmly strokes the snake lightly, then she stops so I can have a turn. The snake remains coiled and calm. I wipe my hands under my armpits as instructed and then step towards the snake.

It lies still and its skin is cool under my fingers.

'It's our dreaming. This snake goes away hunting then comes back,' says Lapuluŋ. 'It's like Yolŋu, it would never harm you,' he continues.

I am moved by Lapuluŋ's words. His eyes grow big as he speaks about *Mundukul*'. With a head of wild greying hair and a thick beard, he reminds me sometimes of a wise Indian sadhu. I am always captivated by his words and knowledge.

'*Bäpi, bäpi.*' The sound of Lapuluŋ's aunt's voice grows louder and more urgent as she moves closer to the snake now. '*Bäpi, bäpi,*' and then she stops and stares into me. '*Nhuŋu lundumirriŋu ŋayi,*' says the old lady.

'May I take a photograph?' I ask.

'*Yow, manymak*, it's *manymak,*' says Lapuluŋ.

I stand underneath *Mundukul*', lightly stroke its cool skin, then take out my camera and snap photos of its long body swirling around, the pole, a backdrop of gum leaves and blue sky.

'He and I are one, Yolŋu and this *bäpi* are one,' Lapuluŋ says.

'*Manymak, ŋayi manymak.*' *Yapa*, the old lady, joins in waving her bony finger to the snake.

'I am the custodian for this *Mundukul*' in this region,' says Lapuluŋ. 'Talk to *Mundukul*,' he continues

'*Waŋi*, "Yow, nhä mirr nhe, manymak *Mundukul*?' says Lapuluŋ.

I repeat the words to the snake and add, 'I don't want to hurt you.'

'*Yow, yupthurru*,' says Lapuluŋ to *Mundukul*'.

*Mundukul*'s body seems to grow longer as it reaches out beyond the stick, and its tongue darts in and out. It is slithering to reach the thin trunk of the palm tree ahead. A welcome breeze from the blue sea creeps up and flows over my face as I wipe the sweat off my forehead.

'*Gu, gu*,' the women encourage the snake from the veranda.

The children stand very still, silent, all eyes glued on *Mundukul*'.

'Careful, come! Like magnet,' says Lapuluŋ.

Almost making it onto to the palm tree, *Mundukul*' changes direction, dropping its head down towards the sandy earth, long sleek body hitting the ground and wiggling off towards the grass ahead, its body making an S-shape in the sand. The kids are following *Mundukul*' closely now, laughing and chatting away.

'See the rainbow on its back.' Lapuluŋ points to the light hues of pink, red, blue shimmering on its diamond-shaped scales. 'The snake is a bit like that cobra in India,' smiles Lapuluŋ. He often makes a reference to India. He knows my passion for yoga and the trips I have made to India and he says we once lived together, the Indians and Yolŋu. 'Our land was once joined.'

I was told *Mundukul* is the Yirritja name for *Mundukul* the rainbow serpent here at Milingimbi, but that would not necessarily be the same name for the Dhuwa moiety or other clan groups across this continent.

All these experiences connect now, experiences with *Mundukul*', the Yolŋu and the journey I have made here to Arnhem Land. Time is flying by. It sounds strange to say this because mostly I feel time isn't passing by at all when I'm with Yolŋu at a ceremony or out bush with the women. The framework of time exists less for me then. But when I think about months, school term dates and deadlines, then time appears speedy, and there is a feeling of pressure, like time is running out, or there is never enough. Hence, the complexities of the meeting of the two worlds in which I dwell. I was scheduled to leave in the middle of the year but decided once again that I'm not ready to go, so I am leaving at the end of 2010, the end of the school year, now.

*Mundukul'* weaves her way up and down the children's limbs. *Gutharra*'s face shines and her white teeth flash as *Mundukul'* slinks over her head.

## 34

# Ḏiltjipuy Mirritjin' – bush medicine

Some of the Yolngu need magic get themselves stronger and when they have lost their magic they have to go to the Balanda doctor to get the Balanda's medicine to help them think clearly.

Sometime Balanda it works and sometimes it doesn't work. That mean they have to go to the bush then. For three days by yourself sitting there and concentrate very hard [find] where's the power gone.

Into that special area – talk to that area so the spirit of the earth, the feeling of the earth it come to you and then you feel free, well and strong and then you can hear the sound of that spirit, not a bad spirit, but a good spirit.

Wandjuk Marika, Wundjuk Marika Life Story:<br>As Told to Jennifer Isaacs

The day is nearly over. My throat aches. I am lying in the lounge room with the middle of my back over a purple bolster on my yoga mat to open up the airways. I focus on my breath to calm my mind and relax my body. Crows squawk outside in my jungle. Soon they'll fly away for the night.

My lungs hurt from coughing. The heaving has reached into my chest. I find I seem to suffer more and heal less quickly in extreme heat. Ginger, garlic and lemon drinks and my own healing techniques are not really changing things. I breathe into my chest; it's tight. I release a long exhalation. What else can I do, I am thinking. There is no doctor on this island and I prefer not to take drugs anyway.

'*Waku, Waku*, are you there?' I hear a voice at the door.

It's my *Ḏändi* and my *waku*. We are in a brilliant choir together on Saturday nights at Scotty, *Wämut*'s house on the other side of my jungle. Scotty is a musician and a music teacher at the school. Wild sandy-coloured hair and blue eyes, he speaks Yolŋu *matha* well and has been working in communities for many years. I first met him in Yirrkala in 2001. I joined in singing with the group standing around him as he played the piano in the Walkabout hotel in Nhulunbuy. I just love it when I hear him playing Beethoven's Moonlight Sonata on the piano. As the melody wafts through my jungle, I'm drawn into its melancholy and moved by it, more so because I am listening to it here on Yurrwi Island in this ancient world. Scotty has a *tanpuru* he brought back from India and sometimes I go round and we have a jam together. I do some Vedic chanting, he plays the tanpuru, and once a Yolŋu guy came and played *yiḏaki* with us too.

Tight black curls around her fleshy cheeks, Ḏäṉḏi comes into the lounge room and hands me a large bottle.

'For *ŋarra? Nhä dhuwal?*' I ask, getting up off the mat and holding my neck.

'*Yow, Waku,*' says my *ŋäṉḏi*, wearing a long blue floral dress. '*Nhuŋu mayaŋ ga rirrikthun?*' she asks.

'*Yow*, but *mayaŋ* means river, *ŋe, muka?*' I ask.

'*Yow, Waku*, river and neck,' smiles Ḏäṉḏi.

I am always fascinated by the link between the names of body parts and bodies of water. Guḻun is stomach, womb or billabong.

'We heard you were sick, so we went out bush for you,' *Waku* tells me.

'*Yuwalk? Yä latju,*' I respond, barking out another cough and receiving the plastic bottle into my hand. I take a sip. The brown liquid slides down my throat. 'It tastes like bark from a tree, Ḏäṉḏi,' I say.

'*Yow, ṉäku*, it's bark from the *gaḏayka dharpa, Waku,*' says *ŋäṉḏi*. 'Drink it up. It will help your cough, *ga yalala* you can wash your skin with it too. Then you can come to back to singing class.'

I take another slug of the bark juice out of the old Coke bottle. 'It tastes smoky,' I say.

'*Yow*, Ḏäṉḏi,' says *Waku*. 'That's from boiling in a pot on the fire for long time.'

'*Wow, manymak*, thank you so much. I'll wash in it and drink it all up, *marrkapmirr*,' I reply.

I love the thought of my ŋä<u>n</u>di and *waku* going out bush, collecting the bark, boiling it up, bottling it and bringing it round for me. They both work as nurses in the clinic but this is far more impressive than receiving a Panadol.

'*Yow, manymak, waku,*' says <u>D</u>ä<u>n</u>di.

'You and me and you and your *waku* here, we are ŋä<u>n</u>di ga waku, yothu-yindi, so we always look after each other. It's the Yolŋu way, *muka*. Now drink it all up.'

I nod and smile at the reference <u>D</u>ä<u>n</u>di makes to how we are all connected. I'm reminded that *yothu-yindi* is indicative of the mother–child relationship, the link between the different relationships. This could be a connection between land, people, songs or totems.

I drink the medicine and within a few days my chest clears, my cough is gone, and I'm singing again.

Long before I came to Yurrwi, I had an interest in bush medicine. My brother Johnnie had a bush food and medicine nursery in Northern New South Wales. Over the years on Yurrwi, the women have pointed out medicines and foods when we were out bush. There are many bush medicines here, and this dry season I have spent time with my *Yapa* Banbaniwuy out photographing a variety of food and medicine. For example, *gu<u>n</u>inyi* is a bush with edible fruit and its roots are used for dyeing pandanus. *Muthir'* is a tree with small black fruit that can be eaten for diarrhoea. After being soaked in water, its inner bark can be drunk as medicine for a stomach ache. The *mapu<u>d</u>umun'* tree holds edible gum and fruit, and its bark is good for treating diarrhoea, pimples and sores. *Yapa* works in the resource centre with Elizabeth *mukul* to produce resources in Yolŋu matha for the students to read at school.

I remember that September in 2006, the searing shooting pain down my leg, the red-hot agony of the pus-filled *mäpa<u>n</u>* low on my left buttock cheek. It started as just a tiny painful speck but grew like wildfire within hours. I remember *Yapa* Jessie standing over me doing an incantation to clear the naughty spirit that had attached itself to me.

I remember asking, 'Where is the *mutamuta*? Please bring me some *mutamuta*,' but the *mutamuta* didn't come and I ended up in the Milingimbi Clinic, barely able to sit on the edge of the chair.

'Oh my God, that will kill you!' I remember the nurse yelping, her face full of terror as she grabbed the phone and called for a plane to medivac me out immediately. But no plane could come that day.

I remember barely making it up the stairs to my house. I remember standing in the bathroom, staring into the cracked mirror, dizzy, eyes blurry, face thin and colourless.

I remember her arriving at my place late that night, armed with extra medication, to find me sitting, high as a kite, with the drip hanging off my arm. She was worried because I hadn't taken so much as a Panadol in at least fifteen years.

I remember sweating silently, my whole body throbbing with intense pain as I flew in the plane across the sky, over the waterways with a young pregnant Yolŋu woman.

I remember how unwelcome I felt in the stark hospital casualty, waiting, waiting and waiting because there was no doctor or hospital bed available.

I remember my boss who lived in Nhulunbuy, with her huge blue eyes and long golden hair like an angel, coming to take me to spend the night in her home. I wasn't operated on until three o'clock the next afternoon, and the bald doctor with the thick-rimmed glasses smiled as he invited me to come back one day to have a skin graft on my butt so there would no longer be a trace of the festering, excruciating, fifteen-headed boil on my sweet arse. But I never went back. And then there was the sequel boil that popped up as I lay recovering on the seaweed-laden beach in Bali on my summer holiday with my friend Kate. But no more about that.

Back in 2007 in *Gopu* classroom with Boyukarrpi, my *gutharra*, we went out and collected mutamuta. The Yolŋu say that your *gutharra* can be a good teacher. Well, it is true of Boyukarrpi; she is a marvellous teacher for the children and for me.

Wutjun is unusually quiet today. I'm not surprised, though, as the boil on his toe looks red and angry and very painful. Gadawulu has one too, on her leg.

'We will go out and get that *nhawi, märi*.'

'*Nhä nhawi, Gutharra?*' I ask, gently prising kids off my ankles in the classroom.

'*Mutamuta.*'

'*Mutamuta!*' I wince a little, recalling the nightmare experience of my boils the year before.

'*Ḏiltjipuy mirritjin'?*' I ask.

'*Yow, ḏiltjipuy mirritjin', muka.*'

'*Manymak,*' I say.

'*Yow*, for that natural environment *djäma* we are doing in Yolŋu *matha* bush medicine and for *märrma djamarrkuḻi*' have that *mäpaṉ* on them. We need to help them with *mutamuta*, so we will all go out together, *warrpam.*'

'*Ma', manymak*. I can take pictures and film a movie and we can make stories with the *djamarrkuḻi,*' I say.

'*Yow, manymak, märi,*' says Boyukarrpi.

'*Yow*, we like to use that bush medicine,' says Maṯay, from up the back of the classroom.

We gather the kids, head out the back gate of the school and walk along the dirt road that leads to the saltpans.

Boyukarrpi, dressed in a red and white floral skirt and a loose blue sleeveless top, stands holding a *yaŋara* in her hand. It has *marwat* branching off the stalk.

'*Dhuwal mutamuta,*' Boyukarrpi says to the small group of Year 1 kids.

I would not have even noticed this plant. It lies very close to the ground on the brown dirt among other bushy green plants.

Boyukarrpi folds forward and scoops her hand under the *mutamuta* leaves so everyone can see. Bits of thin dry grass thread through the plant, so she clears a space around it with a stick. Kids huddle around her, pulling on her skirt. Wutjun pulls off his blue shirt and she picks it up off the ground and throws it over her shoulder. Others huddle close to Maṯay (my *waku*) around a different *mutamuta* plant. Maṯay's hair is swept up on top of her head in a bun with a red scrunchie. She kneels on the ground and digs into the earth.

Scrambling around, bare feet on the earth, the kids giggle and look for sticks so they can help too. They crouch down and intently start digging around the bottom of the plant.

I take photos and find a stick as well.

The children are relaxed outside, fully engaged in what we are doing, speaking their language and learning about their culture.

Wutjun digs his nails into the dirt and pulls out part of the root. He holds it up so I can take a picture of it. It looks like a thin brown twig.

Gaduwula, my *gaminyarr*, waves a thread of *mutamuta* around in the air, and she pulls on its leaves. She is always smiling but I can see her face scrunch up when she feels the pain of her boil. Lots of people get boils in the community.

We collect some roots and walk back to the area just outside the classroom. Kids stick their heads under the running tap to cool down and gulp water. We are all hot, sticky and parched in the heat.

Once again, we huddle around and I film Boyukarrpi giving a talk on *mutamuta*.

'*Mirritjin' napurr gan marŋgithirr. Yolŋu mirritjin' limirruŋ, mäpaṉpuy.*'

The kids peer into the camera screen. Most of them are my *gaminyarr*.

Boyukarrpi peels the leaves off the branches and the kids follow her and pull the leaves off their branches too.

Wutjun picks up the clear bucket and puts it on his head. The kids break up laughing.

'*Yaka,*' says Boyukarrpi. '*Yaka bäyŋu, gapu märram(a)'.*'

He pulls the bucket off his head and gets some water.

Boyukarrpi shakes the clump of dirt off the root and its skin looks red.

She then scrapes the skin off with her nails, revealing a thick creamy-coloured stick underneath. She places it on the concrete. '*Bala*,' she says to the children. Then she thumps the root with a long steel rod. Maṯay is smashing the root with a big white rock. They place the stringy mass in the bucket of water.

'Now we will soak it until it's soft,' says *gutharra*.

Wutjun pulls some soft, stringy bits out and pastes them on his toe. Boyukarrpi makes a poultice of *mutamuta* and places it on Gaduwula's leg. *Gaminyarr* winces then smiles as the thick, pinkish paste is soothing on the boil.

I take more photos. Boyukarrpi and Maṯay wrap bandages around the boils on the kids and they are left there overnight.

The next day, the boils are gone. The scars are there but there is no longer pain or infection. The skin is thick and smooth and the kids seem much happier and lighter. I take more photos for proof.

Boyukarrpi, Maṯay and I work as a team together to translate the film and write English subtitles on it. We print off photos and hang them on the classroom wall, labelled with Yolŋu *dhäruk*.

The children draw pictures of the excursion and we negotiate texts. They match pictures to identify plants. This is a Yolŋu language programme but we do some oral English as well. I encourage the students to use some English words and sentences to describe their drawings.

Boyukarrpi takes the film and resources to Darwin to do a presentation on her teaching studies course. It is very well received and she ends up with her photo in the local newspaper for her work.

## 35

# The spirit of meditation

Mindfulness is the first step in minding your mind.

A.G. Mohan

The month of August has just begun and it's 2010 in my little classroom on the second floor of the primary area. The tall, lean boy grabs the thick roll of sticky tape off my desk, bites a long piece off with his teeth and wraps it across his mouth, shrugging and waving his hands in a manner that says, I can't speak, oh well.

'Please take it off and sit down,' I ask quietly, knowing that if I am too stern he may become volatile.

'*Ŋatha* time, *ŋatha* time,' he yells, an angry frown furrowing his brow.

I usually teach English to small groups of five- and six-year-olds in this small classroom upstairs in the primary section of our community school. But in more recent times, I've been invited to work with students with with yoga and meditation techniques.

'Let's do this first.' I point to a large picture of some native animals and birds.

My plan is to meditate together. I continue to find inspiration from the nine-week journey I took across the ocean from Milingimbi to the south of France at the end of 2007 for studies with the Buddhist Zen master Thich Nhat Hahn. His teachings are about 'mindfulness' and peace. From there, I travelled to Chennai in India and spent five weeks with the wonderful Mohans. Examples of our studies included the psychology of yoga for well-being, the sutras, Vedic traditions and sound therapy.

A.G. Mohan was a dedicated student of Krishnamacharya (often referred to as the Father of Yoga) for eighteen years. His wife, Indra Mohan, also studied with Krishnamacharya and on this course she gave me a personal mantra that I practise daily. The practice of mantra cuts through the mental chatter very quickly, resulting in a calm, clear state from which to proceed.

The thing I love about the teachings of all these mentors is that they inspire confidence in cultivating one's own tools for growth, healing and contentment. This is what I must do for myself. This is a lifelong journey. In my work with other people, I share techniques that will encourage them to cultivate their own practice. When I sit with those who are sick here, I encourage them to become aware of their breath and relax their bodies, allowing nourishment and deep rest. It is amazing what the simple act of breath awareness can do.

Right now, I want to encourage this boy to focus his attention and sit quietly so that some of his pent-up tension and emotion can resolve itself. As a school, we are trying many ways to help him reduce his anger so he can feel at ease with others. This is our third time together and I decide I will start with something simple like looking at pictures of animals and discussing their qualities. I know he will relate to this because he lives in the bush and his tradition has him deeply connected to animals and the earth. I also know that in his tradition there are ways for him to move through the struggle within himself. I cannot take the place of his elders nor his family, but I may have something to offer him too. I will support him as much as I can here at school.

He stands against the large grey desk, eyes bulging at me, arms tightly crossed around his chest.

I look at him and then point to the animals, 'Which one do you like best?'

He relaxes a little and whacks his hand on the dingo.

'*Manymak. Nhaku?*' I ask.

'He can hunt,' he says.

'Ahh, *dhapirrk*. I like the *ŋerrk*,' I say, pointing to the white cockatoo. 'When I was at Laŋarra, they told me *ŋerrk* is a spiritual bird.'

He sits down, interested now, and listens quietly.

'*Nhä dhuwal*?' I point to another bird on the poster.

'*Ḏamala*,' he says.

'Yes, what can eagle do?' I ask him.

'Fly, catch fish.' He rocks back and forth and bites his nails.

'Yes, to catch fish he can focus very well,' I say. '*Ḻiya gaḏaman, nhe marŋgi?*'

'*Yow*,' he responds.

'Now I want us to focus together,' I say quietly.

I hear the kids next door begin to move around and get ready for lunch. Hearing them too, his attention is triggered and it goes into the boxes of toys stored on the light-blue shelves behind where I have stuck the animal poster. He reaches his hand into a box full of animals and drags out the rubber snake. The long, yellow and red, rubber snake is the most popular toy in the box and is now in the tight grip of his hand.

'*Ḏarraku*,' he says, and his plump face becomes fierce again.

'*Yow*, you can play with it now, and then let's leave here for the other children to play with,' I say.

His big brown eyes wander around the room as if he can't hear me.

'*Mel-bambaydhi*, please.'

Thick black curls hang over his eyelashes. He opens and closes one eye at a time. One lingers on me then shuts and then the other opens on the snake.

'*Mel-bombaydhi*,' I say again.

'*Dharraḏayi.*'

He sits again and this time places his hands on his knees and straightens his spine, exaggerating the meditation position, a slight smirk on his face, snake still in hand.

'*Manymak. Ḏir'yun* in and out,' I say calmly.

Eyelids down, his body begins to soften and relax. His spine is straight and he is breathing well, in and out, in and out. The snake falls out of his hand, and lies coiled on the floor.

'Where do you feel angry? Where can you feel it in your body?' I ask as we sit on the orange carpet in the classroom, the air conditioning rattling above us this Wednesday afternoon. 'Close your eyes and feel where it is. Your anger.'

'*Warrpam*'. *Bitjan*.' He lifts his hands and sweeps them over his body. He has no trouble tapping into the places where his feelings are held.

'*Ḏir'yun*.' I watch him sit still, lungs filling with air, belly expanding. He blows the air out his mouth.

'Where is your sadness?' I ask.

'*Ḻiya borin*g,' he responds, his breath slowing down.

'*Nhe ga barririrri?*'

'*Yow, ḏoṯurrk ḏupṯupthun.*' Sweat on his hairline and face scrunched, he places his hand on his heart and pats it quickly up and down.

'Breathe into your sadness. Breathe in and breathe out slowly. Watch your body and your breathing. *Ḏir'yun, bulnha. Manymak, gamiyarr, manymak.*'

This is easy for him. Large tears spill out of his eyes, melting the dark rage in them.

I am relieved to see him relax, to see him cry even. So much bound up inside him. I hope this can bring some peace, help him grow quiet in himself, so that he can move through his deep insecurities.

'*Milkarri*,' he says softly. He smiles and I see the boy who feels safe for a minute.

'*Yow, milkarri*,' I respond.

He pulls himself off the floor and strides to the door without looking back at me. 'Never again,' he shouts, waving his hand in the air. The familiar defensive attitude quickly returns and his chest puffs up. It seems his large size for his age is his power.

I take another long breath out.

'We have only just begun. This will get easier and it will help us.'

But he is gone, out the door.

All these years, I have valued every chance I have had to share yoga but always wish I could do more meditation and breath work with the students at school. For me, education is not only about training the mind to learn information. Training the mind to help us focus and be present in whatever activity we are engaging in will not only help us gain knowledge but also allow us to experience well-being, courage, confidence and vital health in all areas of our lives. As a teacher, anywhere in the world, what I witness is that a child's emotional and mental health and their capacity to learn academically are equally important.

Living on Milingimbi Island has provided an opportunity to deepen my meditation practice. Moving from being a full-time yoga teacher back to school teaching, studying language and culture, yoga practice and teaching, witnessing the deaths of loved ones, new relationships, incessant heat and my body's reaction to it, and times of aloneness, have provided plenty of challenges, and a chance for me to sit before my jungle in the early hour of a new day and allow the currents of madness to run their course, to settle and bring forth a moment of peace, a moment of stillness. Followed by a thought for all beings and for earth itself.

## 36

## The ochres of Munduku*l*'

Our knowledge is uncalculated; our knowledge doesn't depend on modern technology, through the computer. This knowledge comes from the deeper essence within our hearts and we have the stories. Our educational awareness is that we learn from sitting around the campfire. The embers, the charcoal embers is our knowledge, the charcoal embers is a profound knowledge, leaving [a] legacy. In that embers, into far beyond the embers, is that story that connects deeply and [is]mounted within the roots of our culture and into the roots of our ancient people of the past. *Yow*.

Lapuluŋ Dhamarrandji, 2010

The sun shines as we fly across the sky to the home of Baymarrwaŋa, speaker of the Yan-nhaŋu language, my *dhuway*. I am not sure when I'll see her again, so we are making a special trip before I leave Milingimbi in December. We tried to make this trip a few weekends ago but the plane broke down. White puffs of clouds dangle in the vivid blue sky, and our eyes peer down on the clumps of green mangroves and patches of parched, grey saltpans. My *gutharra* Boyukarrpi, the teacher I have enjoyed working with at the school for years now, Wutjun, one of the boys she looks after who is about nine, and a few others are on our way on a seven-seater plane. Six of us are taking this ten-minute flight from Milingimbi to Murruŋga Island.

'*Nhäŋu!*' says *gutharra* Boyukarrpi. '*Djäri.*'

'Rainbow?' I ask.

'*Yow, djäri,*' confirms Boyukarrpi, her round face smiling.

I take a photo of the streaks of purple, aqua, and orange beaming across the sky above the blue-green, milky, crocodile waters.

'*Djäri,*' I repeat.

I flick on the video and scan the camera around the light aircraft, filming the pilot, the various instruments of the plane and my gutharra mala. I zoom in to Wutjun.

'*Yow, Gutharra, nhäkurru nhe ga marrtji?*' I mock interview him

'*Murruŋgalil.*' A half smile grows on his face as he shyly looks into the camera.

'*Nhaku bili?*'

'*Maypal gu.*'

'*Yolthu nhe dhu malthun?*'

'Gwenie.' His large eyes wander to Boyukarrpi.

My skin tingles. Life here is so rich. Spirit has carried me on this journey. At school, it is so easy to stay in the superficial, in the quagmire of unresolved tension, but out here in the wide open space, the wind whispers its secrets, the ground has a profound voice, and the Yolŋu share pearls of wisdom that are natural for them, and yet in our world we are searching for these understandings. I will miss my *gutharra* Gwenie and her whole family. Her father is a strong tribal man and in the many days I've wandered past their home, to and from school, I've felt them watch over me. *Yä* my *gutharramirrinju mala*.

We land safely. This land feels still and strong as we walk along the worn red earth pathway through the bush with our girri (gear): sharp knives to collect oysters, tins, tea bags, freeze dried milk, a yellow plastic jerrycan of diesel oil, and raspberry muffins I baked this morning.

'What was the name of that rainbow, again?' I ask.

'*Djäri.*'

'*Djäri.* Like that Saltwater Band *manikay.* "Djarridjarri",' I say.

'*Mak bay märi,*' Boyukarrpi murmurs, ever patient with my questions.

Baymarrwaŋa's sister, my *gudi*, is walking towards us from the other direction. The first time I met *gudi* was back in the staffroom when I bought Baymarrwaŋa's basket in 2003. Well, this marked the first of a series of meetings. I didn't know she was my *gudi*. Back then, she called me *yapa*. Tall woman, hair swept up in a bun, round cheeks, she wears a black skirt with big brown flowers on it. The elastic at the top of the skirt is stretched around her chest, shoulders bare, typical of Yolŋu fashion on a hot day.

We come across the bright orange tractor on the side of the track. Two lean boys, both my *galay*s, sit on the plastic orange fender on top of the huge tyres.

*Gudi* picks up the yellow jerrycan and refuels the tractor with diesel oil. One of the boys jumps down and peers over her shoulder. The rest of us clamber onto the trailer attached to the back of the tractor. *Gudi* turns on the engine and the tractor jiggles as we ride along the track through the gums, pandanus trees, red anthills to the houses near the beach where Baymarrwaŋa is.

'*Yow, galay marrkapmirr*,' says the old lady with great affection when she sees me. She sits cross-legged on a blue blanket, in a striped floral dress, grey wispy hair, Log Cabin tin under her knee, rolled cigarette between her long fingers.

'*Yow, Dhuway*,' I say smiling. I reach out, take her hand and rub her bony shoulder, eyeing the brown and black dog scratching its fleas crouched behind her. '*Yow, marrkap Dhuway*,' I say.

'*Yow*! Can you take us in that tractor round to the other side where the oysters are?' Boyukarrpi asks one of the boys, promptly making a plan for our oyster collection.

We sit in the shade, but sweat still streams down our faces. I'd love even a slight breeze off the bright blue sea at this point. I pull out some muffins and begin handing them out. Tea bags are boiling in a billy on the campfire.

I am very happy to be with Baymarrwaŋa again, and tell her about the rainbow we saw from the plane.

'What's the name of *Djäri* in Yan-nhaŋu?' I ask her.

'*Doyduyŋu*,' says Baymarrwaŋa.

'*Dhuwal rrambaŋi Mundukul̲*,' pipes up Gutharra Boyukarrpi.

'What?' I freeze. 'That's the Rainbow Serpent!' I shout.

'*Yow, dharrwa yäku ŋayi, märi.*'

Once again, *Mundukul'* is weaving its way into my consciouness. Here we are, a plane ride away from Milingimbi and the essence of the serpent is with us again. With all these years of snake energy, I am inspired and I'd love to have an ochre painting of *Mundukul*. After asking around, I have been told there are only two men allowed to paint *Mundukul* on Milingimbi, and Lapuluŋ, my *waku*, is one of them. The day we visited *Mundukul* at Lapuluŋ's home, I knew he would be the one to paint it.

I reflect on what I have received from this complex life in Arnhem. I've been adopted into an ancient kinship, and experienced the spirit of the land and the Yolŋu, through the children at school, through growing as a team teacher, through the women out hunting and collecting pandanus, through *buŋgul*, through photography, through my connection with the *marrŋgitj*, and through being invited to share the healing, meditation and yoga work in ways that have naturally led me to deeper understandings. When I was growing up and became aware of my intuition and of healing energies, I always felt shy to talk about it. Later, as it became a career for me, I still had a level of discomfort despite working with hundreds of clients. Here, I have been so accepted and encouraged to use these skills to help the community and this has been very healing for me too.

There are days where I experience absolute wholeness. The connections I have made with Yolŋu, yoga and healing fuse together and inspire me. Hopefully, what I have experienced and witnessed can be shared in a life-giving way. Perhaps all of this will remain memories that from time to time wake me up to myself and remind me I am more than just a body struggling along. Perhaps the spirit I see in the photos I have taken will refresh my memory of what I thought was true back when I was a fifteen-year-old reading *Walkabout*. Who knows? Anything can happen.

'Lapuluŋ, *dhiyal(a)*?' I ask the two teenagers glued to their mobiles outside Lapuluŋ's blue corrugated house.

'*Galkurr(u)*,' they murmur, eyes still on the phones.

They disappear and come back out. '*Yow.*'

Lapuluŋ comes out shirtless, in a pair of blue shorts, his long thick greying hair wild on his head. He stands, one hand holding an elbow, the other stroking his long bushy beard. 'You want to see that painting *dhiyaŋ bala ŋama*'? I haven't finished yet.'

We sit on a large, plastic, woven, red and brown African mat in the enclosed veranda of Lapuluŋ's house, that looks out over the grey dry *ninydjiya* dotted with kids playing and laughing. *Waku* places the long bark painting on the mat.

'I like all the colours,' I say, eyeing the rich ochre, red-browns and black.

'I paint only in ochres,' explains Lapuluŋ. 'There are two snakes. *Mundukul'* *miyalk ga dirramu*. This one is swimming in the flowing water. This story of the *Mundukul'* snakes comes from Hardy Island, Luŋgutju. There are two *burruttji* serpents. I'm the *Djuŋgayi*: the custodian of the country that belongs to the Gupapuyŋu Birrkili clan nations. I will paint the other one maybe tomorrow, Saturday morning, and then my family and I will present it to you Saturday *milmitjpa wo munhagu*. Night, I think,' Lapuluŋ explains.

'*Manymak. Ḏarra dhu bathan ŋatha,*' I reply.

'*Dhuwal miny'tji Mundukul'*, ga *dirramu* and *miyalk*. The two snakes are the male and the female. They embody oneness,' says Lapuluŋ, pointing to the ochre painting. 'When the Macassans first came to Hardy Island, they raised a flag. It was blue and white. Blue is the *gapu*. White for the *mulmul*. This signified the coming together of the Macassans and the Yolŋu and the clouds, cumulonimbus. *Waŋupini*. This collaboration was a symbol of unity.The essence of this painting is Yirritja *Mundukul'*. The triangular shapes around the edge signify the rainbow clouds, the cumulonimbus of the rain clouds forming on the horizon of the Murruŋun saltwater ocean. Two Rainbow Serpents were dwelling on that land. Currents of *monuk gapu*, some are calm, some flowing, generated more currents and they built patterns of the rainbow. The current in this painting has important vital power in the *riŋgitj* and in the cycle of the salt water. Seeing the image on this painting is significant. *Mundukul̠* is not just a reptile that crawls or slides on the long grass or climbs the trees. *Mundukul̠* is sacred, you know. It does have a power source. It is really sacred and has strong interconnectedness. The hissing of this snake can create thunder and lightning. We are tuned into the cycle of the profound knowledge that has been passed from our forefathers and their forefathers and their great great grandfathers. This painting represents the formality, the transformation far beyond time in the sense of knowing. Through the painting, we see ourselves, that we are connected, connected into the power outlet, you know, and with this painting it shows the spiritual interconnectedness.'

Unusually, I have no camera or post-it notepad with me. I rummage in my bag and find a pen and two medical certificates I received from the clinic when I was sick. I scribble *waku*'s words down over every small inch of bare paper. I don't want to miss a word he says.

We sit looking at the painting. Lapuluŋ used a tiny *dharpa* to crosshatch white clay and yellow ochre onto the bark. The design around the edge, a series of triangle shapes in black ochre and white, represents clouds. The snake is long, and broader in the centre, ochre in colour. Lapuluŋ will paint the other snake soon.

I look around for a pair of eyes peeping around a corner or someone, anyone, as it is unusually quiet. I can hear a few low voices in the house. Generally, a Yolŋu household is full of people and kids running around but today it is very different.

Pale sunbeams stream through big white clouds as the sky begins to darken. I become glued to Lapuluŋ and his words and to the painting of *Mundukul̠'*.

We don't eat or drink anything, we just sit with the painting and I listen and scrawl words down.

Lapuluŋ looks out towards the saltpans again and begins to tell the story of *Bol'ŋu*, the lightning man: '*Bol'ŋu* is the lightning, the light, the lightning man. If you are lost, he will guide you.' Lapuluŋ cups his hand to his mouth.

'I call him. This is the spirit we are born with, blessed with, this light from beyond. I was out on that *nhawi* with Scotty. He saw this light shine on both sides of the boat and join together. The water around the light and boat was very calm. The water outside, it was rough. I saw lightning man.

His eyes grow big and as he speaks with passion. *Waku* goes on to tell a story of when some of his family were lost in a boat out at sea. 'Everyone one was worrying and asked if I could do something. Bol'ŋu is the one blessed with the power from beyond. I sat in the centre of my knowing with that light and I went there to my son and I could see they were lost at the banyan tree. The children are hungry. I rang the police, who said, "How do you know where they are?" "Just go there," I said and they did, and saved them. I was transported there. That is the power Yolŋu have. They are *gaḏaman*. I had a vision. We the Yolŋu are surrounded by that power, the power of love and humility. So we can be powerful. We are one family. *Ga balanya*.'

I listen and continue to scrawl but running out of space to write. The writing is tiny now.

'We are grounded in the knowledge of the Renaissance, the ancient wisdom that is passed down, like Michelangelo. This profound knowledge is grounded in the embers, the charcoal embers. It is linked to the cosmic knowledge. And it is rekindled as we talk around the fire. Out comes the knowledge. Out of the flames the knowledge of the past. We see the power of the fire and receive it. This painting *Mundukul̲*' comes from that. It is an ancient painting. An old painting; been around a long time. My ancestors passed this painting down over time and I am allowed to paint it. Through *maḏayin* old people, the cosmic knowledge was passed down. This is the way they access power and freedom and knowledge. There is that power here on Yurrwi.'

I walk home this dark night. Several campfires burn brightly outside people's homes. This is not an unusual sight at all but this evening I realise that over the years, I myself have heard so many stories through the Yolŋu as we sit by the fire.

I stand before the pile of books stacked on the shelf ready to return to people I've borrowed from and the library. I pick out the book *The Universe of the Warramirri* that *Wämut* Scotty lent me. It shows paintings and carvings from this area. I lie on my bed looking at two photographs of the snake carvings done by Wurraki and read.

1.The beginning of the Wet Season

The sea God Marryalan is shown as a superhuman who changes the weather under the water. It is December onset of the wet season. He has condensed the vapour from the respiration of sea creatures, and he is transmitting it on high by means of his celestial form, the snakes Ludhay. The sea is hot, the snakes actively extending upwards, each propelled toward clouds by the God.

2.The end of the wet season

It is now April, the end of the wet season or monsoon. Marryalan the Sea God is bringing, the wet season to a conclusion. The sea is now cool. His alternative form, the celestial snake Ludhay, has descended from the clouds into the sea. He is carved in a drooping posture like a mantle around Marryalan's shoulders. Soon he will be incorporated with Marryalan's body.

I fall asleep and dream about being on a tin boat, staring at the horizon. The air is warm and a blue mist swirls around the tinny. I look down. There are snakes slithering in the water by the boat – on the left, snakes moving quickly in fast currents, and on the right, snakes gliding slowly in calm water.

I get up. It's almost midnight. I email Mayrparr, the initiated man. I tell him about *Mundukul'* and the painting. We are back in contact again now and he still guides me spiritually and helps me understand some of the things that have taken place in my life here and in life in general. I consider him a powerful and knowledgeable spiritual teacher.

Even though Mayrparr is a man from a different tribe, it seems all Indigenous people are inextricably linked by the essence of spirit.

Hi Mayrparr

I now have a bark painting, *Ochres of Mundukul*, the Rainbow Ser-

pent. It feels very sacred. It was painted by the *djuŋgayi*, the custodian of this particular painting. He is the caretaker of the past knowledge.
Thank you.
Mary.

And Mayrparr wrote back to me.

Oh Mary! You are so lucky! The *Ochres of Mundukul̲*! Any painting of Marryalan is always very sacred!

I hope you can understand now why the days before summer can be very tense days. That painting will explain to you a lot more than me. During this time life can be intolerable for some people. People generally can read the clouds.

If you can see the Rainbow Serpent as the garland of love between the Sun (the Father) and Mother Earth and we are all fruits of that love, it will start to make sense, especially to you who is very respectable and part of Yolŋu knowledge.

A lot of answers to your questions are depicted in this painting!

Aboriginal paintings take a lot of time to comprehend their full meanings. Please let me know more if you have time. If I was lucky like you, I would keep this valuable painting somewhere it faces the rising Sun.

That is a beautiful Rainbow Serpent painting with so much of spiritual meanings.

All these experiences have culminated in these final weeks here on Yurrwi. I'm about to venture off my island home. Since my early days here, the Yolŋu have shared stories of spirit with me, but in these last weeks it is as if so much has been explained and that I have been shown a glimpse of the bigger picture.

As I pack up my Arnhem home, I sit at night before my *Mundukul'* painting, candles glowing, mala beads draped over my Ganesh statue, and Lakshmi goddess, incense burning, a sense of contentment in my heart. The spirit of this land and my family are embedded in my cells and they will be with me wherever I go from here.

## 37

# My last day on Yurrwi

> When we go and sit down on the land and look around, this is my country, this is my father's country and mother's country. I feel comfortable here, like the family, even though I might be alone, but when you're out there on your country, you are talking to each other, the land misses you when you're gone away. You can feel it, the homesick feeling, you can feel it. 'Oh, my land must be missing me, better go back' and the land is part of you, the whole being, your soil and the ground, are all part of you and when the sacred ceremonies on, on that particular land, it's trying to, in a special way, communicate to the land that this is part of you, you are part of this. It is our Mother Land, it is our backbone.
>
> Yiŋiya Mark Guyula of Milingimbi in the film *Lifestyle Choice? The Land Is Part of Us*

On Monday night, I saw that *ŋalindi* was growing large. Soon the moon will be a huge beautiful shimmering ball, radiant in her silver glow.

'My last Arnhem moon,' I sighed as I stared loving up into the sky.

This Saturday afternoon, I look around my island nest. It is bare without all the sacred art that holds the ancestral power of the Yolŋu. The *märr* that radiates the *waŋarr* through the art works still lingers in this house. *Munhaŋaniŋ'*, agile creatures with big black eyes, scurry across the ceiling. The open slat windows give a wide view to my jungle. The banana trees are thriving and I wonder how I will live in another place if it is devoid of this nature and spirit, this home where I feel the thunder in my heart, breathe the scent of the rain and welcome its touch on my skin. I have followed my heart's calling. It led me to this rich life here. Now my heart calls me to go elsewhere.

It's December, the end of the school year, and my last full day here on Yurrwi Island. I do not know when I will return, perhaps in a year's time, perhaps not. In total I have spent almost seven years here with my Yolŋu family. I fly out tomorrow.

Black clouds loom and billow across the sky and finally nourish us with torrents of rain. The downpour is fresh. The ground dries quickly, as if never even a drop of water fell, and the temperature heats us up again. I sit with my *yapa*s at Ḏarawundhu.

A group of young boys are dancing. Some of them are my *ŋapipi*, some of them my *gaminyarr*. The rhythm from their souls resounds through their bones, limbs, skin, eyes. They energetically dance their spirit. Teeth flash, beaming smiles as the collective thud of their bare feet meets the earth. '*Yow, Waku,*' they yell to me.

Shell necklaces dangle around the necks of my *yapa*s, Yibi Yibi and Mawukuwuy, Linda Slim.

'Island shells, *Yapa*.' Yibi glows. She is dressed up for her birthday and we are having a big party.

I smile, as I know in my heart that tomorrow, though they haven't told me, I'll be wearing those shells. Right now they are being imbued with the vibes of my Yolŋu sisters.

Spots of rain tumble down; mingle with the saltwater spray off the sea and splash on our skin, our saltwater skin. I taste the salt on my lips once again.

*Wäwa* Jo appears, looking gaunt and skinny. A pang ripples through my heart. I am shocked by the look of his bones.

*Wäwa*'s eyes hold mine. With a hint of a smile, his thin warm hand reaches out to me and shakes mine. He sits down on an old red flour tin and stares into space.

Crows squawk and bicker over some scraps near the tin boat on the shoreline.

'*Wäwa, nhä mirri nhe?*' I make conversation but I can't feel *wäwa*.

The boys keep dancing and women fuss about, piling food on a long table covered in a colourful cloth for Yibi's birthday party.

After a while, *wäwa* stands up and walks back to the house. Clearly he isn't well. Our recent conversations have spoken of his illness. Something in me is saying I will not see him again. He is history. He and *Wäwa* Gilbert Gubiyun, of the Gupapuyŋu clan, the elders, the tribal leaders, as was their father before them. I sit silently crying.

Yolŋu eat fresh fish next to me. There is lots of activity but I can't move my focus.

Yibi sits close, stroking my arm, but I can't tear my eyes from *wäwa*.

'*Yaka warguyun wäwa, yaka,*' her voice shakes.

But I am worried about *wäwa*. I am worried about him leaving this plane. I am worried about all the knowledge, wisdom, *manikay*, language, ceremony and history that go with him. Perhaps his spirit will still be passing this knowledge on when he is gone from here but it is so sad to lose our elders from this world.

I hold on to him with my eyes until he walks through the door and shuts it behind him.

Finally, I turn to look at Yibi.

Tears are also spilling down her face. '*Yaka nhe ga warguyun nhuŋu wäwamirriŋu,*' she says again.

But I know she is worrying too.

We sit in silence.

A hum starts in my head. I sit as I have so often, brushed by the breeze on my face as I stare out at the emerald blue-green ocean. Sheets of rain pelt down on the sea, changing the shade from green to grey. My eyes cloud with the tears, but I can hear the *Guku Manikay*. The sound is resounding through my veins just as it did at the *Ḏärra' buŋgul* when I sat with *Yapa* Yibi and all our sisters, aunties, daughters, sons, grandparents, uncles, children, all our *gurruṯumirriŋu mala*.

I remember that time as if it was today, our faces spattered with white clay, yellow ochre stripes streaked across our noses signifying our tribe, the Gupapuyŋu tribe. Our upper bodies were painted with the ancient *Guku* honey dreaming by our *dhuway*s. Haunting wails came through the lips of the sisters sitting close to Yibi Yibi as she crooned the *Guku Manikay* that final day of *buŋgul*. For an instant now, the resonance of her song pulses through me.

'*Yapa, nhaku nhe ga d̠ar̠'taryun' dhuwal manikay?*' I had asked her that day.

'For *wäwa*. I sing for *wäwa*, the old man…our elder.'

I am conscious of the song's vibration now. It is stored in my cells, in my blood and in my bones. It sings in my heart.

*Waŋgany Galanyin* (One together)
*Miyalkthuny ŋuli* (women)
*Riŋgitjhirr milkarri-kurr* (sacred tears)
*D̠irramunydja bil̠ma'* (men, clap sticks).

This *manikay* is a declaration of the deep richness that exists inside the women. It is the language of Yolŋu grief. Women mourn through song and the men play *bil̠ma*. A unique vibration of interconnectedness is created: the Yolŋu themselves, land and spirit, are one together.

I remember that day with *Yapa*. I listened as she sang. My skin moved and my being effortlessly merged into this sense of oneness. I became a part of it and my spirit came to life in a new way.

'And we remember our ancestors,' Yibi Yibi had said.

Then silence. That rich stillness between words that holds the essence of the Yolŋu heart and spirit.

'Your love is here.' The voice of my *waku* shakes me back into the moment. He has been sitting quietly with us the whole time. Earlier, he was dancing with the boys.

His big dark eyes look into me. 'Your love will be with us, *ŋänd̠i*.' He waves his hand out across the sea. 'When you are gone, your love will be here,' he says.

'*Yow, yuwalk, Waku*. Thank you, *Waku*, and you will be with me too,' I respond.

And it is true.

No matter how far I roam, and even when I am alone, I am cocooned in the communal spirit of my Yolŋu family, and held, firmly grounded in my being, by the spirit of Arnhem Land.

# Statements by Yurrwi women

## Jessie Murarrgirarrgi

1 September 2013

*Ḏamurruŋ'puy Mälk* (*Saltwater Skin*) is the *yuṯa yäku* for this book. [Jessie and the author had discussed a few names for the book. Together they chose *Ḏamurruŋ'puy Mälk*.]

When first Mary came to Milingimbi school as a teacher, as the ILSS (Indigenous language speaking students) teacher for ESL, I was just looking at her. I'm singing, 'I am sixteen going on seventeen' and after that she started talking to me and asking me to take her out to go and get pandanus, to learn how to weave, go out hunting to get crabs and I was taking her, just taking her for her own interest and with all other ladies: Paula, Boyukarrpi number 2 and my sister Dorothy Muwalk-muwuy (number 1), going out sitting, collecting pandanus, going out to get *nyoka*, just sitting at the campfire, just talking about Milingimbi or our fathers or our parents' lifetime.

Because I like Mary, she was a yoga lady. I like to go and she can do massage, and when she was doing that I was feeling like way back in my young time, after she was doing healing. She was doing healing. She did lots of healing at Milingimbi. The more she did, the more she learned, too. I like her yoga music, too, and I'm still asking her about that. When I visit her, I'm already tired, and I go to her door, open the door, and that yoga music just already playing and I can go in and I could just relax and listen to that yoga music, like sailing away with a ship. Her room was quiet, silent, and she teach me how to relax or to have a rest. After all that, the work I did, seven days a week, she encouraged me to do less when I was tired and rest. That's why I liked her, because she taught me about relaxing, relaxing, just go, sit on the beach and get something else for yourself, rug, and put it on the sand and just rest and you can feel the air, breeze, coming to you, birds. You could hear the sound of the water; just have time on your own, quiet.

I went to her house and I said, 'I need to get some potato from you,' and I did, couple, and I brought them back to my sister Elizabeth. I introduce Mary to my other family. I said, 'This is *Yapa* Mary. She works at the school but nobody [has] adopted her. Can anyone? I mean, I can adopt her but I want an elder in my family to adopt her.' And my sister Elizabeth adopted her and gave her her own name and with her, she was like our family to all of us, *wäwa, yapa, waku*, all sister[s], brother[s], our son[s], daughters, grandsons granddaughters, all nephew[s], niece[s], and she was like to us, like our own family.

But because of her job taking her away, far away country: Bali, India, Bhutan, throughout Australia, overseas. She could ring us, we could ring her: 'Where are you?' Just saying hello and how she is, finding out how she is getting on. With our hearts we could still touch her or contact her even here, when she has holidays back at home: 'Where are you?' We could still say, 'Hello, Merry Christmas, Happy New Year to you,' all the little bits and pieces, or we say, '*Yapa*, you know so so, they passed away, *ŋäthi*.'

So, something was connected to us and to her and it doesn't matter that she travels around, our communication in spirit was travelling around with her, and that's how I, we, knew about her and me. I learn from her how to relax, about yoga, healing and even though she was teaching me, I have been teaching others, doing the same thing and doing the same thing when she left, helping others relax. This is what *yapa* taught me: how to help people where they aching or paining, and she said to me, relax, just close the door and be on your own. Even she taught me to eat nice food for our body, and that's how I learn, that's how I know my *yapa*.

Even year after years going past, even if she doesn't ring me, I can ring her. 'Hello, where are you?' *Yapa*'s favourite word she used is *gurrupurungu*, and I was going see my sister Yibi and say, '*Yä, Yapa Yibi, gurrupurungu* Mary, can we ring? Wonder where she is. I can say hello.' And she does and we both call, her and me Ganyawu, we talk a lot about Mary and the Djambaŋ, Ganyawu's aunties and mothers and others, because she was like close family to us even though she was busy doing teaching.

That's how I knew about Mary McCarthy, and she came back yesterday from Mäpuru. When she was at Mäpuru, me and *yapa* said that's our family too, that's our blood family because of our mother's totem, *ŋändi*'s side. Our mother *ŋathi*, their father, they had *waŋgany* father, all *djamarrkuḻi*' there and *waku ga nhina* [sat] there, they family. *Yow.* Like from two *ŋathi*s.

Mary's story is a story. That story, we need that story in the library just to teach other teachers or friends or other Europeans coming in and telling us, and we could keep that one story in the library. We might keep that for our Yolŋu *matha*, and *yow yapa ga wäwa*'s story and their lifetime, and *waku* too, and I love what she is doing and it's not just for herself. Something that she lived Milingimbi for seven years, and seven years was something she thought was good to do, and she is going out and sharing and I'm happy.

*Ma'!*

## Judith Maḏupinyin Ganyawu (author's gäthu – brother's daughter)

30 August 2013

(Translation support by Gwen Warmbirrirr)

I'm Ganyawu.

I work at the office at the school. *Yow nhawi*, I'm going to tell you a story about Mary McCarthy. She came here to Milingimbi in 2003. *Yow*, she came to Milingimbi, to Yurrwi. She was working as a teacher at the school.

We didn't know that she was coming here, but she came here to work at the school. The boss from the department had sent her here to work as a teacher. *Yow*, we don't know that she had *ŋayaŋu*, the heart for Yolŋu people, she had closeness to Yolŋu people.

*Yow*, when she came, she was adopted by Yibi Yibi. *Yow*, she was adopted by Yibi Yibi. I didn't know that she was adopted by my *mukul bäpa*, my aunty Yibi Yibi and Mary became my aunty as well, my *mukul bäpa* and our friend. *Yow*, when Mary was adopted by Yibi Yibi, she became a part of us, our family.

*Yow*, she became a friend, our ḻundu, and family. She was meeting *dharrwa* old women and she worked with them with *gunga djäma*, pandanus gathering *ga* stripping, and she met with my mother[s] like Munguli, Gamuti, Djämbutj, Ḏarandarrawuy, Judy, Liku's wife, Sandra, Jackie's wife, Djuwandaŋur's mother. And she was like a friend and a family.

*Yow*, she knew everyone in the community, she came here to teach our *djamarrkuḻi'*, the children here at Milingimbi school, but she was like family.

*Yow*, she learned. She was taught by Dorothy Muwalkmuwuy, Jessie's sister, to make pandanus baskets made out of pandanus leaves and she was taught by those old ladies *ŋarraku ŋäŋḏi 'mirriŋu mala*, my aunties and my mum.

*Yow*, she went with those old ladies, my aunties and my mother Munguli *ga* she was learning Yolŋu ways of hunting. She knew how she was connected to the Yolŋu people and that's how we became her family, even though her family was long way but she became one of us, she became a family and a friend, learning all these Yolŋu ways of hunting *ga* how to make a basket made out of pandanus, *yow*.

*Yow*, she was well adapted to us, to the Yolŋu families, and she learnt a lot of all those things they had taught Mary. She was part of us, even though she was from a long way, she was a *balanda miyalk* but she became our family.

*Yow*, Mary taught the older ladies all the healing *djäma*, healing through yoga and always sharing healing, learning more too, and that's why we loved her and she knew everything that she was taught from these Yolŋu people, she learned through the older ladies here at Djämbaŋ and all my aunties.

Mary was like my aunty, like Yibi Yibi, ga Muwalkmuwuy and Linda Slim, Mawukuwuy, yow, she was like my own *mukul bäpa* on my father's side. She was my father's sister in Yolŋu ways. She learnt well. I was surprised. I didn't know Mary was adopted by Yibi Yibi. I knew her from my mother and my aunties and from my *mukul bäpa* Yibi Yibi and that's why I was so close to her. Like she had the heart for Yolŋu people.

When I heard that Mary was adopted to Yibi Yibi I was so happy, my heart jumped for joy that I knew that I had another *mukul bäpa*, a *balanda mukul bäpa*. *Yow*, my whole body was happy from head to foot because I knew that Mary was in my family, in my father's side family. Yeah, she was my *mukul bäpa*. And that's why I knew her and that's why I love her.

*Yow*, that's why I need to show her *yindi'*, great respect for she became my *mukul bäpa*, my aunty, and I had to welcome her into my home and into my house. She can come any time and sit with us under the *Djambaŋ* tree.

*Yow*, that's why I had to show her that respect, because I call her *mukul bäpa* like Yibi Yibi, like, Mawukuwuy, like Jessie, like all the others married to Mary's *wäwa*[s] *ga yapa*[s]. *Wäwa*[s] *ga yapas*.

Yibi Yibi gave her her own name, Yibi Yibi.

She gave her *bäpurru ga bundurr* and she taught her *Rom'*. Yolŋu culture and language. Yibi Yibi introduced Mary to all my other fathers, my uncles and aunties and that's why Mary learnt a lot from my uncles, aunties and my father, all the Yolŋu *Rom'*, Yolŋu culture, Yolŋu ways hunting. She learnt a lot.

She became our real family in Yolŋu ways when was adopted.

She came from somewhere, we don't know, she was somebody but we knew she was Mary, our *mukul bäpa* and a family and a friend. We don't know where she came from but she became one of us, she was like Yibi Yibi and Mawukuwuy, she was like all the other aunties and uncles and she taught our kids and she taught the older ladies and she taught us, she became one of us.

*Yow*, when she came she learned everything, Yolŋu culture. She learnt *marrŋgitj djäma ga* she learned from my mother's side of my family and *bäpa* side family. They taught her, she taught them. She knew everything of Yolŋu culture. They were teaching her all the culture, all the Yolŋu *Rom'*, *ŋarraku* family, my family were teaching her and she taught them. They were teaching each other.

Like this time now, Mary is like a Yolŋu person. She's like a Yolŋu black colour like *ŋarra* Ganyawu, she was like a Yolŋu person in a white skin. She was a Yolŋu person in a white skin, she had the heart for Yolŋu people, she had the ways, thoughts, feelings, thinking for Yolŋu people. She was like Yolŋu.

*Yow*, like we love her so much, all around here in Milingimbi, everyone knows her and everyone loves her because she had the heart for Yolŋu people and that's why they love her. They love Mary because she was like one of us.

She was a *manymak miyalk*, she was friendly to everyone, she loved Yolŋu people, she loved Milingimbi and she loved the community and that's why we love her.

She's *manymak miyalk*, happy *miyalk*, when she goes away to see her friends and family, she always had her thoughts and heart for Milingimbi and she sometimes rings us to find out how we are and she rings and says, '*Nhämirr nhuma Yolŋu mala, marrkap mala.*'

When she was here, she was teaching everyone and the Yolŋu people taught her.

*Yow*, she's a *manymak miyalk*. *Latju. Yow*, she was always *manymak* from the beginning and now that she is finishing up her *djäma* here at Milingimbi she was always *manymak miyalk* and will always be *manymak miyalk*.

When she gets worried, she rings and says she is coming back to Milingimbi.

*Yow*, she was learning all the *buŋgul*, she's dancing Yolŋu, *ga* Dhuwa *ga* Yirritja *buŋgul, ŋayi marŋgi miyalk. Yow, Rom'* she learned.

She doesn't say but she is Yolŋu, yow, because she loves the Yolŋu and that's why she does the dancing and learning culture.

Mary taught the kids and she brought her knowledge of yoga *djäma* and healing *djäma* to the community. She brought something new to Yolŋu people so that's why when people got sick they came to her and knew that she had brought in something that can help and teach Yolŋu.

It's *manymak* for Mary to make that *dhäwu* into a book, so that when we die the children that are growing up or are yet to come to Milingimbi will know that story of what Mary had been doing here with the Yolŋu people here. Those children will know that story.

All the photos that she had been taking, she needs to put them into that book and what she had been learning from all the Yolŋu people here, it's okay for you, Mary, to put it into a book, so everyone will know that *djäma* that you did here. It will teach other young generations.

I'm happy for me from Ganyawu, for you to share that *dhäwu*, what you have learned from the Yolŋu people. Everyone here will know about it and all the world will know about that *djorra'*.

And those people who are gone before us already know what you are doing, and you can share what they were teaching you, and you were lucky that you could sit with them and learn from them while they were here. We are all happy about it.

*Yow, bilin.*

## Gwen Warmbirrirr speaks about religion and Yolŋu
11 January 2016

Mary McCarthy: Can you talk to me about religion and Yolŋu, *Waku*?

Gwen: *Yow, Ḏändi*. Religion came to the Yolŋu people, it was brought in by the mission. Before the mission came, Yolŋu had their own identity, their own *nhawi*, spirituality. People can take two pathways, one for their identity and one for their spiritual pathway. That's what I believe. Nowadays they are doing that. But before, our Yolŋu people had identity, their own identity, to identify themselves as Yolŋu people, and their spiritual identity connects them to the land and to everything around them, the environment. Sometimes when a person is reading, looking at the Bible, and those stories are different in the Bible. That made people change sometimes, change their thinking about how we exist in this world, you know? And that's why sometimes people need to understand where we are coming from and where we have been there, like long time ago we were the creation of God, and all our places and areas, even though that is our identity but still need to think about someone, our bigger God source. The world before that was created by him and for him and through him, yow, but we are Yolŋu people, we are still Yolŋu people. In a *bäpurru* we have connections to that *buŋgul*, we need to understand who we are and who we were made of. At the *bäpurru* we do connect Yolŋu ways of life into religious ceremony. Yolŋu have religious ceremony in their own ways, but to Christianity ways, it's different from Yolŋu ways, even though one is the Christian way, though that there are two kinds of religious spirituality. One is the Christian way where we believe this through reading the Bible. We believe there is a way we can connect to God through spirituality.

Mary: So how do you meet the two, *Waku*?

Gwen: To *ŋarrakal*, to my understanding, I don't mix them, because Yolŋu is Yolŋu ways and Christianity is Christianity. I don't mix them. To Yolŋu, if I'm a Yolŋu I do it in Yolŋu way, but if I'm going to the church, it's different.

Mary: Thank you, *Waku*. I'd like to understand more about this. Maybe we can talk more about it again one day.

Gwen: *Yow, manymak, Ḏä<u>nd</u>i, marrkap.*

# Glossary

All words listed are in the Djambarrpuyŋu or Gupapuyŋu languages unless otherwise stated.

**Pronunciation**

ŋ = ng as pronounced in song.

ä = long a as in father.

d̠ l̠ n̠ t̠ = retroflex consonants formed with the tongue curled backwards against the palate

' = glottal stop.

**Vowels**

short vowels – a as in about, i as in bin

long vowels – ä as in father, e different in length to English (try lengthening the in as in bin)

u as in put; o as in pore

**Consonants**

b, g, k, l, p, m, n, t, w, y – as in English

dh, th, nh – pronounced with tongue between teeth

dj – as in jug

tj – somewhat similar to ch as in church

ny – as in news

ng – as in song

(To learn more, go to www.learnline.cdu.au/yolngustudies)

# Yolŋu words

**A**

| | |
|---|---|
| arrawa | home (Burarra language) |

**B**

| | |
|---|---|
| baba'mirri | miss, make a mistake, behave in a silly way |
| babalamirr | anything |
| ba<u>d</u>ak | wait, still |
| bala | there, away, that way, direction away from speaker |
| balgurr | name of tree used for grass skirts, string |
| ba<u>n</u>umbirr | morning star |
| Baŋa<u>d</u>itjan | a skin name, mälk |
| bäpa | father and his brothers (uncles), father in sense of minister of religion |
| bäpi | snake |
| Bäpurru | clan group name, funeral ceremony |
| barrarirri | scared, frightened |
| barrku | far away, away off, distant, long (distance), move back, move away |
| bäru | crocodile |
| bathan | cook |
| bathi | pandanus basket |
| bäydhi | never mind, don't worry |
| bäyŋu | nothing, none |
| bi<u>l</u>ayn | plane |
| bili | because, since |
| bili(n) | (are you) finished, (I've) finished) or (I've completed the work |
| bilitjbilitj | coloured parrot |
| bi<u>l</u>ma | clap stick(s) |
| Birrimbirr | soul, human spirit |
| birrka'yun | try, test |
| Birrkili | clan nation |
| bitjan | like this |
| bitjarr(a) | this is what he/she said |
| bittja (') | photo, picture |
| Bol'ŋu | lightning man, lightning power, thunder |
| bondi | hurry, quickly |

| | |
|---|---|
| Buku-lup bungul | cleansing ceremony with water |
| bul'manydji | shark |
| bulangitj | excellent, good (Yan-nhaŋu language and many others use this word) |
| buliki' | cow |
| bulu | more |
| bun'kumu | knees |
| bunapi' | trepang, sea cucumber |
| bundurr | totemic name given to clan; special name given to person relating to clan territory or totems |
| bungawa | leader, boss, manager |
| bungul | ceremony |
| Burarra | name of language |
| burruṯji | snake, water python |

## D

| | |
|---|---|
| ḏaḏa'yun | cleanse, purify in ceremony (for example, house of a dead person by burning branches around it) |
| ḏamurruŋ' | saltwater, brackish water |
| ḏetj | grasshopper |
| dhäkay-ŋäma | feeling about something, feeling for the land, deep feeling within or experience of land, ancestors, law |
| dhapirrk' | great, fantastic |
| dharpa | 1. tree, branch, stick 2. hooked stick to pull pandanus |
| dhäruk | words |
| dhäwu | story, news |
| dhipal(a) | here |
| dhiyal(a) | here |
| dhiyaŋu bala | now |
| dhu | future marker |
| dhukarr | road, path |
| dhulumburrk | purple water lily In kin terms, my manyi |
| dhumumu | used to make black dye for weaving pandanus roots; inedible fruit quinine bush, *Petalostigma pubescens* |

| | |
|---|---|
| dhumungur(') | grandchild's (female gutharra's) husband, avoidance relationship, grandchild (in opposite moiety) |
| dhunupa | straight |
| dhuŋa | don't know |
| Dhuwa | name of moiety |
| dhuwal(a) | this |
| Dhuwala | name of language |
| Dhuwala'mirri | name of Wäwa Jo's language |
| dhuwali | that (near the person addressed) |
| dhuway | husband (real or classificatory), brother-in-law, sister-in-law, first cousin (in opposite moiety), 'mate' |
| ḏimiṯimirr | spikes, thorns from pandanus fronds (in hands from collecting pandanus) |
| ḏiltji | bush |
| ḏirrpu(') | root of waterlily, baman'puy ŋatha (food people ate long ago) |
| ḏirramu | man, boy |
| ḏiyamu | shellfish found in shallow mud or sand |
| djäl | want, like, love |
| djäma | work |
| djamarrkuḻi ' | children |
| djambaŋ | tamarind fruit/tree |
| Djambarrpuyŋu | name of clan and language |
| djanda | goanna |
| djäri | rainbow |
| djawaryun | be tired |
| djirripum(a) | (a) stroke, massage |
| djorra' | book, paper |
| djuŋgayi (buŋgawa) | leader, boss, land owner, manager |
| djutjutjnha | keep on going, off you go, goodbye |
| ḏoṯurrk | heart |
| Doyduyŋu or Wunaŋu | totemic lightning snake ancestor who created the waterhole at Milingimbi, also Mundukuḻ Wunaŋu |
| ḏupṯupthun | beating (of heart) |

# G

| | |
|---|---|
| ga | and |
| ga balanya | like this |
| gadaman | strong, knowing, clever |
| galay | wife (real or classificatory), 'mate', brother-in-law, sister-in-law, first cousin (of opposite moiety), her sisters and brothers (mother's brother's child) |
| galigali(') | an instrument used to produce a clapping sound at specific ceremonies |
| galka | sorcerer |
| galki | close, close by |
| galkurr(u) | wait (for) |
| galpu' | woomera, spear thrower used at Därra' and Dharpa ceremony |
| Gamalaŋga | name of language and clan |
| gaminyarr | grandchild (of opposite moiety), first cousin once removed, grand-niece, grand-nephew |
| gamunuŋgu' | white clay (some say gamu) |
| ganydjarr | power, strength, speed |
| ganyu | star |
| gaŋga | careful |
| gäŋu | carry (it), bring (it), take (it) |
| gapu | water |
| gäthu | grandchild (of opposite moiety), first cousin once removed, grand-niece, grand-nephew, father's child, nephew or niece of your brother child, son, daughter (of father), niece, nephew, daughter-in-law (of woman), great-grandparent of same moiety |
| gara | spear |
| gäthur(a) | today |
| gay'wu | string for dilly bag |
| girri' | gear, clothes, things |
| giyalaram(a) | process of stripping pandanus |
| godarr' | later, tomorrow |
| godjula | beach (Burarra language) |
| gopu' | fish, marlin |

| | |
|---|---|
| gora | shy |
| gu | come |
| gudurrku | brolga |
| guku | honey |
| guku manikay | honey song |
| gulun | waterhole, billabong, womb, stomach |
| gunda | rock |
| gundirr (') | red ant hill, used to burn in fires for some ceremonies; can be used to send away mosquitoes |
| gunga | pandanus |
| gunga djäma | pandanus work |
| guŋga'yurru! | help! |
| guninyi | edible fruit that is used as a medicine for coughs, and roots as a dye for pandanus |
| guŋurru | purple colour made from grey ash mixed with yellow (from two different trees) |
| Gupapuyŋu | name of clan and language |
| gurul | visiting; go to see someone |
| gurrpan | call by relationship |
| gurrugurru | shelter for the body, a general term sometimes used but there are different names for different tribes |
| gurruŋ | avoidance relationship, son-in-law (female-ego), 'poison cousin', second cousin, mother-in-law or her brother |
| gurrumattji | magpie geese |
| gurrupan | give |
| gurrupuruŋu | oh, poor thing; term of affection |
| gurrutjutju | hawk (Yirritja) |
| gurrutu | kin, family |
| Gurryindi | name of clan nation and language |
| gutha(') | younger brother/sister, younger first cousin |
| gutharra | grandchild (of the same moiety), marratja |
| gutharra (marratja)' | grandchild (of the same moiety) marratja, grandchild of your male gäthu |
| guyaŋa | thinking |
| guyiŋarr | cold |

## H
| | |
|---|---|
| huntinglil | hunting |

## I
| | |
|---|---|
| ininjaya | where are you? (Burarra language) |

## L
| | |
|---|---|
| lakaram | tell |
| lalu | parrot fish |
| larrtha | mangroves |
| latjin | mangrove worms |
| latju | beautiful, nice |
| -lil | suffix – to |
| limurr(u) | we, inclusive |
| limurruŋ | ours, belonging to us |
| litjalaŋ | ours |
| liw'maraŋal | surround, around |
| liya | head |
| liya rathala' or rathala | headache |
| luka | eat, drink, consume |
| lundu | friend |
| luplupthun | wash, swim, bathe |

## M
| | |
|---|---|
| ma' | okay; go on; get on with it |
| madayin | sacred |
| mak | maybe |
| mak bay | maybe, might |
| mala | group |
| mälk | skin |
| manda | they (two); dual term used to address two people |
| malthun | follow, join, go with |
| Mandayala | name of ceremony |
| manhdhapidi(') | shellfish medicine for ear problems |
| manimani | bracelet or necklace from seeds |
| manymak | good, thanks |
| mäpan | boil |
| maranydjalk | stingray |
| maralkur | avoidance relationship, grand-uncle, mother-in-law's brother; an abbreviation is mukul-rumaru |

| | |
|---|---|
| märi | maternal grandmother, grand-uncle, paternal grandfather, mother's mother and her siblings (grandmother and great-uncle) |
| märi'mu' | paternal grandfather, grand-aunt |
| marŋgi | know, identify |
| marŋgithirr(i) | teach |
| märr | spiritual essence |
| märriyaŋ | gun |
| marrkapmirr | term of endearment |
| märrma | two |
| marrŋu | possum |
| marrtji | go walk |
| marrtjin | past tense go |
| marwat | long thin leaves, hair |
| matha | language, tongue |
| mayali' | meaning of something |
| mayaŋ | river, neck |
| maypiny | leaves for smoking ceremony |
| mel | eyes |
| mel-bambaydhi | close (your) eyes |
| menduŋ | snail |
| midiku | yapa, sister |
| miku | red ochre used as body paint |
| milkarri | tears, crying song |
| milmitjpa | afternoon |
| milmitjpa wo munhna gu | afternoon or night |
| mimi | spirit |
| miny'tji | colours, design, painting |
| mirritjin' | medicine |
| mirithirr(i) | very, loudly, a great deal |
| -mirriŋu | kinship marker |
| -'mirriŋu | kinship proprietive; for example. bäpa'mirriŋu: one's (true) father |
| miyalk' | woman, girl |
| miyapunu | turtle (collective term, general name) |
| mokuy | spirit |
| mol | name for the colour black |
| monuk | salt water |

| | |
|---|---|
| momu | father's mothers and her sisters; paternal grandmother, grand-aunt |
| mori' | father |
| muka | is that right? indeed! definitely! (question or agreement indicator) |
| mukul | 1. aunty, grand-aunt, mother-in-law (of mother); 2. avoidance relationship, grand-aunt, or real mother-in-law (of male) |
| mukul bäpa | father's sister |
| mukul rumaru | mother-in-law and her sisters (mother's brother's wife), male märi's daughter, avoidance relationship, grand-uncle, mother-in-law's brother; an abbreviation is mukul-rumaru (female dhuway's child (FSOC) |
| muḻmuḻ | white foam |
| mumalkur | wife's mother's mother, male märi's wife. avoidance relationship, grand-aunt, mother-in-law's mother |
| mumalkur | avoidance relationship, grand-aunt, mother-in-law's mother |
| mundukuḻ' | water python, sometimes referred to as rainbow serpent |
| munhagu | night |
| munhaŋaniŋ(') | gecko |
| munydjutj | green bush fruit |
| mutamuta | plant used as medicine to make a poultice for boils |

## N

| | |
|---|---|
| napurr | we (not you) |
| nhä | what |
| nhaku bili | what for? |
| nhäkurr(u)(') | where to? |
| nhäma | look, see; for example, nhäma nhe ga? |
| nhämirr(i) | how are (you)? |
| nhäŋal(a) | I looked, saw |
| nhäŋu | Look! This here |
| nhäpuy | what about |
| nhätha | when? |

| | |
|---|---|
| nhawi | what's its name, thing |
| nhe | you |
| nhini | sit (request) |
| nhumalaŋ | all of you (non-inclusive); nhuma for short; yours (plural) |
| nhuŋu | yours |
| ṉinydjiya | saltpans |
| ṉirriwan | oysters |
| ṉonḏa | longbum mud creeper |
| nyoka' | mud crab |
| nyumukuṉiny | little |

## ŋ

| | |
|---|---|
| ŋali | us together, you and me |
| ŋaḻindi | moon |
| ŋäma | listen, hear |
| ŋama' | mother or ŋäṉdi |
| ŋäṉdi | mother and her sisters (aunties) or ŋama' or ŋamala (aunty also) |
| ŋänitji | alcohol |
| ŋäŋ'thun | ask |
| ŋapipi | mother's brother(s), uncle(s), grand-uncle, aunt, great-grandparent of (opposite moiety), great-grandfather, great-grandmother, grandson, grandaughter |
| ŋarali' | cigarette |
| ŋarra | I |
| Ŋärra' | law, ceremony |
| ŋarraku | mine |
| ŋatha | food |
| ŋathi | maternal grandfather, grand-uncle |
| ŋäthi | cry |
| ŋathiwalkur | avoidance relationship, grand-uncle, wife's mother's mother's brother |
| ŋayaŋu | feeling for Yolŋu; heart and feeling in heart |
| ŋayi | he, she, it or here (you are) |
| ŋayipa | love, like (Burarra language) |
| ŋerrk | white cockatoo; Yirritja totem |
| ŋuli | usually, always, often, that/there, recently |

| | |
|---|---|
| ŋunha bala, ŋunhala | over there |
| -ŋur(a) | at (suffix) |
| ŋurru | nose, point |

## P
| | |
|---|---|
| puy | about (suffix) |

## R
| | |
|---|---|
| rägudha | mussel |
| raki' | rope, string |
| räli | come |
| raypiny | fresh water, sweet good taste |
| rerri' | sick |
| riŋgitj | place which is sacred to special people. |
| rirrikthun | sick |
| Rom' | Law |
| roɲiyirr(i) | return, go back |
| rrambaɲi | the same, together |
| rrupiya | money |
| rumaru(') | tabooed (relative, avoidance kin, for example, mother-in-law) |
| rumaru (mukul) | avoidance relationship, grand-aunt, mother-in-law |
| rumbal | body |

## S
| | |
|---|---|
| sha / shibay / djibay | go away (generally to dogs) |

## W
| | |
|---|---|
| wäk | crow |
| waku | mother's child, nephew or niece of your sister, child, son, daughter, niece, nephew, son-in-law, first cousin, aunt, grand-uncle, great-grandparent (of opposite moiety), great-grandfather, great-grandmother, grandson, granddaughter |
| wakuluŋgul' | mist, morning fog |
| waltjan | rain |
| walu | sun, time |
| wandirr(i) | run travel |
| wanha | where? |
| waŋa | speak, say, talk |

| | |
|---|---|
| wäŋa | home, place, land, house |
| waŋan | said |
| wäŋa-waṯaŋu | landowner |
| waŋarr | ancestral totemic beings, totem dreaming |
| waŋgany | one |
| Wangurri | name of language/clan |
| waṉi | speak! (command) |
| waŋupini | cumulonimbus clouds |
| warguyun / warwuyu / wargugu / warwuwu | worry, grieving |
| Warrabunbun | mimi spirit |
| warrakan | animals, meat |
| Warramiri | name of clan and language |
| warrpam' | all, everybody, the whole lot |
| wata | wind, gentle breezee |
| waṯaŋu | traditional owner |
| waṯu | dog |
| wäwa | similar age brother; wäwa older brother; also a general term applied to a male outside the gurruṯu system |
| wäy! | hey! |
| weṯi | wallaby |
| winyiwinyi | little bats |
| wiripu | different |
| wititj | snake, olive python – Dhuwa moiety |
| wo | or |
| Wunaŋu or Doyduyŋu | totemic lightning snake ancestor Mundukul̲-Motj, also Mundukul̲ |
| wurrpan̲ | emu |

## Y

| | |
|---|---|
| yä | oh yes; ah! |
| yaka | no, not |
| yäku | name |
| yalala | later |
| Yalakun | place name |
| yapa | sister (of male), elder sister (of female); general term sometimes used for non-Yolŋu women when their relationship is not known. |

| | |
|---|---|
| Yan-nhaŋu | name of language |
| yaŋara | tail, leg |
| yätj(kurr) | bad, no good, evil, sick |
| yindi(') | big |
| yiriŋaniŋ(') | red seeds for manimani necklaces |
| Yirritja | moiety name |
| Yirrkala | place name |
| yolku | whose |
| Yolŋu | people of north-east Arnhem Land |
| yothu | child |
| yothu-yindi | identifies as a mother-child relationship, expresses the link between different relationships (for example, people, clan groups, places, totems |
| Yothu Yindi | band |
| yow | yes, greeting |
| yupthurr(u) | get down |
| yuṯa | new, fresh, young |
| yuwalk | true |

## Yolŋu reciprocal relationships

### Dhuwa mälk

| female | male |
|---|---|
| Galiyan, Galikali | Burralaŋ' |
| Wamuttjan | Wämut |
| Bilinydjan | Balaŋ' |
| Gamanydjan | Gamarraŋ' |

Each pair above is brother and sister.

### Yirritja mälk

| female | male |
|---|---|
| Buḻanydjan | Buḻany |
| Gutjan | Gayak, Guyuk, Gudjuk |
| Ŋarritjan | Ŋarritj |
| Baŋaḏitjan | Baŋaḏi |

Each pair above is brother and sister.
Yirritja marries Dhuwa. Dhuwa marries Yirritja.

## Seasons

February–March     *Mayaltha*     Flowering season
Within the Wet, before bush foods are ready around March.

March–April     *Mi<u>d</u>awarr*     Fruiting season
Just after the Wet when bush foods are ripe, animals are fat, seafood is plentiful and the wind blows from the east.

May–July     *Dharratharra'*     Early Dry
In the Dry season when it is chilly and there are plenty of yams and bush food, cold weather.

August–October     *Rarranhdharr' mirri*
Late in the Dry season when it is very hot, fresh water is scarce, animals are getting thin and feet are scorched when walking. Stringybark blossoms signal wild honey.

October–November     *Dhulu<u>d</u>ur(')*     Pre-wet
End of the Dry, very hot, humid. It is the build-up to the Wet season. There are black clouds and thunder but not necessarily rain. Plants develop new shoots.

December–January     *Bärra' mirri*     Growth season
Winds blow before the Wet.

## Yoga terms

| | |
|---|---|
| Adho Mukha Svanasana | dog pose |
| Anjali Mudra | 'The palms are not flat against each other but are shaped like the bud of a flower' (*Yoga Reminder*, A.G. Mohan) |
| Asana | posture, pose |
| Dharana | one of the eight limbs of yoga: concentration |
| Ganesha | Hindu deity; remover of obstacles |
| Garudasana | eagle pose |
| Isvara Pranidhana | the practice of connecting with the divine within us with trust |
| Kundulini | awakening from the base of the spine |
| Kurmasana | tortoise pose |
| Lakshmi | Hindu goddess of prosperity and compassion |
| Mantra | series of syllables or words, used as a focus to calm or steady the fluctuations of the |

| | |
|---|---|
| | mind and repeated to create a new set of latent impressions |
| Marjaryasana | cat pose |
| Meditation | fix attention steadily on a subject of your choice to change the state of mind and see clearly. |
| Nadi Shodana | Pranayama; alternate nostril breathing |
| Niyamas | internal discipline |
| Prana | breath of life |
| Pranayama | the practice of pranayama is used to extend and regulate the breath and remove impurities of the mind |
| Santosha | one of the Niyamas: contentment |
| Saraswati | Hindu deity; teacher, communication, music |
| Sesha | serpent, kundulini shakti |
| Shavasana | corpse pose |
| Surya Namaska | salute to the sun |
| Tadasana | mountain pose |
| Tara | Tara goddess; compassion, truth; mantra can be used |
| Tratak | candle gazing to increase Dharana (concentration) and a spiritual practice |
| Uttanasana | standing forward bend |
| Vishnu | Hindu deity; part of a trilogy; preserver; |
| Viparita Karani | legs up the wall |
| Vipassana meditation | a practice of fixed attention on the breathe, 'to see reality as it is, not as it appears to be' |
| Virabhadrasana | warrior pose |
| Vrksasana | tree pose |
| Yamas | behavioural observances |

## Yoga teachers mentioned

| | |
|---|---|
| A.G. Mohan, Indra Mohan | Krishnamacharya, teachers of Svastha Yoga |
| Tirumala Krishnamachrya | 'the father of modern yoga', 1888–1989 |
| Thich Nhat Hanh | Vietnamese Zen Buddhist Master based in the south of France at Plum village |

# References

## Books

Almaas, A.H., 1998, *Essence with the Elixir of Enlightenment: The Diamond Approach to Inner Realization*. Weiser Books.

Baymarrwaŋa, Laurie and James, Bentley, 2014, *Yan-Nhaŋu Atlas and Illustrated Dictionary of the Crocodile Islands*.

Byron, Lord, 1881, *Poetry of Byron, Lord Byron, 1788–1824*, Chosen and Arranged by Matthew Arnold. Macmillan, London.

Campbell, Joseph, 1995, *Reflections on the Art of Living: A Joseph Campbell Companion*. Selected and edited by Diane K. Osborn, Harper Perennial.

Cawte, John, 1972, *Healers of Arnhem Land*. UNSW Press, Australia.

—, 1993, *The Universe of the Warramirri: Art, Medicine and Religion in Arnhem Land*. University of NSW Press.

Davis, Stephen, 1984, *The Hunter For All Seasons: An Aboriginal Perspective of the Natural Environment*. Milingimbi School Literature Production, NT.

Donaldson, Mike, 2012, *Kimberley Rock Art: Volume 2: North Kimberley*. Wildrocks Publications, Mt Lawley.

Gilbert, Kevin, 1999, *Black from the Edge*. Photographs, Eleanor Williams, Hyland House.

Hakanson, Donni, 1998, *Oracle of the Dreamtime: Aboriginal Dreamings Offer Guidance for Today*, cards. Journey Editions.

Hanh, Nhat, Thich, 2015, *Breath is the Bridge: Meditation Practices for the Miracle of Mindfulness: An Introduction to the Practice of Meditation*. Ebury Publishing, London.

Isaacs, Jennifer, 1980, *Australian Dreaming: 40,000 Years of Aboriginal History*, Lansdowne Publishing, Sydney.

Marika, Wandjuk, 1995, *Wandjuk Marika Life Story: As Told to Jennifer Isaacs*. University of Queensland Press, St Lucia.

Marshall, James Vance, 1979, *Walkabout*. Puffin, first published by Michael Joseph, 1959, as *The Children*.

Mohan, A.G., 1993, *Yoga for Body, Breath, and Mind: A Guide to Personal Reintegration*. Shambala Publications, Boston and London.

Mohan, A.G., 2015, *Yoga Reminder: Lightened Reflection*. Svastha Yoga.

Mundine, Djon OAM, 2000, *The Native Born: Objects and Representations from Ramingining, Arnhem Land*. Museum of Contemporary Art in assocociation with Bula'bula' Arts, Ramingining.

Piccoult, Jodi, 2015, *Change of Heart*. Hodder & Stoughton, London.

Rilke, Rainer Maria, 2012, *Letters to a Young Poet (1875–1920)*. Merchant Books.

Reid, Janice, 1982, *Sorcerers and Healing Spirits: Continuity and Change in an Aboriginal Medical System*. Books Australia.

Sendak, Maurice, 1963, *Where the Wild Things Are*, Harper & Row

Thompson, Donald, 1983, *Donald Thompson in Arnhemland*, compiled and introduced by Nicolas Peterson. Curry O'Neill Ross.

Tweedie, Jill, 1998, *Aboriginal Australians: Spirit of Arnhemland*. New Holland, Sydney.

## Language

Baymarrwaŋa, Laurie, and James Bentley, 2014, *Yan-Nhaŋu Atlas and Illustrated Dictionary of the Crocodile Islands*.

Christie, Michael J., 2001–2008, Yolŋu Languages and Culture, Gupapuyŋu Books and CDs pack, Charles Darwin University.

Greatorex, John, Yolŋu–Matha Dictionary, online resource, Charles Darwin University, http://yolngudictionary.cdu.edu.au/

Lowe, Beulah, 2004, *Yolŋu–English Dictionary*, Aboriginal Resource and Development Services Inc., Darwin.

Zorc, R. David Paul, 1996, *Yolŋu–Matha Dictionary*. Charles Darwin University, Batchelor, NT.

## Songs

Mac, Johnnie, 'Highway', 'One Farewell'.

## Films

Baymarrwaŋa, Laurie, 2012, Senior Elder of the Year. Senior Australian of the Year awards.

Guyula, Yiŋiya, Mark, 2015, *Lifestyle Choice? The Land is Part of Us. The Yolŋu people of Arnhem Land*. ABC, *The Sydney Morning Herald*. Our Say. Primal Vision Films.

*The Intervention: Riyawarray, Common Ground*. A film by the Yolŋu People of East Arnhem Land.

Nair, Mira (director), 1997, *Kama Sutra: A Tale of Love*. Distributor: Trimark Pictures.

# Acknowledgements

This book and I have been on a long journey together and I am really grateful to all those involved with its making and for friends and family who have been here in some way as I have worked hard to complete this memoir.

I would like to thank
- Ginninderra Press for publishing this book with support and respect;
- my parents, Betty and Lenard McCarthy; despite there not being much education on this topic when I went to school, my parents encouraged me to learn about Australia's First Nations people from a young age;
- all my Yolŋu gurruṯumirriŋu mala, Yolŋu family for your consistent, incredible generosity, hearts and spirit in holding space for me to learn, grow and share in this profound life with you all;
- Waku Gwen Warmbirirr, for sitting down with me on her visit to Byron Bay and going through the whole book with me – the spelling, stories, discussions needed and phone calls to Yolŋu family in Arnhem Land;
- Gäthu Judith Maḏupinyin Ganyawu and Yapa Rebecca Nunydjulu for, to this day, always answering my messages out of the blue on the phone or Facebook Messenger, helping me spell names and answer questions about family;
- the balanda teachers and friends I shared this life with on Yurrwi Island, Milingimbi Homelands and in Yirrkala;
- Scott Wilson and Jeremy Cloake for inspiring me and supporting me in getting to Arnhem Land in the first place and always offering encouragement to this day;
- Mayrparr, a profound mentor, teacher and guide;
- author Sarah Armstrong, a wonderful writing teacher, mentor and friend, always offering me sincere and great encouragement;
- Robyn Kirley, editor, proofreader and dear friend;
- Helen Williams, an encouraging editor;

- Charles Darwin University Yolŋu Studies unit for language support;
-  friends I made in Bhutan and Sri Lanka who expressed interest in this journey and supported my writing journey whilst I was travelling and teaching yoga;
- friends who took the time to read excerpts or the entire book in its early stages, Cheryl Oliver, Christopher Driscoll and Jean Campbell;
- Kira Kay for offering guidance whilst I was living life in remote Arnhem Land;
- Byron Bay Writers Festival for inviting me to pitch the book at the festival in 2014 and invited me two opportunities to 'meet the literary agent';
- Melissa Ladkin, for reading this book and giving endless encouragement and love;
- Byron Amaya for taking the time to help me with the cover design;
-  my family Tim and Jenny McCarthy Johnnie and Michelle Mykee McCarthy and Aunt Margot, bless her soul;
- friends may not be in the remote Yolŋu life, but are here on this journey with me and much appreciated – Kate Rourke-Sutton, Sally-Anne Brown, Leanne Cramp, Jacque Sullivan, Kimberley Mitchell, Jean Campbell, Tashi Martel, Jo Buchanan, Fiona Kalazich, Loretta Vanessa, Kim O'Brien, Ron Snodgrass, and my teacher, Indraji Mohan;
- yoga for always being there.

www.ingramcontent.com/pod-product-compliance
Lightning Source LLC
Chambersburg PA
CBHW071804080526
44589CB00012B/680